Praise for

# *I'M DYING UP HERE*

## by William Knoedelseder

"Written with a journalist's strong narrative sense, *I'm Dying Up Here* chronicles the tight-knit community of artists who cracked open the world of funny entertainment and the event that shattered their camaraderie. . . . Knoedelseder's ability to sniff out the human stories behind the headlines is what makes this rowdy chapter in stand-up such a good read. It's a bittersweet tale told with humor and economy."
—*Dallas Morning News*

"Full of dishy, I-was-there detail about people who went on to become famous—and occasionally rich—being funny on TV."
—*Washington Post*

"Knoedelseder skillfully layers powerful dramatic details, and readers will shelve the book alongside those other key classics on comedy."
—*Publishers Weekly*, starred review

"A revealing and entertaining look at the 1970s Los Angeles comedy scene and the labor dispute that ended its most glorious era."
—*Shelf Awareness*

"In *I'm Dying Up Here*, his candid look at standup comedy's 1970s golden age, ex–*Los Angeles Times* reporter William Knoedelseder says boomers raised on Milton Berle and Henny Youngman began seeking 'their own countercultural heroes of humor.' They found them—Letterman and Leno, Richard Lewis and Andy Kaufman—working for free at the showcase Comedy Store on Sunset Strip. But then came a laughter stoppage: The unpaid comedians went on strike in 1979, and a troubled comic named Steve Lubetkin killed himself. The funny business, we learn, is deadly serious."
—*AARP The Magazine*

"One of the most eye-opening and informative books ever written about standup comedy. . . . One of the books of the year for any student of American television and pop culture. . . . A little-known story has now been told very well in perfect context. And when you finish the book you may feel as if you finally understand every comedian you see on TV for the first time." —*Buffalo News*

"A lively new book. . . . Knoedelseder reminds us that comedy is a dicey calling." —*Daily Variety*

"Fact-packed, highly readable history . . . peppered with plenty of portraits of struggling young comics, some destined for national fame, others headed to obscurity and, in a few cases, early death." —*Booklist*

"Illuminating." —*New York Times Book Review*

"Always amusing and deftly written—Knoedelseder is a good reporter and a self-effacing writer happy to turn the spotlight over to comedians, who relish it. He captures the frenetic atmosphere that comics create and the tangy camaraderie of can-you-top-this all-nighters at Canter's deli on Fairfax." —*Palm Beach Post*

"An important contribution to America's cultural history—and a helluva good read by an outstanding reporter." —*Huntington News*

"Knoedelseder, who was around in those days as a reporter on the *Los Angeles Times*, interweaves the fascinating stories of the tragic, unknown Lubetkin and the performers who were to become household names, set against the basic contradictions of working the Comedy Store." —*Irish Times*

"*I'm Dying Up Here* lays bare the bad and the ugly of Hollywood; from what good there was, like primordial muck, emerged the funniest guys and gals around." —*DigitalCity.com*

"This book is a biography of Comedy . . . the story of how the stand up comedy world migrated from New York City to Los Angeles, from the small, dark clubs where most of the great comedians got their start to the stage of *The Tonight Show with Johnny Carson* where careers were literally made or broken based on one 5-minute set on the show. . . . So well written and important that it should not only be read, but should be developed into a movie or a mini-series in the next few years." —*Artoftalk.tv*

# I'M DYING UP HERE

## HEARTBREAK AND HIGH TIMES IN STAND-UP COMEDY'S GOLDEN ERA

# WILLIAM KNOEDELSEDER

**PUBLICAFFAIRS**
*New York*

PublicAffairs books are available at special discounts for bulk purchases in the
U.S. by corporations, institutions, and other organizations. For more information,
please contact the Special Markets Department at the Perseus Books Group,
2300 Chestnut Street, Suite 200, Philadelphia, PA 19103, call (800) 810-4145,
ext. 5000, or e-mail special.markets@perseusbooks.com.

Designed by Trish Wilkinson
Text set in 12-point Goudy

Library of Congress Cataloging-in-Publication Data

Knoedelseder, William, 1947–
   I'm dying up here : heartbreak and high times in stand-up comedy's golden
era / William Knoedelseder.
      p.   cm.
   Includes bibliographical references and index.
   HC ISBN 978-1-58648-317-3 (alk. paper)
   PB ISBN 978-1-58648-869-3
   1. Stand-up comedy—United States—History—20th century. I. Title.
PN1969.C65.K56 2009
792.7'60973—dc22                                                    2009013751

10 9 8 7 6 5 4 3 2 1

*Dedicated to the memory of
Irv Letofsky and Howard Brandy,
and to the girl of my dreams.*

# Contents

# Acknowledgments

I started doing the research for this book thirty-one years ago, when my editor at the *Los Angeles Times*, Irv Letofsky, called me into his office and said there was something happening on the local comedy club scene that had the feel of Greenwich Village in the early 1960s. He thought stand-up comedy was about to explode nationally in the hands of a new crop of young performers working at the Comedy Store and the Improvisation. He thought the *Times* should establish a comedy beat. Was I interested?

For the next two years, I had stage-side seats at the best show in show business. I was at the Comedy Store the week that Robin Williams first erupted on to the LA scene, and I spent a quiet afternoon at the beach with him in his final hours of obscurity before *Mork & Mindy* hit the air. I sat slack jawed one evening as Andy Kaufman performed his entire stage act, complete with three costume changes, for an audience of two on the patio of my house and then wanted to wrestle my eight-months-pregnant wife. I spent a surreal night on the town with Kaufman's alter ego, Tony Clifton, and was present on the set the day Clifton was fired from his guest-starring role in *Taxi* and then wrestled off the Paramount Studios lot by security guards. I met and wrote about

Jay Leno, David Letterman, and Richard Lewis before the world knew who they were. I watched the funniest people of my generation get up on stage alone and try and fail and triumph. And I laughed my ass off.

I am grateful for the help and inspiration provided by the following people: Jimmy Aleck, Dottie Archibald, Alison Arngrim, Jo Anne Astrow, Mike Binder, Steve Bluestein, Elayne Boosler, the late Bernie Brillstein, Ken Browning, Johnny Dark, Lue Deck, Tom DeLisle, the late Estelle Endler, Ellen Farley, Budd Friedman, Gallagher, Argus Hamilton, Charlie Hill, Jeff Jampol, Bill Kirchenbauer, Jay Leno, Mark Lonow, Barry and Ginny Lubetkin, Jamie Masada, Dennis McDougal, Barbara McGraw, John Mettler, the late George Miller, Judy Orbach, Susan (Evans) Richmond, Phil Alden Robinson, Brad Sanders, Ross Schafer, George Shapiro, Mitzi Shore, Wil Shriner, the late John Stewart, Susan Sweetzer, Bennett Tramer, Marsha Warfield, Ellis Weiner, Dr. Robert Winter, Ann Woody, Bob Zmuda, Brian Ann Zoccola, and Alan Zwiebel.

I would like to offer special thanks to the following:

- Tom Dreesen for his generosity and many, many hours of time
- my friend and brother Richard Lewis for that and so much more beyond this book
- my dear friend and agent for life, Alice Martell, for always believing
- all the people at PublicAffairs, especially founder and editor at large, Peter Osnos, and my very cool editor, Lisa Kaufman, for their saintlike patience
- Dayan Ballweg, for his encouragement and great title
- and most of all my family—Bryn, Matt, Colin, and Halle—for their unquestioning love and support as I struggled to figure things out and find my way back to where I always should have been.

# Prologue:
# A True Comic

They slipped into the nightclub quietly, one by one, stepping carefully at first as their eyes adjusted from the bright afternoon light outside: a soft parade of mostly middle-aged comics come to pay their respects to a fallen comrade.

George Miller had died the week before from complications due to a blood clot in his brain. He was sixty-one and had battled leukemia for seven years. An obit in the *Los Angeles Times* summed up his career with the headline "Stand-up Comedian Was Often on 'Letterman.'"

In fact, Miller had appeared as David Letterman's guest fifty-six times over two decades. That may not sound like a lot to a layperson, but professional comedians considered it a feat of Barry Bondsian proportion. No other comic could boast such a record. Miller also had logged thirty-two appearances on *The Tonight Show Starring Johnny Carson*. It hadn't made him rich or particularly famous, but it had kept him working longer than many of his comedy peers—performing in small clubs around the country, occasionally opening in Las Vegas for middle-of-the-road music acts, making a living by making people laugh. Miller had stood alone in front of a crowd and cracked wise most every night for more than thirty years. That's not an easy thing to do.

So, on Sunday, March 16, 2003, his friends turned out to honor him at the Laugh Factory on Sunset Strip, where Miller had appeared regularly in recent years. Their names and faces ranged from vaguely familiar to instantly recognizable. Among them were Richard Lewis, the perpetually angst-ridden comic who appears regularly on *Curb Your Enthusiasm*; Tom Dreesen, a veteran of sixty-one *Tonight Show* appearances and Frank Sinatra's longtime opening act; Mike Binder, the comic turned filmmaker who created, wrote, directed, and starred in the HBO series *The Mind of the Married Man*; Elayne Boosler, the comedienne credited by her colleagues with breaking down the gender barriers for her generation of female stand-up comics; the ubiquitous Jay Leno, arguably the most successful stand-up of their generation; and Mort Sahl, an elder hero to every performer in the room and, as Master of Ceremonies Dreesen noted, "the only comic George ever paid to see."

Letterman was a notable no-show. He was hospitalized in New York with a case of shingles, and all present took his absence as a sign of just how sick he really was. Dave and George had been best friends since 1977, when they both lived in the same apartment building across the street from the Comedy Store, just a few blocks down the street. Dave had paid for all of George's medical expenses during the last few years of his life and had even picked up the cost of a two-bedroom apartment and a twenty-four-hour on-call nurse. When it appeared that George was dying in 2000, Dave got him admitted to an experimental leukemia treatment program at UCLA by donating nearly $1 million to the medical center. The treatment involved a new "miracle" drug called Gleevec that stabilized George's white blood cell count and saved his life, at least for a time.

In a way, it was probably a good thing that Letterman didn't make it to the memorial, given that Leno did. The tension of having them both in the same room might have proved a major distraction. Once good friends, they'd had a famous falling out in 1991, when NBC chose Leno over Letterman to succeed Johnny Carson as host of *The Tonight Show*, and time had not healed the wound. Neither man ever talked publicly about the rift, but their mutual friends in the room knew both sides by heart:

Leno expressed bewilderment that Letterman blamed him for the fact that NBC offered him the gig after deciding—for whatever reasons—that Dave wasn't right for it. That's the way the showbiz cookie crumbled, he figured; it was all in the game. What was he supposed to do, turn down the opportunity of a lifetime?

The way Letterman saw it: yes. Dave thought their sixteen-year friendship should have precluded Jay from lobbying for, and making a secret deal to take over, the show that he himself had always dreamed of inheriting. As much as Dave coveted the job, he couldn't imagine going behind Leno's back to get it. He didn't know if he would ever be able to trust Jay again.

These were treacherous waters for their fellow comics to navigate. *The Tonight Show Starring Jay Leno* and *The Late Show with David Letterman* were the twin peaks of the stand-up comedy business—the best TV exposure a comic could get. So, no one wanted to appear to take sides in the Dave-Jay thing for fear of losing both a friend and a potential buyer. Truth be told, given the opportunity, most—if not all—of them would have done what Leno did, but they probably would have felt worse about doing it. Nobody blamed Jay, but everybody understood why Dave felt betrayed. Letterman was nothing if not loyal to his old friends (the joke among them was that he hadn't made a new one since 1979). In addition to Miller, he regularly brought on longtime pals Tom Dreesen, Richard Lewis, Johnny Dark, and Johnny Witherspoon. And it was, ironically, Letterman's frequent booking of Leno on NBC's *Late Night* all during the 1980s that had helped propel Leno to the top rank of stand-up comedy and ultimately put him first in line for Carson's crown.

In contrast, Leno rarely featured stand-up comics on *The Tonight Show*, explaining to his old friends that the network didn't think they drew viewers, that the research showed people even tuned out when comics came on. The comics didn't buy it. They thought that, as host, Leno should buck the network brass and book anyone he thought was funny, just like Carson had before him. Fair or not, the knock on Jay was that he wouldn't go out of his way to help a fellow comic.

And yet, here he was, one of the busiest men in show business, spending a Sunday afternoon at the Laugh Factory, mixing easily with the old gang and reminiscing with obvious affection about a guy he hadn't hung out with in twenty-five years.

"George and I had nothing in common," Leno said. "Not one thing. Cars? [Leno collects them; George drove his mother's battered Chrysler LeBaron with cracked Corinthian leather seats and a peeling vinyl top.] Drugs? [Leno never did them; Miller never stopped.] But George always made me laugh," he said. "He was a true comic—not a sitcom actor or an improv performer. He was a classic stand-up; it was what he was meant to do."

He noted that their relationship had been conducted mostly by phone in recent years, with George calling frequently to critique his *Tonight Show* monologues or to apologize cheekily "for not being able to get me on the Letterman show. He suggested I send a tape."

One by one, Miller's old pals followed Leno to the microphone to share their favorite George joke or anecdote. The famously garrulous Dreesen explained why he was chosen to emcee by telling Miller's favorite joke about him: "The cops stopped Tom Dreesen the other night and asked him, 'You wanna talk here or down at the station?' Dreesen said, 'Both, and in the car, too.'"

Native American comic Charlie Hill launched into a call-and-response with some of Miller's best-remembered bits.

"Why are so many people drinking diet cola?" he shouted. "Because they are fat and thirsty," the crowd hollered back.

"A cow on speed . . . (rapid fire) Moo-moo-moo-moo-moo."

"How much does [comic] Paul Mooney weigh? . . . 200 pounds; 180 without cologne."

"Last night I was watching an Elvis Presley movie on diet pills and Xanax . . . because that's the way Elvis would have wanted it."

"I went to see the movie *Accidental Tourist* and something horrible happened in the middle. . . . It continued."

The dialogue quickly devolved into a kind of shorthand that only they understood, as people in the audience began calling out their own favorite lines to uproarious reaction:

"Then the head waiter came over . . . " (guffaws, whooping).

"I'm chewin' and he's lookin', and I'm chewin' and he's lookin' . . . " (hands slapping on tables, tears of laughter).

"Yesterday I was sitting at Denny's having a waffle . . . " (falling out of their chairs).

And finally, some one shouted out, "one hundred eighteen," which they all apparently considered the funniest number in the universe.

The "George stories" were more accessible to an outsider. Ross Schafer told of the time one of Miller's girlfriends broke up with him. "So, George took this picture of Jesus she had on her wall and wrote on it, 'Rot in hell,' and put it on the windshield of her car. The woman called the cops, who showed up at George's apartment and told him that the woman feared he was making a threat because it was a picture of Jesus. 'Oh, gee,' said George. 'I thought it was Dan Fogelberg.'"

Johnny Dark recalled the time that Miller got into an argument with the manager of his neighborhood Starbucks and was told to get out and never come back. "Oh, my God," George had wailed. "Where am I ever going to find another Starbucks?"

Elayne Boosler remembered a middle-of-the night phone call the week she moved to Los Angeles in 1976:

"A voice says, 'Hi, it's George Miller. You met me last night at the Comedy Store. You've gotta come out to the corner of Sunset and Sweetzer and give me some money so I can buy some drugs.'

"I didn't even have a checking account in those days," Boosler went on, "and I had $75 in cash to my name. But for some reason I got in my car and drove there, and he was standing by the curb. I rolled down my window, he reached in and took the money, and I drove away. Years later his punch line to me was, 'You handed me $75 when you didn't even know who I was . . . so I consider you an enabler and the reason that I have a drug problem today.'"

Miller's drug consumption was conspicuous even among this drug-experienced crowd. Quaaludes were his favorite in the early days; he preferred prescription Soma in later years. It was the dope as much as the leukemia that killed him because he'd get so high that he'd forget to take his life-preserving medicine. Dreesen, Letterman, Gary Muledeer, and Laugh Factory owner Jamie Masada had tried to stage an intervention with him in the months before he died—to no avail. Letterman flew to Los Angeles to be there, but when Miller saw them all together, he said, "Oh, this is that intervention shit, isn't it? We'll I'm not going for it."

"George, you have to get straight," Letterman told him. "You have to get well or else."

"What does that mean?" Miller shot back nastily. "That you're not going to put me on your show anymore?"

For Letterman it was like a sucker punch to the gut. He left hurt and angry, and he and Miller didn't talk to each other for weeks afterwards—the only time in their long friendship that had ever happened.

Naturally, none of this was mentioned at the memorial, where one of the biggest laughs of the night was prompted by Kelly Montieth's drug-referenced quip, "George probably doesn't know he's dead yet."

When it seemed for a second that Dreesen was steering dangerously close to sentimentality, saying, "I'm going to miss George's criticism of me," Elayne Boosler pulled him back from the brink by calling out, "I'll fill in for him," to which someone in the back of the room added, "And when she dies. . . . "

The exchange kicked off a volley of high-spirited heckling, with insults and put-downs caroming around the room—"Yeah? It won't be the first time you've used my material"—all goosed along gleefully by a beaming Leno, dressed as of old in well-worn jeans and a rumpled denim shirt and standing shoulder-to-shoulder with Mike Binder, with whom he'd had a painful parting of the ways more than two decades before.

In that moment, they all seemed transformed. The years fell away. Suddenly, it was the mid-1970s. They were twenty-something, bubbling with ambition and bursting with dreams. No one was rich; no one was famous. No one had been to rehab; no one had died. Dave and Jay were still pals. They were all having the time of their lives. And no one had any inkling of what was about to happen.

# Blood Brothers

Richard Lewis was scared. On a cool April evening in 1971, he was on the way from his apartment in Hasbrouck Heights, New Jersey, to midtown Manhattan, driving through the Lincoln Tunnel in his silver Chevy Vega, a car with more electrical problems than he had neuroses. No mechanic could figure out what was wrong with the car. Typically, the tape deck would begin to slow down, causing the high-pitched vocals of Procol Harum to drop to the deepest of bass, and then the headlights would dim, alerting him to the fact that he was a mile or so from hell, when the engine would die. Which could be a big problem in the tunnel.

But that's not what he was afraid of. Earlier in the day, Lewis, a twenty-four-year-old Ohio State graduate with a degree in marketing, had finally decided what he wanted to be in life, what he had to be: a stand-up comic. And that scared the shit out of him.

Lewis had been funny as far back as he could remember, the class clown from kindergarten on. He fell in love with laughter at the age of five and gobbled up whatever comedy early television had to offer—*The Colgate Comedy Hour* with Dean Martin and Jerry Lewis, *Texaco Star Theater* with Milton Berle, *Your Show of Shows* with Sid Caesar, *The Ed Wynn Show*. By age nine, he had memorized the *TV Guide* schedule and was a discerning enough consumer of comedy to prefer Steve Allen to Ed Sullivan on Sunday night. He tried not to miss Oscar Levant's weekday afternoon show and stayed up late to catch Alexander King and Shelley Berman on Jack Paar.

Humor provided solace from the sense of isolation he felt growing up as the baby of his family with a considerably older brother and sister who consequently paid little attention to him. His father, William Lewis, known in northern New Jersey as "the King of Caterers," was devoted to his business and was seldom home. His mother was lonely and often depressed. The only time "Richie" felt connected to his parents was on the rare occasions when he would lie between them in their bed watching *The Honeymooners*. But the feeling lasted only as long as the show. So, he sought comfort in the company of comedians he found first on television and later on record albums: Jonathan Winters, Mike Nichols and Elaine May, Lenny Bruce, Mel Brooks, and Carl Reiner. He came to think of himself as a rebel, laughing at authority, like Holden Caulfield.

He experienced an epiphany one day at Dwight Morrow High School in Englewood, New Jersey. During an assembly in the school gymnasium, he was mocking the people on stage under his breath and cracking up everyone around him when the principal suddenly stepped to the microphone and halted the proceedings. He directed the students to file out of the gym homeroom by homeroom until only Lewis's homeroom remained. Then he ordered the class to file out row by row until, out of the original nine hundred kids, only Lewis was left in the gym, whereupon the principal looked down at him and said, "Richard Lewis, you are *the* troublemaker of this school."

Most teenagers would have been mortified, terrified, undone by such a singling out. But Lewis appreciated the absurdity. His first thought was, "Hey, I might be able to make a living at this."

At first his plan was just to write comedy. In college he started jotting down funny premises and jokes in a notebook that he carried everywhere he went. He fantasized about transitioning directly from student life to that of a staff writer for a TV star like Sid Caesar, which was how Woody Allen had gotten his start. When that didn't happen upon graduation, he hung around Columbus, Ohio, for nearly a year, doing odd jobs, afraid to return home to New Jersey and face his father's inevitable questions about finding "a real job."

What finally moved him out of Ohio was the news that one of his comic heroes, Robert Klein, was going to host a summer "replacement" show on network TV. A friend tracked down the address of Klein's manager, Buddy Morra, who was with the prestigious firm of (Jack) Rollins and (Charles) Joffe, which also managed Woody Allen and Dick Cavett. Lewis mailed off a package of material he wrote specifically for Klein and followed up a week later with a phone call to Morra, who'd been impressed enough with what he read to pass it on to Klein. Morra told Lewis to call him the next time he was in the New York area, and he'd arrange a meeting with the comedian. Lewis couldn't get back to New York quickly enough.

The meeting proved to be life changing, but not in the way Lewis had expected. "I read your stuff, and it's really good," Klein told him. "But I got into stand-up to express *myself*, so I only do my own stuff on stage. I don't get off doing other people's premises."

Lewis was disappointed but also buoyed by the praise and the fact that Morra had promised to hook him up with some older comics who were always looking to buy good stand-up material. The best known of them was Morty Gunty, a big star in the Catskills who'd appeared numerous times on TV. Over the next few months, Lewis earned a few hundred dollars writing jokes for Gunty and the others, but he was frustrated that they invariably turned down what he thought was his best stuff, the most personal material that expressed how he felt about the world around him. The obvious solution was to perform the material himself. But he couldn't even think about that because of the conversation it would require with his father, whose approval he craved. What was he going to say? "Hey, Dad, I've decided to chuck the college education that you worked so hard to pay for in favor of becoming a stand-up comic?" Writing comedy was one thing—that was being a "humorist." Performing comedy was something else entirely— that was *show business*, and they were not a show business family. He couldn't imagine his father saying, "My son, the comedian," with any pride. As a result, he was uncomfortable with the idea himself and felt guilty even considering it.

But all that ended on April 12, 1971, when William Lewis died of a heart attack (his fourth) at age fifty-seven. After the first wave of shock and grief, Richard realized that he was finally off the hook. He didn't have to face the conversation that he so feared. His father's death had freed him to find his own comic voice. Two weeks later, as he emerged safely from the Lincoln Tunnel in his haunted Vega, he said to himself, I'm writing jokes for Richard Lewis now. . . . But how am I ever going to get up on that stage? He headed uptown toward the only place he knew that might hold the answer to that question.

The Improvisation, at the corner of Forty-fourth Street and Ninth Avenue, was the comedy center of the universe. Established in 1963 by a former ad man named Budd Friedman, it was the only nightclub of its kind, a casual, chaotic cabaret where comedians and singers alternated sets and on any given night you might catch David Brenner and Jimmie Walker working out new material for *The Tonight Show*, Robert Klein blowing blues runs on his harmonica, Bette Midler doing some impromptu warbling in the bar accompanied by Dustin Hoffman on the piano, David Frye climbing out of a limousine in front with a drink in his hand, or Woody Allen arriving in a raincoat and fedora and dramatically instructing the doorman to "whisk me to my table."

It was 8:30 p.m. on a Monday when Richard Lewis first walked into the Improv. Monday was "open-mike night," when anyone with the will or compulsion to do so could get up onstage and perform five minutes of material in the wild hope of impressing Friedman and being asked back to perform as a regular in the Tuesday-through-Sunday rotation. Lewis had no intention of getting up on stage, however. He was there purely for research purposes. For all his love and knowledge of stand-up comedy, he had never seen it performed live.

The first comic he saw was a handsome, shaggy-haired Jewish kid about his age whose name he didn't catch but who was everything he wanted to be as a performer—cool, hip, confident, sexy. He particularly liked the way the guy handled a heckler: "So, you come here to work out your heckles in a small club, right? Thinking that pretty soon you'll get really good at it and maybe someday you'll be in Vegas heckling the biggies?"

Between shows an hour later, Lewis saw the comic sitting alone in the back of the room, nursing a beer and looking morose. "Jeez, you were really great," he said sincerely.

The guy's eyes lit up. "You're kiddin' me," he said. "I thought it didn't go so well."

"Naw, man, you were the best, hands down," Lewis said. "I *aspire* to be that good." They shook hands.

"I'm Richard Lewis."

"Steve Lubetkin."

Both felt an immediate connection. Lewis confessed that he was thinking about becoming a comic but had no idea how to go about it. Lubetkin said he knew a lot. "I'd be happy to show you the ropes," he said. They wrote their phone numbers on cocktail napkins.

In the ensuing weeks, Lubetkin proved even better than his word, guiding Lewis on a tour of every bar, restaurant, disco, or strip club that allowed self-proclaimed comedians to entertain, or irritate, its customers. The itinerary included such oddball venues as Dan Lurie's Gym & Health Spa on Long Island and Gil Hodges's Grand Slam Lounge in Brooklyn, which abutted a bowling alley so that punch lines often had to compete with the crash of falling pins.

Lewis especially loved the Greenwich Village clubs that Lubetkin introduced him to—Café Wha, the Village Gate, Gerdes's Folk City—where Warholian hipness permeated the walls and the smell of grass and sound of Dylan still wafted in the air.

The Village was Lubetkin's turf; he was born and raised there. His father, Jack Lubetkin, owned Ye Olde Treasure Shoppe at 1 West Eighth Street, right off Fifth Avenue. Opened in 1948, the year Steve was born, the Shoppe was one of the original Eighth Street establishments that catered to a beatnik clientele, selling antique furniture and jewelry and leather bags, belts, and sandals that Jack made by hand in the back. By the late 1960s, the Shoppe had become a Village institution, with customers often lined up outside waiting to get in.

Growing up, Steve and his older brother, Barry, worked alongside their father, as did their mother, Evelyn. The brothers didn't get paid, but they were allowed to take money from the till whenever they needed. Jack Lubetkin fostered a loose, irreverent atmosphere in the store, entertaining customers with his constant shtick. "Excuse me, madam," he'd say to an indecisive browser, "but I have a rather weak heart, and I've been watching you looking around, and it's upsetting me, and I don't want to faint, so could you please leave?" Then, he'd wait a few seconds before winking at the flummoxed woman to let her know he was just teasing. One of his favorite bits was playing off the family's flatulent pet bulldog, Caesar. Every time Caesar farted with a customer nearby, Jack would rebuke one of the boys—"Steve, how many times have I told you about that?"—then they'd all break up.

The family lived above the store, which was set back from the street in a quaint little arcade that looked as if it had been lifted straight out of colonial times. The boys' bedroom overlooked the arcade. One block away, Washington Square Park served as their playground when they were little and their political classroom as they got older—a multiethnic, multiracial marketplace of free-thinking, loud talking, and public protesting.

Free expression was encouraged in the Lubetkin household. At their weekly "Sunday Breakfast Club," the four would sit around the dining table and decide such family issues as whether to buy a pool table or a new car or what TV shows to watch. The two boys had an equal vote with their parents. The Lubetkins were culturally rather than religiously Jewish. Evelyn tried to keep a kosher kitchen, and both boys were bar mitzvahed, but if the family went to temple at all, it was only on Yom Kippur and Rosh Hashanah. Jack Lubetkin was a conservative Republican who as a young man had battled the Nazi bunds in Yorkville (now New York's Upper East Side) before World War II. He was forever thankful that his parents had emigrated from Russia in the late 1800s. A distant cousin, Ziviah Lubetkin, had been one of the leaders of the Warsaw rebellion and now lived in a Holocaust survivors' kibbutz in Israel. Leon Uris's novel *Mila 18* was dedicated to her. Steve often boasted about being related.

All in all, it would have been a storybook childhood if it hadn't been for Evelyn Lubetkin's slow, agonizing death from ovarian cancer at the age of forty-four. Steve was twelve at the time and took it harder than anyone. Barry, who was seventeen and later went on to earn a PhD in psychology, always believed that the tragedy of their mother's death had driven Steve to become a comedian, that his little brother figured if he could just learn to make other people laugh then he could laugh again himself.

Steve Lubetkin and Richard Lewis made one another laugh a lot. They got each other's sense of humor completely, no doubt because they had so much in common: a middle-class Jewish up-bringing, a deceased parent, a degree in marketing, a part-time entry-level job in advertising, an intense interest in sports and girls, and, above all else, a love affair with stand-up comedy.

In the first week of their friendship, Steve took Richard to a tiny West Village dive called the Champagne Gallery. "You're gonna love this joint," he said. "It's as far off the beaten path as you can get."

With its not-ready-for-*The-Gong-Show* lineup of wannabe comics and weirdos doing whacked out performance art, the Champagne Gallery made the Improv seem like Vegas. "This is like a variety show at Christmas in a mental institution," Lewis said.

"That's why it's the perfect place for you to start doing stand-up," Lubetkin responded. "It is safe here. There's no pressure."

Lewis made his debut at the Champagne Gallery a week later, on a Sunday night, with Lubetkin and forty other people in the audience. In stand-up parlance, he killed. He felt it as it was happening, a high like he'd never experienced before. He'd finally done it; he'd gotten up on stage and made people laugh. He'd passed the test. He was a stand-up comic.

From that night on, Lewis and Lubetkin were nearly inseparable. Using the Improv as their hub, they hopped from joint to joint, sometimes hitting four or five places in a single night, plying their trade, testing material, trying to develop their acts. They'd do sets at a club called the Metro in Forest Hills, hustle out to Pip's in Sheepshead Bay, and eventually wind up back at the Improv with $20 apiece to show for their night's work, enough for dinner and a couple of beers before they headed home for a few hours sleep followed by eight hours of day job.

Steve continued to do open mike nights at the Improv and eventually graduated to occasional late-night spots during the week. But Richard held off trying for the Improv on the advice of David Brenner, who took a liking to him after meeting him in the bar and became something of a mentor. "Wait until you've put together twenty minutes of killer material," Brenner told him. "Then call me, and I'll tell you if you're ready."

Lewis waited six months before he invited Brenner to see him at the Champagne Gallery. Lubetkin was in the audience as usual, and once again Lewis came off the stage feeling like he'd killed. Still, he needed to hear it from Brenner. The older comic greeted him with a serious face, placed his arm around his shoulders, and walked him outside without saying a word. Then, he turned to him and broke into a smile. "You're ready," he said. It was the most joyous night of Lewis's life.

The following Monday, he showed up at the Improv for open mike night. As it happened, he was the last to go on, and his performance brought down the house. He was still taking his bow when Budd Friedman bounded onto the stage to bask in the applause. "It looks like we've found a new all-star," the club owner announced to the standing, cheering crowd.

In the following weeks, Lewis and Lubetkin were on a sustained high. Against long odds, the two best friends had become performers at the Improv. They were brothers in comedy, embarked on a kamikaze mission to make it in show business and never look back. They would live on the streets if they had to, but nothing was going to keep them from accomplishing their goals—unless, of course, by some unforeseen circumstance, they somehow "got fucked over by the business." That was always the nagging fear in the back of their minds. In an attempt to guard against that possibility, they took out a small insurance policy. One inebriated night at the corner of West Fourth Street and MacDougal, in faux *Godfather* grandiosity, they took a blood oath that whoever made it first would help the other one.

It was a pact that would haunt Lewis in the years to come.

# The Hippest Room

Lewis and Lubetkin arrived on the stand-up scene at a propitious time. As the 1970s dawned, the baby boom generation was turning to comedy as a favorite form of entertainment. The boomers had stood the music business on its ear in the late 1960s with their embrace of progressive rock 'n' roll. Now they were looking for their own countercultural heroes of humor.

The first one they found was George Carlin. A former disc jockey turned clean-cut, coat-and-tie nightclub comic, Carlin went through a kind of "road-to-Damascus" conversion in 1970 when he was fired by the Frontier Hotel in Las Vegas for, in his words, "saying 'shit' in a town where the big game is called 'crap.'" That quip was the opening line of his groundbreaking 1972 album, *FM and AM*, which pictured him on the cover dressed in bell-bottom jeans and sandals, with shoulder length hair and a beard. His follow-up album later that year, *Class Clown*, included the now legendary routine "Seven Words You Can Never Say on TV" ("shit, piss, fuck, cunt, cocksucker, motherfucker, and tits"). Both albums quickly went gold, meaning they sold at least 500,000 copies, which was considered huge at the time.

After Carlin came Robert Klein, whose best-selling 1973 debut album, *Child of the Fifties*, established him as the hippest and brainiest chronicler of upper-middle-class uptightness.

Richard Pryor made it a triumvirate. He'd been a middling success as a kind of nonthreatening Bill Cosby imitator until one night in Las Vegas in 1970 when he stopped his routine in midsentence, stared at the audience for a few seconds, and asked, "What am I doing here?" Then he walked off the stage and disappeared from the mainstream comedy scene for several years. He spent the time reinventing his act at small black clubs—the so-called chitlin circuit—and reemerged in 1974 with the Top 40 album *That Nigger's Crazy*, which introduced the style of incendiary, race-based, and profanity-laced material that would earn him accolades as one of the most brilliant and influential stand-up comics of all time.

Carlin, Klein, and Pryor were in their early to mid-thirties, but they managed to tap into the sensibility of an audience at least a decade younger. They proved that stand-up comedy didn't have to be structured around jokes, setups, and punch lines. It could be conceptual, observational, absurdist, sociopolitical, and scatological all at the same time. That was a mix that struck an immediate chord with the college crowd.

The first evidence that a youth renaissance was underway in American comedy could be seen in the age of the patrons at the Improv and the hopefuls who lined up to audition for Budd Friedman. Monday was the club's official amateur night, but after midnight during the week, if the crowd was thin and no headliner comics were waiting to go on, Friedman would let anyone try out on stage for a couple of minutes.

On one such night, a long-haired college student from Boston walked up to the usually brusque club owner and whined, "Mr. Friedman, my name is Jay Leno, and this is the third night in a row that I've driven down here from Boston to go on, and I keep not getting on. I really wanna go on. Could you *please* put me on tonight?"

Friedman looked at him in disbelief. The kid was wearing glasses, a big-collared, open-neck shirt, and bell-bottom jeans secured by a wide leather belt with a huge turquoise-studded buckle, and he was affectedly cupping a curved tobacco pipe in his right hand.

"Wait a minute," Friedman said. "You're telling me you drive all the way down here, four hours, don't get on, drive all the way back and then turn around and come back again the next day?"

Leno nodded. "You're on next," said Friedman. Leno did five minutes, after which Friedman told him "You can come back any time."

That same night, a seventeen-year-old senior at the Fiorello LaGuardia High School of the Performing Arts also passed his first audition and was added to the regular lineup. He had recently changed his name from Freddie Pruetzel to Freddie Prinze, and he promptly dropped out of school.

Andy Kaufman was twenty-three and living with his parents in Great Neck, Long Island, when a local music club owner called Friedman and said, "You really should see this guy." Kaufman showed up at the Improv in his "foreign man" character and introduced himself to Friedman in badly broken English.

"Where you from, kid?" Friedman asked.

"An island in the Caspian Sea," Kaufman replied in the voice of a five-year-old. Friedman didn't get the joke because he didn't know there are no islands in the Caspian Sea, but he put Kaufman on anyway and watched as he stumbled through a series of egregious celebrity impressions while members of the audience either giggled nervously or stared in slack-jawed silence. After what seemed like an eternity, Kaufman announced, "Now I would like to do the Elvis Presley," and ripped into a dead-on impersonation of the King singing "Treat Me Nice." The crowd went wild over the extended put-on and Kaufman became an instant Improv regular.

Elayne Boosler had no thought of doing stand-up when she first walked into the club. She was a twenty-one-year-old part-time dance and acting student who was looking for a waitress job so she could move out of her parents' house in Brooklyn and get an apartment in Manhattan. Friedman insisted that all his waitresses (there were no waiters) had to be able to double as singers so that there was always someone on hand to fill in between comics. He didn't think a comic should follow a comic onstage. Fortunately for Boosler, there was an opening, and she managed to sing well enough to get the job.

From the start, Boosler felt as if she had entered an alternative universe. What she knew about stand-up she'd learned from watching Ed Sullivan and *The Tonight Show* growing up. She knew Jackie Mason, Shecky Green, and Jackie Vernon; she knew Totie Fields, Phyllis Diller, and Joan Rivers. The material was invariably hangdog, self-deprecating, married. She enjoyed it and laughed at it, but it bore no relation to her life. Now she was watching attractive young men onstage every night talking about sex and dating, their mothers and school. Oh, my God, she thought. This *all* relates to me. I think just like that. It was a level of funny she never knew existed. She couldn't stop laughing.

From her vantage point working tables, seating customers, and sometimes singing between acts, Boosler got to see not only the stage performances but also the creative process. She saw that the guys were driven by their creativity. Whenever a singer was performing in the back room, the comics would be gathered at the bar in front—running lines, critiquing, feeding off one another, jotting down ideas on cocktail napkins. It wasn't unusual for a comic on stage to suddenly fish into his pocket, pull out a wadded napkin, and start reading from it.

One night, after Boosler had been working for a few weeks, Andy Kaufman took her aside and told her she was more funny than tuneful. "In fact, you should never ever sing again in public," he said. With his encouragement, she began working on a stand-up routine. They were soon a romantic item, and Boosler was eventually accepted as the sole female member of a boys' club that included (in addition to the aforementioned newcomers) David Brenner, Steve Landesberg, Jimmie Walker, Richard Belzer, Ed Bluestone, and Michael Preminger.

Brenner, at age thirty-six with a dozen *Tonight Show* appearances under his belt, was the grand old man of the group and a generous mentor, especially to Richard Lewis. They were sitting in a neighborhood deli one day when Lewis lamented that if he could only put together $1,000, he could quit his three part-time jobs and devote all his time to working on his act. Brenner quickly wrote him a check for the grand. "Congratulations," he said, "now you are a full-time comedian." Lewis quit all the jobs.

Another night, Brenner and his girlfriend drove Lewis home to the guesthouse he rented in the backyard of a home in Paramus, New Jersey. Lewis was mortified when they insisted on coming in because it was a twelve-by-fourteen-foot, one-room hellhole with orange curtains and mushrooms growing through the walls. He was in the bathroom checking to make sure there was no pubic hair on the porcelain when he heard Brenner say to the girl, "Tell him you love the place."

All the younger comics were poor, partly because the Improv didn't pay them. Budd Friedman couldn't afford to when he first opened the club with a borrowed $3,000 and only seventy-four seats. Over time, not paying had become a tradition. The Improv was considered a "showcase club" where performers could get up on a professionally equipped stage, create without interference, and potentially be seen by agents, talent scouts, and other very important people in show business. The club was a favorite after-hours hangout for performers and producers from the nearby Broadway theater district. It wasn't unusual to see the likes of Danny Aiello, Vincent Gardino, Jason Robards Jr., and Albert

Finney in the audience or drinking at the bar. One magical night found Dudley Moore and Christopher Plummer playing duets on the sixty-six-key piano, while a slinky Tuesday Weld draped herself across its top.

In the early 1970s, the Improv was the hippest room in town, possibly in the world, which was why comics didn't complain about working there for free. If you were a regular at the Improv, you could get paying jobs at all the little clubs in the area. And if you played enough of those places, you could earn enough to almost not starve. In a way, the comics didn't think of the Improv as a real nightclub. It was more like their own gym where they worked out and got in shape for the big game. And the big game was always *The Tonight Show*.

At the time, Johnny Carson was the prime arbiter of comic worth in America. If he thought you were funny and put you on his show, then you were instantly marketable, positioned to land relatively high-paying gigs as an opening act for pop stars in Las Vegas or rock bands on tour. If Carson didn't think you were funny, then you were dead in the water, consigned to eke out a living in small clubs. Not surprisingly, Carson was a common obsession among the comics. Putting together five minutes of solid, clean material for Johnny was their mission in life, whether they were trying to get on for the first time or the tenth. Other TV shows featured stand-up comedians, but only *The Tonight Show* launched careers.

Of all the young comics he'd seen, Budd Friedman thought that Jay Leno might be the best of his generation. He was particularly impressed with Leno's work ethic. Leno kept up the commute between Boston and New York—every weekend and often during the week—while he finished his senior year at Emerson College. He had a part-time job at a car dealership that sold Rolls Royces and sometimes had to travel to Rolls Royce headquarters in Paramus to pick up new cars. On those occasions, he risked getting fired by stopping in New York to perform a set or two at the Improv before heading back to Boston.

Leno was relentless in his pursuit of new stand-up venues, pitching himself like a door-to-door salesman to any place that offered a raised platform, a microphone, and a few chairs. He worked everywhere from skuzzy strip clubs in Boston's notorious Combat Zone to earnest folk clubs in Cambridge. He got his foot in the door of the latter by offering an unusual deal to the reluctant club owners. "Here's a $50 bill," he'd say. "Put it right there on the bar, and let me go on. If I don't do well and people start to leave, then you can keep the fifty." He never lost the money.

Leno reminded Friedman of Robert Klein, whom the club owner respected above all other comics. Leno had the same casual observational style and no gimmick. Other young stand-ups sweated to develop twenty minutes of solid material, but Leno seemed able to walk on stage and riff for hours if he had to. He made it look easy, like he was making it up as he went along, and sometimes he was. Already the other comics at the Improv were starting to quote him to one another. "Did you hear what that guy from Boston said last night?"

Friedman liked Leno so much that he was thinking about becoming his manager. But first he wanted to see him perform someplace other than his own club. The problem with the Improv was that it didn't reflect the rough-and-tumble real world of stand-up comedy. People came there expecting to laugh, which usually made for a supportive, forgiving audience. You could kill at the Improv and still bomb at the Hilton with the same material. As Rodney Dangerfield liked to joke, "If you do well at the Improv it means you ain't got no act."

So Friedman drove to a little jazz club called Lennie's on the Turnpike outside of Boston, where Leno was opening for Buddy Rich. The place was packed with fans of the famed drummer, and Friedman was happy to see Leno holding his own with the much older crowd that hadn't come to see a comic. But he couldn't figure out why Jay kept hopping up and down during his routine. He moved closer to the stage and saw that a patron in the front row was trying to pound on Leno's toes with his balled up fist. Friedman had seen some weird stuff during his years in the nightclub business but never anything like this. What amazed him the most was that Leno kept his composure and timing while managing to avoid most of the blows. He decided right then and there to manage him. It turned out that the toe-pounder was the owner of the company that manufactured the cymbals Buddy Rich used, and he wanted this hippie comic off the stage so his product could be seen in action. (Leno would write later in his autobiography that on his first night of opening for Rich, an impatient fan of the drummer jumped up on the stage during his set and punched him out. And for this, he was paid $75 a night for two half-hour sets.)

Incidents like that were another reason comics didn't mind playing the Improv for free. You didn't get paid, but at least you didn't get hurt. The club was gaining a reputation among young comics all across the country as a place where you could work in a collegial atmosphere and not have to dodge projectiles from the audience. What's more, word was going around that talent scouts from *The Tonight Show* came in regularly looking for new blood.

All that sounded almost too good to be true to Tom Dreesen in Chicago, so he and his comedy partner, Tim Reid, hopped a Greyhound bus to New York to see for themselves. Arriving in Manhattan, they checked into a shared room at the Warwick Hotel and then went directly to the Improv. They met Jay Leno standing outside with a handful of young hopefuls waiting to audition for the first time. Always affable, Leno introduced them to the others, and Dreesen and Reid immediately felt a sense of camaraderie in the group that they'd not experienced before among comedians. There was no wariness or posturing on anyone's part, none of the edgy competitiveness common among the old-school comics they'd met on the road. Leno was a font of useful and funny information about club owners he knew and clubs he'd worked all over the Northeast.

Dreesen and Reid had their own colorful tales to tell. Together since 1969, they billed themselves as "Tim and Tom," the world's only black-and-white comedy team. They worked charities, churches, and any room that would have them, from Playboy Clubs to chitlin-circuit hotspots like the High Chaparral in Chicago and the Burning Spear on the Southside, the 20 Grand in Detroit, the Sugar Shack in Boston, and Club Harlem in Atlantic City. In the black venues, Dreesen was often the only white face in the crowd, and they killed with a routine they called "Superspade and the Courageous Caucasian," in which Reid introduced his partner as "the world's fastest human from parking lot to the stage." Then he'd attempt to teach Dreesen "how to be a brother" so that he would survive the night. Dreesen, of course, would screw up all the mannerisms and street jargon to great comic effect.

In one of their most far-fetched bits (at the time, anyway), Dreesen played a reporter interviewing the first black man elected president of the United States:

Dreesen: What's the first thing you are going to do when you take office?

Reid: Enact a law that dead people can't vote in Chicago.

Dreesen: What's the second thing you are going to do?

Reid: Enact a law that living people can't vote in Mississippi.

(The interracial repartee didn't always go over with the audience, however, and when that happened, the consequences could be painful. One night at the Golden Horseshoe in Chicago Heights, an offended white patron walked up to them after their set and smashed out his cigarette on Reid's face. Another time, while they were performing at the University of Illinois, Dreesen got hit in the face with an ice ball thrown from the audience.)

The irony of the street-savvy black dude/naive white boy act was that Reid had a college degree in business and was formerly a marketing rep for the Dupont Corporation, while Dreesen was a high school dropout from some of the meanest streets in America who had survived a childhood that even Charles Dickens couldn't have conjured. He was the third oldest of eight children, four boys and four girls, who were raised in a rat-infested shack in Harvey, Illinois, with no bathtub, shower, or hot water; to bathe they boiled water in a pan. All four boys slept in one bed. Their parents, Walter and Glenore Dreesen, were dedicated drinkers. The shack sat in the shadow of half a dozen steel mills in a neighborhood that supported eight taverns. Glenore was a barmaid in one, and Walter was a patron of them all.

Tom went to work at age six, shining shoes in the bars. Every day after school he'd make the rounds, from Sparrows Tavern, to Al's The Corner Club, to Fuzzy's, to Mudryck's, to The Curve Inn, to Johnny's Gay Club (long before the word took on its current meaning). His last stop was always Polizzi's Tavern, where his mother worked. As he waited for her shift to end, he'd watch with rapt attention as the owner, Frank Polizzi, held forth behind the bar, telling the best stories he'd ever heard. Tom marveled that Polizzi's vocabulary, inflections, and imitations of various accents could make strange sounds come out of the customers' mouths. He didn't have a TV; he'd never seen a comedian. This was his first exposure to comedy and laughter, and he was mesmerized. He'd take Polizzi's stories back to the playground at Ascension grade school and try them out on his Catholic playmates. He didn't understand some of the stories; he just knew that Polizzi's customers had laughed at them.

Frank Polizzi was a big, tough, good-looking, charismatic guy who was married to Tom's mother's sister, which made him Tom's uncle. Tom would learn as a young man that Polizzi was also his real father. His mother had had a fling with her brother-in-law, and he had been the result. That finally explained why he was the only Dreesen kid who wasn't fair-haired and blue-eyed. Walter Dreesen went to his grave without figuring it out, however.

At fifteen, Tom ran away from home and was arrested and briefly jailed in Hammond, Indiana, before being sent back to Harvey. At sixteen, he quit school because he could no longer stand the taunts from his classmates about his shabby clothes. On his seventeenth birthday, he finally escaped the poverty by joining the navy, where for the first time in his life he slept in a bed by himself, ate three meals in the same day, and experienced a hot shower.

Dreesen and Reid met in 1968 when Dreesen was attempting a wider launch of a drug-education program for kids that he'd developed as part of the Jaycees in Harvey, where nearly 80 percent of crime was drug related. Reid attended a meeting at which Dreesen was presenting his program to a community group. After the meeting, he introduced himself and said he'd like to work with Dreesen on it. The program became a huge success, eventually spreading to all fifty states and dozens of foreign countries. And Dreesen and Reid proved a big hit with the kids, to the point that an eighth-grade girl said to them one day, "You guys are really funny together; you oughta become a comedy team." So they did.

At the Improv, Dreesen and Reid arranged a so-called showcase audition for Craig Tennis, the talent coordinator for *The Tonight Show*. Other than giving them a time slot, Budd Friedman wasn't particularly friendly or accommodating. They asked for two microphones and two stools, but when they got up on stage, there was only one of each, so they had to hand the single microphone back and forth, which wreaked havoc with their timing. Tennis said afterwards that he liked their act and thought they showed promise, but he didn't think they were ready for *The Tonight Show*.

On the bus back to Chicago, they were disappointed about the audition but also energized by their overall experience at the Improv—and full of ideas. There was no comedy club in Chicago, no stage where comics could try out new material, experiment without fear, and dare to fail. "We need a place where we can be bad," Dreesen kept saying. Within weeks, he convinced a Chicago club owner named Henry Norton to let him take over his place on Monday night and put on a lineup of stand-up comics. "Comedy on Monday Night at *Le Pub*" was patterned after the Improv, with Dreesen in the Budd Friedman role as emcee. In a classic case of "if you build it, they will come," young wanna-be comics started coming out of the woodwork to audition, and a small stand-up community began forming where there'd been none before.

# Mitzi's Store

In the spring of 1972, NBC set off a shockwave in the entertainment industry with the announcement that after eighteen years as a New York institution, *The Tonight Show* was moving from New York City to the Los Angeles suburb of Burbank.

Over the years, a large proportion of the show's guests had been drawn from New York's creative ranks—Broadway actors, singers, dancers, and songwriters; novelists, magazine writers, and newspaper columnists; and, of course, comics—all of whom wondered what was going to happen with those guest spots now that Johnny was going Hollywood. Comedians were particularly concerned. Many of them lived in New York—had moved there—because of *The Tonight Show*. Now, the center of power had shifted to Los Angeles. The Improv was a great place to work out, but would the dynamic be the same with *The Tonight Show* 3,000 miles away?

Steve Lubetkin fretted more than most. He worshipped Johnny Carson, often telling the story of how he once ran into the Great Man on the street as he was getting out of his car. Steve went up to him, introduced himself, and said he was a stand-up comic and that he hoped to be on the show some day. Carson was friendly, shook his hand, and wished him luck. As Steve walked away, he couldn't help it—he blew Johnny a kiss. Now Lubetkin worried that Carson's move west would make it more difficult for him to realize his career goals. What was *The Tonight Show* going to do, send someone back to New York a couple times a year to scout for East Coast talent? How was he ever going to get noticed?

He talked about his worries with Richard Lewis, but Richard didn't seem all that concerned. He was too busy. Freed from day-job hell by David Brenner's largesse, he'd worked his way up to head-liner status at the Improv, getting prime-time slots on the week-ends. When he wasn't writing or performing, he was enjoying one of the by-products of his new status: women, lots of them. Every night when he came off the stage, he'd hit the bar, and there they'd be, waiting for him. They didn't even seem to mind having to schlep to his crummy guesthouse in Paramus to have sex with him.

Steve wasn't doing nearly as well. For one thing, he was still living at home with his father. He'd appeared on one local TV show, *The Joe Franklin Show*, but he was stuck in place at the Improv, still relegated to occasional late-night spots during the week. Richard had eclipsed him.

After weeks of worry over what would happen with Johnny gone, Lubetkin decided what he had to do: He was going to follow *The Tonight Show*. He was moving to Los Angeles. His destiny was waiting there; he was certain.

On April 10, 1972, a few weeks before *The Tonight Show*'s West Coast debut, an old-school comic named Sammy Shore opened a small club on Sunset Strip in the building that once housed Ciro's, the famed Hollywood nightspot of the 1930s and 1940s. The launch of Shore's ninety-nine-seat club passed unnoticed by the media and most of the comedy community. But together, the two events were about to bring big changes to the business of laughter.

When Shore and his partner, Rudy DeLuca, were trying to come up with a name for their new venture—the Fun Spot? Sammy Shore's Club?—Shore's wife Mitzi piped up from the kitchen, "Why don't you call it the Comedy Store?" It would become one of the most recognizable brand names in show business, but it was a misnomer in the beginning. The Comedy Co-op would have been more accurate.

Shore had forged a successful career as a warm-up act for such mainstream nightclub performers as Ann Margaret, Tony Bennett, and Sammy Davis Jr., and he was coming off a five-year run opening for Elvis Presley in Las Vegas and on tour. But he was not a businessman. He saw the Comedy Store as a place where he and his comedy pals could hang out and entertain one another between real jobs on the road. He had a rent-free deal with the owner of the building and a vague agreement to split whatever was left over from cover charges and drinks after expenses. But it really didn't matter to Sammy. Profit was not part of his equation. This wasn't about making money; it was about having fun.

And the Comedy Store was riotous, free-form fun in those early days. No one, not even Shore, knew who would be performing on any given night. It all depended on who was in town and happened to walk in the door. It might be anyone from Norm Crosby to Buddy Hackett to Jackie Vernon or a dozen other Shore contemporaries. Flip Wilson showed up regularly, arriving in his blue Rolls with license plates that read "Killer" and awarding a hundred-dollar bill to the evening's "ugliest comic." Redd Foxx was the biggest star on TV at the time with his *Sanford & Son* sitcom, so he got extra-special treatment: Whenever Redd came around, Sammy immediately cleared the stage for him to go on. Foxx could do an hour off the top of his head—and often did. Shore never cut him off.

If the night was going well, Sammy let it go on and on. He'd stop letting people in the door and send the bartender home at the legal closing time of 2:00 a.m., but the show sometimes continued until as late as 5:00 in the morning. The comics went behind the bar and poured their own drinks. Sammy didn't charge them. How could he when they were working his place for free?

Filling in the gaps between the big names was a resident troupe of younger improv performers, the Comedy Store Players, which included Valerie Curtin (who would become a successful actress and screenwriter), her husband-to-be Barry Levinson (later the prolific writer, director, and producer of such films as *Diner* and *Wag the Dog*), Craig T. Nelson (of TV's *Coach*), and Pat Proft (who went on to mint money as the creator of the *Police Academy* movie franchise).

The arrival of *The Tonight Show* brought in even more talent. New York–based comics like David Brenner and Robert Klein started stopping by to try out their new material on a West Coast audience the night before they appeared on Carson. *Tonight Show* talent coordinator Jim McCawley dropped in once or twice a week. It was like the Improv, but with better weather.

One day Shore got a phone call from TV producer James Komack asking him to "put this Mexican kid on for me tomorrow night. I want some people to see him." Shore had never heard of Freddie Prinze (who was not Mexican but rather half Puerto Rican and half Hungarian, or "Hungarican" as he liked to say), but he put him on at 10 p.m. the next night as requested. The people that Komack wanted to see Prinze turned out to be *The Tonight Show*'s Jim McCawley and some NBC executives.

As he watched Prinze's set, Shore had to admit the kid was young, fresh, and impressive, and he could tell that the TV guys liked what they saw. But the middle-aged comic felt a twinge of jealousy as he watched the proverbial big break wash over a performer not yet out of his teens. Look at this little shit, he thought. And I'm having trouble trying to get a deal for a damn talk show.

What happened next has become the stuff of show biz legend, much like the discovery of Lana Turner at the lunch counter at Schwab's Drug Store. On December 6, 1973, Prinze appeared on *The Tonight Show*. His friends at the Improv were gathered around the TV on the bar, watching as he broke through the curtains. Freddie did an engaging five-minute set that so tickled Carson that the host immediately waved him over to the panel to chat. Jaws dropped at the Improv, where the crowd of compulsive Carson watchers instantly recognized that they were seeing history: Never before had Johnny done that for a young comic making his debut on the show. Comments around the bar ranged from "Holy shit," to "I can't fucking believe this," to "Right on, Freddie."

Within weeks, NBC announced that it had signed Prinze to star in the title role of a new NBC sitcom called *Chico and the Man.* Overnight Freddie had become rich and famous. He was only nineteen. (The next time anyone saw him at the Improv, he was climbing out of a limousine wearing a purple velvet suit, two babes on his arms, high on quaaludes, and headed for big trouble.)

Few comics failed to notice one more thing about Prinze's *Tonight Show* debut: Johnny introduced him as "a young comedian who's appearing here in town at the Comedy Store." That statement put the Comedy Store on every comic's map and created a new equation in their heads: One set at the Comedy Store plus one appearance on Carson equals the whole world. If it happened to Freddie, then it could happen to any of them. You could almost hear the suitcases being packed.

Sammy Shore's bags were packed, too. As 1973 came to a close, he had to return to Las Vegas to fulfill a contract with the Hilton left over from his days with Elvis. He would be working solo in the lounge for several months, which posed a problem: Who was going to run the Comedy Store while he was gone? Rudy DeLuca was going to work as a writer for *The Carol Burnett Show.* The only person he could think of to take over was his wife, Mitzi. They'd been married nearly twenty years and had four children, ages six to nineteen. She had been the quintessential long-suffering showman's wife, raising the kids alone while he was on the road and sometimes hauling them along with her to wherever he was performing, which is how the youngest, Pauly, came to pee on Elvis's pant leg. Careerwise, Sammy was no Bill Cosby, but he'd been a good provider. The Shores owned a beautiful home on Doheny Drive in Beverly Hills that was built by Cecil B. DeMille for his daughter and over the years had been the residence of Dorothy Lamour,

Joan Blondell, Andy Williams, and Carol Burnett. But Sammy knew that Mitzi had ambitions beyond homemaking. She had been a career girl when he met her: Mitzi Lee Saidel, the twenty-year-old secretary to the owner of the Pinewood Resort in Elkhart Lake, Wisconsin, where he was the social director. She was attracted by his Jewishness. "I grew up as the only Jew in Green Bay," she joked. Everything about her was different from any other woman he'd ever met—from the way she dressed (vaguely bohemian, dramatic), to the way she talked (in a piercing nasal voice that once heard can't be forgotten), to the way she thought ("When everyone else goes right, she goes left," Sammy always said). And she was smart as hell. She'd done fairly well as the proprietress of the Pickle Barrel, a funky clothing store/gift shop that Sammy financed for her across the street from the Comedy Store. But it bored her, so they closed it down after eight months.

Sammy knew that Mitzi loved comedians, finding them endlessly fascinating. So he asked her, "Why don't you take over the Store while I'm in Vegas? Run the place. It'll be fun for you." She said okay with no visible excitement. But once he was gone, she jumped on the opportunity like a dog on a bone.

She turned her attention first to the growing number of young comics who'd been coming in night after night and sitting in the back hoping to get on. Under Sammy's whoever's-famous-goes-first rule, they rarely got a chance. But Mitzi saw potential in the youngsters, both as performers and as a labor pool. She immediately set them to work at $2.50 an hour redecorating the club to her specifications. She had them paint the entire room black— walls, ceilings, tables—and ordered that the stage be lit with a single spotlight. "That way, all of the audience's attention is focused on the comic," she explained. She removed the bar from the room and put it in the back by the kitchen so that patrons had no access to it and had to order their drinks from cocktail waitresses, who then brought them to the tables. She initiated a two-drink minimum. Taking a page from Budd Friedman's playbook, she established Monday as "Potluck Night," when anyone could get up on stage for a few minutes to try out. And she instituted a system of nightly lineups, featuring a dozen or more young comics, starting with beginners doing five-minute sets in the early evening and then moving to increasingly polished performers and longer sets as the night went on and the crowd grew. No one stayed onstage more than twenty minutes. She put on two shows a night, clearing the room after the first to make way for another paying audience. Each show was stitched together by an emcee and tightly timed with an amber light that warned performers they had sixty seconds to wrap it up and get off the stage. Comics were supposed to check with the club on Monday to get their assigned time slots for the following week and to take the stage on the minute. Mitzi made the comics run on time.

And she made herself into the impresario, personally putting together each night's lineup and determining the order and length of more than a hundred sets per week, based on her knowledge of each comic's act. Unlike Budd Friedman, she believed that a comic *could* follow a comic if you carefully managed the mix of material and the pacing, always building to a big finish at the end. "You have to produce the show," she said. "You can't just let it happen."

The one thing she didn't change was Sammy's policy of not paying the comics. The way she saw it, the Comedy Store was a place for them to find opportunity, not their employer.

After a month in Vegas, Sammy arrived back in town and was astonished by the changes Mitzi had wrought. For starters, the place was packed; there was hardly an empty seat. The bar was gone, the room was black on black, and the only thing you could see clearly was the young comic onstage. Instead of a middle-aged bartender, young waitresses slung drinks right and left. Mitzi sat at the cash register just inside the entrance, barking instructions. Everything was very neat and clean, with plants hanging all around. Fucking plants! He greeted her with his best, "Hi, Honey,

I'm home," and she looked at him and said, "Yeah, hi, Sammy, could you give me a minute and step out of the way there." Then she turned to a young comic he'd never seen before and said, "Okay, you are going on at 10:15 for fifteen minutes and then you get off, understand?"

Sammy felt the ground move under his feet. "Oh, my God," he thought. "She's finally found something she's been looking for all her life, and she doesn't need me anymore. She doesn't want to get off that seat. I'm history."

He was right. Within months they were in divorce proceedings. Mitzi hired hotshot divorce attorney Marvin Mitchelson, who would later pioneer the concept of "palimony" for unmarried cohabitants. In the end, Mitzi got the house and the club. Thanks to Mitchelson's penchant for publicity, it was reported that Sammy "lost" the club. In fact, he voluntarily relinquished his share of ownership in exchange for a reduction in alimony from $1,100 to $600 a month. Though ridiculed as "the man who gave away the Store," he really didn't care that much about the club. It had been fun, but he felt no emotional connection to it. No one had discovered *him* there. And he thought Mitzi deserved it. After all, she'd turned it into a business.

Steve Lubetkin was one of the first of the New York Improv comics to head west. "All the action is out in California," he told his father. "If I'm really going to do something with this, then I have to go to the Comedy Store."

Jack Lubetkin and Steve's brother, Barry, were concerned. Jack couldn't see how you could make a career out of comedy when it didn't pay a living wage. Ten or twenty bucks for a night's work? You could do better at McDonald's. Barry knew Steve had talent—he'd seen him on stage many times and been filled with pride that his little brother could get up in front of a room full of strangers and make them laugh. But he also knew that Steve was a fragile soul, sensitive to rejection, with a tendency toward sadness. He'd seen how Steve reacted whenever he bombed: he'd be angry and hurt, and you couldn't even talk to him for a few minutes. Steve had never really been away from home. He'd gone to college on Long Island. How would he fare in a tough town like Los Angeles?

But Steve was determined and convincing. He pointed to Freddie Prinze and Jimmie Walker, who'd just been cast in a new sitcom called *Good Times* after auditioning at the Comedy Store. "I *know* these guys; they're my *friends*," he said. "I can do that, too."

So, Jack Lubetkin flew to Los Angeles with Steve to help him find an apartment for between $100 and $200 a month. They settled on a one-bedroom with a few pieces of shabby furniture in a building located where La Cienega Boulevard dead-ended at Sunset Strip. It was a dump, but to Steve it was better than a penthouse on Park Avenue because he could walk to the Comedy Store in eight minutes. He was there the very next Monday night, standing in line with several dozen others waiting to take their first step toward comedy stardom: auditioning for Mitzi Shore. He couldn't quite believe it when he got on that night or that he did as well as he did. But Shore said to him afterward, "You're funny. Come back next week." He did, and every night in between. Soon he was getting weeknight time slots, not prime-time spots but more than Budd Friedman ever gave him. He quickly became part of Shore's inner circle of young male comics who doted on her and ran her errands. She invited him to dinner at her house, and he was among the few she allowed to join her in her special booth at the club. In his mind, she became as important to his future as Johnny Carson. He felt like he was finally on a roll, in the right place at the right time. It was all going to happen for him, he was sure of it.

Lubetkin fell right in with other recent comedy émigrés, including George Miller, who'd come down from Seattle the year before and lived in an apartment building directly across the street from the Store. Johnny Dark lived in an apartment a few blocks away on Laurel Avenue. Dark, a Philadelphian, had come to Los Angeles from Atlanta, where he'd been the drummer and lead singer in a lounge band called the Johnny Dark Thing. Now he was trying his hand at stand-up, and Mitzi Shore liked him. Dark's wife, Suzy, was a waitress at the Comedy Store, which meant that she got paid, but he didn't. Half a dozen other Comedy Store performers lived in Dark's building, including Steve Bluestein, who was a buyer for Macy's by day, and Alan Bursky, the youngest comic ever to appear on *The Tonight Show* (he was eighteen at the time but looked twelve). Bursky's parents, Herman and Helen, managed the apartment building, which would eventually house more than twenty comics and become known as Fort Bursky.

With their new TV shows being produced in Los Angeles, Freddie Prinze and Jimmie Walker started showing up at the Comedy Store all the time, either to perform or hang out. Prinze moved in with Bursky. Another Improv alum, Steve Landesberg, began coming into town regularly to do showcase auditions at the Store, trying to land a TV job.

It was all getting too much for Jay Leno. Back in Boston, he was watching *The Tonight Show* when Carson introduced another "young comedian who is appearing here in town at the Comedy Store." It was Walker. Leno had performed on the same bill with Jimmie many times at the Improv and other clubs, and he'd done as well, if not better, with the crowd. So why was Jimmie now performing ten feet away from Johnny while he was sitting on the couch in this crummy apartment? He would later describe it as a "pivotal" moment in his life and career. He stood up and announced to the empty room. "That's it. I'm going to the Comedy Store." He booked a flight to Los Angeles, and the next day he withdrew his $1,500 in savings, packed a single bag, and walked out of his apartment, leaving the door open behind him. "Take whatever you want," he told the neighbors.

In Los Angeles, he instructed the cab driver, "Take me to Sunset Strip." He spent his first night in town sleeping on the couch of a comedian pal, Billy Braver, who lived in the same building as George Miller. For the next few weeks, he lived like a vagabond, bouncing from couch to couch, crashing for several days at Freddie Prinze's place in Fort Bursky, even sleeping on the back stairs at the Comedy Store several nights. The police stopped him one night at the corner of Hollywood and Vine.

"Where do you live?" one cop asked him.

"I'm a comedian, and I don't really live anywhere yet," he said. They told him to get into the squad car, and he rode around with them for the whole shift, telling jokes.

All in all, Leno's transition was fairly painless. He quickly won over Mitzi Shore and became a regular at the Comedy Store, getting prime-time spots in the lineup. He vowed to himself that he wouldn't take a straight job to support himself. He was going to sink or swim as a comic.

Richard Lewis made his first foray to Los Angeles in February 1974. He flew in to do a paid gig at the Ice House in Pasadena and took a bus from the airport to Lubetkin's apartment. The first thing Steve did was walk him over to the Comedy Store to show him around. Lewis was shocked by how many comics there were—standing in the back hallway waiting to go on or hitting on girls as they came out of the restroom, gathered in groups around the front entrance or in the parking lot, sitting in cars smoking pot. It was almost overwhelming. Steve's fixation on Mitzi Shore, about whom he talked incessantly, seemed a bit extreme, but he appeared to be in his element, happy and confident. Which was surprising, considering that, according to Steve, he'd just been rejected by *The Tonight Show*.

Once again, it had been a case of almost but not quite. The way Steve told it, a *Tonight Show* talent coordinator had caught him at the Comedy Store and asked him to call the office the following week. But the next night, the same guy happened by a little club where Steve was trying out some new material that didn't go over with the audience. So, when Steve called, he was told, in effect, "Never mind."

"Oh, man, I'm sorry," Lewis said, trying to imagine the disappointment of being turned down by *The Tonight Show*. But Steve shrugged it off, saying he wasn't that upset about it because he had something bigger in the offing.

"I'm making a movie," he said. "I wrote it, and I'm starring in it. It's called *Dante Shocko*, and it's a bizarre comedy about this guy who competes in a Man of the Year contest to see who's the best athlete, chess player, lover, killer, and a bunch of other things."

"You're making a fucking movie?" Lewis replied, astonished.

Not only was he making it, Steve said, but he was also helping to raise the money and auditioning actors for the supporting roles. He was hooked up with an experienced producer and director, and they were hoping to sell the movie to a major Hollywood studio. He had even conducted his own market research into its earning potential: He had asked nine of his friends to watch Mel Brooks's smash hit *Blazing Saddles* and to mark down each time they laughed and to note exactly what kind of laugh it was. Then he asked them to do the same thing while reading his *Dante Shocko* script. The result, he reported proudly, was that while *Blazing Saddles* elicited an average of 7 "killer laughs," 15 "mediums," and 27 "chuckles and strong smiles" for a total score of 49, *Dante* produced an average of 60 killers, 106 mediums, and 126 chuckles for a total of 292. Which meant that *Dante* was five times funnier than a movie that had grossed more than $100 million at the box office. "It's staggering to think what *Dante* can make," he said.

Steve never ceased to amaze Richard. First, he had the balls to just pick up and move to Los Angeles, and now he was trying to be the next Woody Allen or Mel Brooks. Lewis admired his friend's courage, his drive and ability to dream large, but he worried about him, too. It seemed that Steve's expressing himself creatively was never a means to an end, a step toward a certain career plateau. Rather, it was as though Steve viewed each gig, each set, as a test that he took too seriously. For Steve, every night was *Hamlet*.

Lewis did well at the Ice House, so well that *Tonight Show* talent coordinator Craig Tennis contacted him the next day. "I caught your act last night," Tennis said. "We'd like you to be on the show." It was the call every young comic dreams of getting. He immediately phoned practically everyone he knew back East. "I'm going to be on *The Tonight Show* in two weeks!"

For his national TV debut on March 27, Lewis wore an aqua blue, Western-style leisure suit with a yellow turtleneck. It was an era-appropriate outfit, but, as he would say later, "I looked like a Jewish marionette that was stalking the Muppets." Lubetkin and Steve Landesberg accompanied him to NBC Studios in Burbank and sat in the green room with him during the taping. With time starting to run out, Carson and actor George Peppard became engaged in an interminable and decidedly unfunny discussion of their respective smoking habits, puffing on cigarettes the whole while. At one point Peppard said to Carson, "Well, John, my cancer is slower than yours." You could have heard a pin drop in the audience. With seven minutes remaining in the show, Lewis got his cue. At the curtain, he froze for a second, but Landesberg literally put a foot in his butt and pushed him through.

Lewis had his five minutes down pat. He'd run the lines a thousand times, until he could do the material in his sleep—from the shiny yellow raincoat his mother made him wear to school "so child molesters could see me through a dense fog" to his high school coach "Moose Blechas," who wouldn't excuse a kid from gym class for any reason: "But, Coach, I have the *measles.* . . . Walk it off!"

Sensing correctly that the smoking conversation had left the audience down, he tried to get them back up, working the room as if he were at the Improv, playing to the three hundred people present instead of the millions watching at home. As a result, on the small screen he seemed to be trying too hard, looking off camera and waving his arms frenetically.

When he was done, Carson smiled and clapped politely but didn't invite Richard over to the panel or even give him the big okay sign. Word came the next day that Carson was upset with

Craig Tennis, saying, "You brought that kid on too early. He wasn't ready." Johnny thought he "needed a little seasoning" before he could come back.

Lewis was devastated. After three years of working day and night, he'd finally gotten his big break, and he'd blown it. He knew Carson was right. On TV, if you move around a lot, you look like an amateur. "I was like some escaped mental patient from a comedy jail," he wailed to Lubetkin.

Lewis flew back to New York in a funk, knowing he was going to have to serve some time in purgatory before he got back on *The Tonight Show*. He returned to headlining at the Improv and watched as two former headliner pals of his scored big in Los Angeles.

*Chico and the Man* and *Good Times* were smash hits out of the box, making Freddie Prinze and Jimmie Walker the breakout stars of the 1974 television season. Their characters' trademark expressions—"It's not my job" in the case of Prinze's Chico and "Dy-no-mite" from Walker's J. J. character—entered the American lexicon, picked up and repeated by millions of young viewers. The word quickly went out from the TV networks to all Hollywood agents and production companies: If you want a show on the air in the 1975 season, then bring us your young and hungry stand-up comedians.

With that, the Great California Comedy Rush was on in earnest, and few would be able to resist its pull. Not even Budd Friedman and the Improv.

# Tom, Dave, and George

America's only black-and-white stand-up comedy team broke up in early 1975 when Tim Reid told Tom Dreesen that he needed to strike out on his own. Dreesen probably should have seen it coming, but he didn't. He was devastated and scared. He had a wife and three small children to support (ages four, seven, and ten), and without Tim, he had no act; he was just another white comic with barely five minutes of material.

As he sat downing beer after beer in his favorite Chicago hangout, the Sulky, Dreesen pondered his choices. He either had to find a new black partner or come up with an hour's worth of new material, which could take months, even a year. Or he could do what his wife wanted him to do: give up his comedy dream and take a steady, stay-in-town job in a local factory. He pushed his beer across the bar and got up off the stool.

"Is that it, Tommy?" the bartender asked. "Are you quitting for the night?"

"No, I'm quitting for good," Dreesen replied. He was referring to the alcohol, not to comedy. He'd made up his mind. He was going to go it alone, and he didn't want anything to get in the way.

Tim and Tom's last appearance together was at a club in Houston. The split was amicable. (Reid soon gained fame as the pimped-out disc jockey Venus Flytrap in the TV series *WKRP in Cincinnati*.) Dreesen hopped a plane from Houston to Los Angeles, where the twin beacons of *The Tonight Show* and the Comedy Store beckoned. He told his wife he'd only be gone for two weeks, just enough time to establish a beachhead, and then he'd be back for her and the kids.

He hustled up free lodging by house-sitting for a girl singer he knew, Pat Hollis, who was going on the road for a few weeks. For transportation, he used his thumb, hitchhiking from Hollis's house in West LA to the Comedy Store. He'd been there before, when he and Reid played the Los Angeles Playboy Club in 1973, so he knew the drill. On his first Monday night in town, he lined up with all the other hopefuls on the sidewalk in front of the club. It didn't matter that he'd been a working comic for nearly six years. He had to prove his worth with five minutes of material in front of Mitzi Shore. If he passed muster, then he could use the Comedy Store stage as a springboard to Carson. If he didn't, then he could always be a factory worker in Chicago. No pressure or anything.

It took him a month of Mondays and every day in between to get an audition with Shore. "Well, you're funny, and you've got some polish from working before," she said (he had never heard such a voice). "We can use you here."

The break came not a moment too soon. Pat Hollis had come back off the road and told him he had to leave. Her boyfriend was very jealous and didn't like the idea of her sharing her house with another man. So, Dreesen moved into an old Nash Rambler that was sitting up on blocks in the alley behind Hollis's house. Fortunately, it had a fold-down front seat, so he could sleep. Thanks to his childhood training, he knew how to bathe in the restroom sink of a nearby gas station. And he survived on one meal a day at Kentucky Fried Chicken, where the "Corn and Cluck for Under a

Buck" promotion offered two pieces of chicken, a small ear of corn, mashed potatoes, gravy, and coleslaw for ninety-nine cents. His only break from the Colonel's cuisine came the day he hitched over to Jay Leno's house. Leno wasn't home, but the pretty girl who opened the door invited him in anyway.

"You hungry?" she asked. "Want something to eat?"

"Yeah, sure," he said.

She looked in the refrigerator. "How 'bout a steak?"

Dreesen almost laughed out loud. Good old Jay, the Charlie Hustle of stand-up. In town only a matter of weeks and already he had a nice place to live, a good-looking girlfriend, and enough work to afford steak. The one the girl served Dreesen turned out to be the last one in Leno's fridge, which made it taste even more delicious.

Mitzi Shore put Dreesen in the regular lineup—early and late spots, not prime time—and agreed to let him emcee occasionally. After a few weeks, he decided it was time to return to Chicago and round up his family, so he hatched a plan to pay his way back home. Pretending to be the manager of a hot new stand-up comic named Tom Dreesen, he called the booking office of a new talk show in Edmonton, Canada, which was paying comics $300 per appearance and flying them round-trip first class. He told them that Dreesen had been on *The Merv Griffin Show* and *The David Frost Show* (he didn't mention that he'd appeared as part of a team) and was now a rising star at the Comedy Store. They not only booked him but agreed to fly him home to Chicago rather than back to Los Angeles after his appearance. Once in Chicago, Dreesen talked the owner of Mr. Kelly's nightclub into letting him open for Fats Domino for two weeks at a whopping $750 a week. He needed every cent of that money to convince his wife to pack up the kids and return with him to Los Angeles.

The Dreesens drove across the country in tandem in a pickup truck and a beat up VW bug. They rented an apartment in the

San Fernando Valley for $225. Tom immediately applied for unemployment and food stamps and went to work at the Comedy Store, a state-funded stand-up comic.

A few months later, in May 1975, twenty-eight-year-old David Letterman and his wife, Michelle, left Indiana and drove to Los Angeles in tandem, he in his 1973 half-ton Chevy pickup, "Old Red," and she in their 1972 Oldsmobile Cutlass. The pair had met and married when they were students at Ball State University in Muncie, Indiana, where he majored in radio and television. After college, David became a minor celebrity in his hometown of Indianapolis as the host of a 2:00 a.m. movie show and a substitute weekend weatherman on WLWI-TV. It was there that he pioneered the concept of irony in weathercasting, making up fictitious weather phenomena and spicing up the daily temperature readings with wry comments like, "Muncie, 42 . . . Anderson, 44 . . . always a close game,"* which didn't always go over well in rural central Indiana, where most folks liked their weather straight. He also used the station to incubate what would later become some of his trademark late-night bits—making fun of management and using staff members and passers-by (sometimes cruelly) as unwitting foils.

Unlike Dreesen and the others, Letterman wasn't moving to Los Angeles hoping to make it big as a stand-up comic. Performing live was not his thing. He'd been required to make all manner of public appearances as part of his TV gig in Indianapolis, and he'd hated every minute of it. The prospect of an upcoming event would cause him to lose sleep for a week, so that he constantly questioned himself, If it were in me to do this, then wouldn't it be easier?

---

*Caroline Lathan, *The David Letterman Story: An Unauthorized Biography* (London: Franklin Watts, 1987).

Letterman's ambition in going to Los Angeles was to land a job *writing* for television, preferably for Johnny Carson, his hero. He'd gleaned from watching *The Tonight Show* that performing at the Comedy Store was a good way to get Carson's attention, so he saw the Comedy Store as a necessary evil. Two months earlier, he'd flown to LA on a reconnaissance mission. Even though it was a Tuesday night, the Sunset club was jam-packed. The first comic he saw perform was George Miller, who was doing a routine about working in a Hollywood mailroom where the workers rated the executives as stamps; one guy was known as a "five center," another as "air mail." The punch line was about the stupidest executive of all: "Imagine what it's like to be known as 'postage due.'" It was a really dumb joke, but the crowd laughed, and Letterman did, too, thinking to himself, Oh, hell, I can do this.

On his first Monday night in Los Angeles, he jumped right back into the fire, lining up with the other hopefuls waiting to audition for Mitzi Shore. His turn came just before midnight. As he stepped onto the stage, he was immediately unnerved by the white-hot intensity of the spotlight. It felt as if he were standing on a train track with a high-speed bullet train bearing down on him. The next five minutes seemed to take forever, and afterward, he was sure he'd bombed. But Shore apparently saw something she liked in his Midwestern manner. "That was nice," she said. "You should come back."

He didn't realize that meant he had passed the test; he thought she was just being polite. He went home feeling relieved that he hadn't blown it completely and clinging to the hope that someone from the club would call him soon about trying out again. In the meantime, he spent his time writing new material and hanging with the comics who gathered in clumps every night in the parking lot of the Sunset club. The first comic he introduced himself to was Dreesen because he seemed the most approachable.

More than a week passed with no call from the Comedy Store. When he felt comfortable enough around the other comics, he confided that he was concerned that he hadn't heard anything. He wasn't going to, they told him, because that wasn't how it worked. Based on what Mitzi had said to him, he was supposed to call in to the club during the day on Monday and inform them of his availability to work the following week. Then, if Mitzi really thought he was ready for the Original Room, someone would call him Tuesday afternoon with assigned time slots. If he didn't get a call on Tuesday, then he should show up again for Monday night tryouts. That was Mitzi's system.

Letterman likened it to trying out for the high school basketball team: If you didn't make the cut, nobody told you directly. Your name just didn't appear on the list the coach posted on the bulletin board. He felt like such a freshman.

He phoned in his availability the next Monday and held his breath. Sure enough, he got a call back on Tuesday assigning him time slots for the week. They weren't in prime time, but they were a start. The other comics quickly took notice of him because he wasn't like anyone else. For starters, he didn't tell jokes. He used everyday experiences as the setup and then supplied his own punch line, like the dreaded call from the mechanic telling you there's a lot more wrong with your car than you'd thought: "Yeah, Dave, this is Earl down at the garage. . . . We were adjusting the dials on your radio . . . and the engine blew up. . . . Yeah, it killed one of our guys."

The other comics also noticed that Letterman didn't sound like the rest of them. He didn't have the staccato cadence and hard sell delivery that usually came with being a club comic. He sounded more like a broadcaster—smooth, controlled, conversational—in the style of Carson, Steve Allen, and Jack Paar. That, combined with his caustic wit and ability to turn the tables on hecklers, created a presence on stage that belied his limited experience and cued his fellow comics that a major talent had arrived. It also helped to offset his appearance: the Hoosier clothes and scraggily red beard that Jay Leno said made him look like "either Dinty Moore or Paul Bunyan's son."*

Johnny Dark thought Letterman was a "hayseed" when he first met him. They were standing in the hallway by the Comedy Store restroom waiting for Letterman to go on. Letterman introduced himself, called him "Mr. Dark," and said how much he admired his act. Dark then watched as the scruffy newcomer took the stage and faced a crowd that had been tough all night. "They are going to eat this kid," he thought.

Instead, Letterman took it right to them. "So what do you puds want to talk about tonight?" were the first words out of his mouth. From opposite sides of the room, two men heckled him simultaneously. He fired back, "Are you two guys sharing a brain?" The crowd roared. After that, he owned them. Johnny Dark was awed.

Given Letterman's cocksure stage manner, other comics were surprised to discover that offstage he was shy and socially ill at ease. Fellow Midwesterner Tom Dreesen took an instant liking to him. They were both married, lived in the San Fernando Valley, and had their days free, so they quickly bonded over sports activity. Dreesen invited Letterman to play racquetball and join in pickup basketball games at the Van Nuys YMCA. When Dreesen put together a Comedy Store basketball team, the Bombers, he drafted Letterman as the power forward. Tim Reid, Jimmie Walker, and Johnny Witherspoon also played on the team, as did Paul Mooney's twin sons, Daryl and Dwayne, who would only pass to one another, which meant that their teammates constantly had to steal the ball from them.

Dreesen worked hard to draw Letterman into his ever-widening social circle of comics. It wasn't easy because Letterman was a

---

*Jay Leno with Bill Zehme, *Leading with My Chin* (New York: Harper-Collins, 1996).

loner, almost to the point of being a recluse. He was comfortable
hanging out with Dreesen one-on-one, shooting hoops, and having a sandwich, but he was uneasy in the kind of larger group situation that Dreesen was constantly engineering. But Dreesen pulled
him along, counseling, "Always remember that your fellow comics
will get you more work than any agent or manager ever will." Their
routine was to meet up at the Comedy Store before the show
started, catch everyone's set, and then, because the Store didn't
have a bar to hang out in, move to either Theodore's, an upscale
coffeehouse on Santa Monica Boulevard in West Hollywood, or
Canter's Deli in the Fairfax District, where they'd laugh and swap
stories until 3:00 or 4:00 a.m. The group usually included Johnny
Dark, George Miller, Jay Leno, Steve Bluestein, Johnny Witherspoon, Jimmie Walker, and whomever else Dreesen could round
up. On weekends, they'd sometimes cross over the Hollywood
Hills to a San Fernando Valley club called the Show Biz that was
owned by Murray Langston, who later gained some fame by putting
a paper bag over his head and performing as the Unknown Comic.
One of the waitresses at the club was a then unknown Debra
Winger, a serious comedy groupie who had a crush on George
Miller at the time. At the Show Biz, comics would perform impromptu, and when business was good, Langston would throw
some money their way. Leo Gallagher was a Show Biz regular in
the days before he ditched his first name and began using his
"sledge-o-matic" to splatter audiences with smashed fruits and
vegetables.

It was a late-shift life guaranteed to wreak havoc with mar-
riages, as Letterman soon learned. With Michelle working during
the day as an assistant buyer for the May Company, the couple
rarely saw one another. When the inevitable split came and Michelle returned to Indiana brokenhearted, Letterman was guilt-
ridden and anguished. He soon moved into an apartment just
down the hallway from George Miller, and the two quickly became fast friends.

Miller was a true eccentric. Born George Dornberger (a "Nazi name," in his opinion), he was the only child of a single mother, Helen (his father abandoned them when George was a baby), with whom he maintained a lifelong love-hate relationship. Miller and his mom adored one another but fought constantly. He thought she was the funniest person he ever knew, and he frequently made merciless fun of her in his act, especially her penchant for worrying about his and everyone else's well-being. "George, it's been raining, and you know what happens," she once cautioned. "It gets cold, and then you have ice." Another time, she supposedly lectured a teenager who was sitting on the bus with his arm hanging out the window, "Young man, that's a very good way to lose an arm." In George's act, the teenager replied sarcastically, "Why, thank you very much, ma'am. Could you suggest a few other ways?"

If there had been a contest for worst-dressed comic, Miller would have won walking away. As far as anyone could tell, he'd worn the same rumpled brown sport coat and baggy corduroy pants every day for years, and he apparently owned a closet full of hideous shirts. The only wardrobe upgrade he ever invested in was an occasional new pair of deck shoes. Miller spent money on two things: his phone bill, which was often huge because he spent hours each day talking to comedian friends all over the country, invariably asking, "Are you bombing, too?" and food, which was something of an obsession with him. He talked about food all the time, questioning people constantly about where they'd eaten last and what they'd had. He seemed to know the daily special at every chain restaurant in the country: "It's pea soup Tuesday at Coco's." And he only ate one kind of cuisine—American home-style comfort food. His favorite bread was white, and he preferred to have a side of mashed potatoes and gravy with every meal. Basically, Miller ate what a teenager would eat in the 1950s.

Miller was an accomplished pool hustler and, despite his couch potato ways, not a bad shot on the basketball court, as

Letterman learned one day when George suckered him into shooting free throws for money. Letterman was stunned to find himself suddenly down $100 that he could not afford.

"I don't understand," George said. "If you were so concerned about losing the money, then why did you bet?"

Letterman looked at his doughy friend and replied, "Because it never occurred to me that I would lose to *you*."

Letterman found Miller's myriad idiosyncrasies endlessly amusing. But what he liked most about George was his wry wit and superb joke-writing skills. Miller was a master of the one-line setup and quick punch line, a kind of joke haiku that always cut to the core but was never mean-spirited. He was an irascible character but still sweet natured. "George goes for the jugular," Elayne Boosler liked to say, "but never with his teeth, only with his gums. He'll gum you to death."

For his part in the friendship, Miller seemed to like nothing more than to tweak Dave's natural state of unease. One evening he was having sex with a girlfriend on his couch when Letterman walked into the apartment without knocking. Letterman was horribly embarrassed, which Miller thought was a hoot. From then on, he made a point of always making love to the girl on the couch with the door unlocked in the hope that Letterman would walk in on them again. He got Dave one more time, but after that Dave always knocked.

Letterman would downplay his relationship with Leno in later years, but he was drawn strongly to Jay in the early days. The initial attraction was professional rather than personal. He admired, even envied, Leno's onstage craft. Letterman was never comfortable in the nightclub arena, always thought his performances were subpar, and constantly felt like an imposter in the company of real comics like Leno, Miller, and Dreesen. Leno, on the other hand, had confidence to burn and never seemed to sweat a blown line or a bad audience. Everything rolled off his back.

Letterman loved Leno's attitude and marveled at his ability to sell even a mediocre joke to a crowd. "Jay is absolutely the best at observational stuff," he told the *Los Angeles Times* in one of his earliest press interviews. "He has an amazing ability to take every-day stuff to the stage and make it work nine times out of ten." Letterman observed about Leno's act that he won over the audi-ence by treating them as if they were a group of his hip friends. They were all in it together, laughing at the absurdities of the world.

Leno was equally impressed with Letterman. He noted that Letterman was not one to work the room or prowl the stage, but he was a superb wordsmith who radiated smarts and constantly came up with some of the most original material he'd ever heard.

They quickly formed a mutual admiration society, watching and learning from one another. Night after night at the Comedy Store, when they weren't onstage, they were standing together in the back, taking it all in, studying everything. Their fellow comics came to think of them almost as a team, connected by an amper-sand like Abbott & Costello or Martin & Lewis. The consensus in the comedy community was that Leno & Letterman (or vice versa) were destined for big things.

Proving Tom Dreesen's dictum about comics getting each other work, Letterman landed his first paying job in Los Angeles work-ing with Leno as a joke writer for Jimmie Walker. They were each paid $100 a week and expected to come up with fifteen acceptable jokes. Their employer was actually Walker's company, shamelessly named Ebony Genius Management, which was run by Walker's managers, Helen Gorman and Jerry Kushnick, who eventually married. They quickly signed Leno and Letterman to talent con-tracts but saw Letterman primarily as a writer, not a performer. (Leno remained with Helen Kushnick until 1991, when her er-ratic behavior threatened to cost him his job as host of *The Tonight Show*. He reluctantly fired her at NBC's insistence.)

Letterman's next break came courtesy of Tom Dreesen. A TV
producer named Ron Greenberg recruited Dreesen to round up
some young comics to help in auditioning potential hosts for the
pilot of a new TV game show called *Throw Me a Line*. The comics
would act as stand-ins for a *Hollywood Squares*–type panel of celebrity guests that was to include Zsa Zsa Gabor, Jack Cassidy, and
Jan Murray. Their job was to throw funny lines back at the auditioning hosts, who included such daytime TV veterans as Jim
Lange of *Dating Game* fame and Lloyd Thaxton. For the first half-
hour run-through, the comics included Dreesen, Letterman, Leno,
Johnny Dark, and Elayne Boosler, who had just moved to town.
They were paid $6 each, and all of them performed well except
Letterman, who was so flat that Greenberg told Dreesen he didn't
want him back for the second session the next day. "This guy
doesn't get it. Find somebody else," he said.

But Dreesen dug in for his friend. "No, no, I promise you he
does get it, and he is *very* quick. He was just off today. He'll be
great tomorrow, I guarantee it."

Outside the studio Dreesen found Letterman leaning against
a parking meter, looking dejected. "I'm sorry," he said. "I was
awful."

"Don't worry about it," Dreesen said. "Just knock 'em out
tomorrow."

The next day Letterman tore the place up. The auditioning
host was Lloyd Thaxton, who Dave addressed variously as Boyd
and Floyd and even Hemorrhoid. When Thaxton read out one of
the scripted questions, "Why would someone wear garlic around
their neck," Dave ad-libbed in a Hoosier accent, "Because it goes
real good with a brown sport coat." Letterman was so sharp that
he raised everybody else's game, and the session proved a riotous
success (for everyone but Thaxton, who didn't get the gig). Jan
Murray and Jack Cassidy had stopped in to watch, and Murray
said to Greenberg, "These kids are wonderful. What do you need
us old farts for? You should shoot the show with them."

In the end, the "kids" were paid $150 each and sent on their way. But Letterman had made an important impression. An NBC development executive named Madeline David sat in on the Thaxton session and came away convinced that the network should try to develop a TV show with him.

In the meantime, Mitzi set him up with a gig at an IBM corporate retreat in Marina Del Rey. In an elaborate put-on dreamed up by some creative-services director, Letterman was hired to pretend he was a corporate goon brought in by the top brass to announce management layoffs. It was a task ideally suited to Letterman's borderline-cruel sense of humor. Armed with some names and a little bit of biographical information, he was to stand on the stage and call out the employees who'd been selected by their bosses for a roasting. He spent a couple of days writing the material and twenty minutes delivering it. The pay was $100.

Much more lucrative—but far more painful—was an engagement his managers, the Kushnicks, arranged at a club in Denver called the Turn of the Century. He opened for singer-actress Leslie Uggams, who was touring a musical variety show that featured three male dancers. The gig was two shows a night for ten nights, and his pay was $1,000. That was the good part. The bad started with the fact that he was expected to do a forty-five-minute set, and he only had twenty-five minutes of good material. On opening night, he got through the first set okay, but then the club owners announced to the crowd that they could all stick around for the second show. With no material in reserve, Letterman was forced to repeat his act verbatim to virtually the same audience that had sat through it an hour before. And so it went for ten excruciating nights. One night, he was trying desperately to fill minutes with some "So-where-you-from?" banter when a patron in the back called out wearily, "He's from *Denver*. I'm from *Denver*. We're *all* from Denver. We're *in* Denver."

He didn't think it could get worse, but it did. On the Fourth of July, some clown celebrated by setting off fireworks at his table.

Things reached the level of Grand Guignol the day the club owner's wife, a former dancer, had the dance floor refinished. When Uggams's dancers hit the slick new surface that night, they all went flying, and the singer refused to go on, which meant that Letterman had to perform back-to-back identical sets to the same increasingly surly crowd. It was a humiliation on the scale of a public proctological exam, and he took the whole episode as further proof that he did *not* have the right stuff to be a stand-up. Guys like Tom and George and Jay could bull their way through stuff like that without breaking a sweat and laugh about it an hour later. Not him; he brooded.

As part of his Denver deal, the club was supposed to provide him with limousine service. But after opening night, the owners cancelled the car, and from then on he walked to and from work, a mile and a half along the interstate highway between the hotel and the club, alone.

# All About Budd

On October 11, 1975, at 11:30 p.m. Easter Standard Time, *Saturday Night Live* (*SNL*) premiered on NBC. The soon-to-be-famous · cast did not comprise stand-up comedians. The Not Ready for Prime Time Players—John Belushi, Dan Aykroyd, Gilda Radner, Chevy Chase, Larraine Newman, Jane Curtin, and Garrett Morris—were all improvisational actors, a different breed of cat. But stand-up comics would be the first beneficiaries of the *SNL* phenomenon. The debut show featured guest host George Carlin, then at the height of his *Class Clown* fame, and introduced special guest Andy Kaufman to an astonished national TV audience. Kaufman's appearances on three of the first four *SNL* shows established him as the hottest (and oddest) of the new crop of stand-up comics.

*SNL* quickly became a cultural icon, ushering in a new era of sex, drugs, rock 'n' roll, and laughter, a time when stand-up comics were treated like rock stars. But the fact that *SNL* was broadcast live from New York didn't stem the tide of comic migration west. Funny kids from all across the country were pouring into Los Angeles and lining up to audition at the Comedy Store like immigrants being processed through Ellis Island. Their number would eventually swell to an estimated three hundred and include Robin

Williams from San Francisco; Howie Mandell from Toronto; Bob Saget from Philadelphia; Michael Keaton from Pittsburgh; Billy Crystal from Long Island; Skip Stephenson from Omaha; Arsenio Hall from Cleveland; Tim Thomerson from San Diego; Marsha Warfield, Jimmy Aleck, and Brad Sanders from Chicago; Johnny Witherspoon and Mike Binder from Detroit; Jeff Altman from Syracuse; Sandra Bernhard from Scottsdale; Argus Hamilton from Norman, Oklahoma; Gary Muledeer from Deadwood, South Dakota; and Kip Addotta from Rockford, Illinois.

After watching his best comics pack up and leave one by one, Budd Friedman finally made his move. He leased a building on Melrose Avenue in West Hollywood, just a mile from the Comedy Store. He wasn't worried that the market might not support two comedy clubs. A new showcase club called Catch a Rising Star had opened in New York the previous year, and business at the Improv had not suffered. In fact, both clubs were booming, with the best comics playing both places nightly.

News that there would be a West Coast Improv caused a ripple of excitement in the Los Angeles stand-up community. It meant more time slots, more opportunities for exposure to agents, managers, and TV executives. Jay Leno, Richard Lewis, and Michael Richards (who went on to fame as Cosmo Kramer on *Seinfeld*) lent Friedman a hand in painting the inside of his new place, for which they were paid $3 an hour (their comedy services they would continue to provide for free). The first bartender Friedman hired was Les Moonves, who is now chairman and CEO of CBS.

In many ways, Friedman was the antithesis of Mitzi Shore. A Korean War vet who'd been wounded in the famous Battle of Pork Chop Hill, he was barrel-chested and bombastic, resembling a TV version of a marine drill sergeant. He wore his considerable ego on his sleeve, or, more aptly, around his neck in the form of a monocle that appeared more affective than effective. In addition to giving himself top billing at his club—the logo above the door read "Budd Friedman's The Improvisation"—he took the stage to introduce

every act, delivering his own mini performances that were sometimes funny and just as often rambling and overlong. Jay Leno
once interrupted him by shouting from the back of the room,
"That's enough. This is boring." A comic could say things like that
to Budd and not worry about hurting his feelings. At least, a *good*
comic could.

Unlike Shore, who avoided the spotlight at her club, Friedman
strode the Improv like the frustrated actor he was, mixing with
patrons in the bar and dining room between trips to the stage to
introduce the performers. On a typical night, the garrulous proprietor logged (some would say hogged) more stage time than any
comic. He reveled in the spotlight. You'd never hear *him* say he
was doing it all for the comics. The Improv was all about Budd; it
said so right above the front door.

Shore was not happy about Friedman's expanding his franchise
into her territory. She was in the middle of her own expansion,
having just opened a second Comedy Store on Westwood Boulevard in West Los Angeles, not far from the UCLA campus. In
terms of location, she held the high ground in West Hollywood,
literally and figuratively. Sunset Strip was a brightly lit tourist des-
tination with loads of foot traffic and carloads of young people
cruising on the weekend, plenty of restaurants, and half a dozen
hotels within a stone's throw of her club, including the Continental Hyatt House right next door. The Improv was a mile down the
hill from the Comedy Store, on a stretch of Melrose Avenue that
was a comparative dark alley: You had to want to go there. Friedman apparently had a penchant for choosing less-than-hospitable
locations. The Hell's Kitchen neighborhood surrounding the New
York Improv was, to paraphrase a Mike Preminger joke, "a great
place to hang out, if you're a bullet."

Despite her advantage, Shore still felt threatened by Friedman. She was accustomed to having a monopoly. So, in an attempt to kill Budd's baby in its crib, she put out the word to her
comics that they couldn't work both clubs; they had to pick one

or the other. Always sure of himself, Jay Leno was the first to call her bluff, saying that if that was the case, then he'd just work at the Improv. Shore instantly caved. Leno was too big a draw, too good a performer, to bar from her stage. For those with similar star clout, it became a matter of preference. David Letterman and George Miller stayed exclusively with the Comedy Store, as did Jimmie Walker, even though he'd gotten his big break at the New York Improv and invested in the new one. (Friedman would never forgive him for not playing the LA club, calling him "the most ungrateful comic I've ever known.") Freddie Prinze, Tom Dreesen, and Andy Kaufman worked both places at will.

For less established comics, however, it was a dicey proposition to displease Mitzi Shore. So in an abundance of caution, most of them, including Steve Lubetkin, stayed with the Store, which offered many more time slots than the Improv in any case. Friedman didn't respond in kind to Shore's attempt to cut off his talent supply; he never punished a comic for working at the Comedy Store. But the seeds of enmity had been sown, initiating a bitter rivalry for the hearts and minds of a generation of stand-up comedians.

Richard Lewis's relocation to Los Angeles came courtesy of Sonny Bono. The singer and his ex-wife were hoping to recapture some lightning in a bottle by launching a new Sonny and Cher TV show on ABC, and Bono hired Lewis as a regular on the LA-based production.

Lewis found an apartment on La Brea Avenue north of Sunset, a block from Hollywood High School. The second-floor one-bedroom cost $140 a month and came equipped with a nightly soundtrack of hookers and johns arguing about money on the street below.

The TV gig turned out to be less than Lewis expected. He was cast not as a stand-up but rather as a member of a comedy/variety troupe. The show's humor was broad and involved lots of singing and dancing. During the first week of rehearsals, he injured his knee doing kicks in a dance number. He was given a single line on the first show and had to appear in a scene made up as a Greek statue—half-naked in a toga and spray-painted gray from head to toe. After the taping, he sat in the makeup room staring at himself in the mirror. "This is so humiliating," he said aloud. "I just can't do it. I quit."

Sonny Bono's manager heard his comment and walked over and stood next to him. "You can't be serious," he said. "This is a *network* show. If you leave now, you'll regret it the rest of your life."

Lewis contemplated their absurd reflection in the mirror for a few more seconds before bolting from the room. He went to his apartment and washed off the greasepaint, then hit the Improv, where he did an inspired set. An agent from the William Morris Agency was in the audience and called him the next morning. Within twenty-four hours of walking out on Sonny and Cher, he was signed to one of the biggest talent agencies in Hollywood.

Steve Lubetkin's personal life took a turn for the better on a spring day in 1976 when he walked into his neighborhood grocery store. As usual, he hadn't had anything to eat that morning, so he headed straight for a card table set up at the end of an aisle where a young woman was handing out food samples. Her name was Susan Evans. A vibrant redhead with a master's degree in speech interpretation, she was working with actor-director Victor French as a member of Company of Angels, an equity-waiver theater on Melrose Avenue, all of which apparently qualified her to dish out small cups of ice cream in a Hollywood supermarket.

Lubetkin reacted to the hair, the ice cream, and the girl the way any young comic would—he started doing his routine, and within a few minutes, he had Susan Evans laughing so loudly that other shoppers started forming a circle around the two of them, and she feared she would be fired. Fortunately, it was time for her lunch break, and they were able to take their cute meeting outside to a little patch of grass under a browning palm tree. She was instantly attracted to him, with his long, dark hair, rakish moustache, and warm smile that seemed to draw her in. His personality was positively vivid; she'd never met anyone like him or laughed so hard.

He showed up at the same time the next day and over lunch invited her to dinner that night at his place. When she arrived at the address he gave her, she discovered that he really didn't have a "place" but a room in someone else's apartment. The only furniture in his room was a mattress on the floor. He had access to the kitchen, but he had no food in the fridge, no money to buy any, and no clue how to cook it if he did. So, she shopped for dinner and cooked it, too, an inauspicious first date, but she didn't mind because he was so charming and appreciative, telling her that he'd had only a handful of home-cooked meals since his mother died when he was twelve. He talked to her about Mitzi Shore and *Dante Shocko* and his show business dreams.

Over the next few weeks, they became inseparable. He took her to the Comedy Store, where she met Letterman and Leno, who were clearly the big men on that campus. He introduced her to Mitzi, who didn't seem at all like the warm, nurturing mother figure he'd described. After a couple of months, he moved in with her, arriving at her single-room apartment with a small, cheap suitcase stuffed with his clothes, a cardboard file box full of notes and jokes, and a cassette recorder. It was everything he owned.

# Six Minutes,
# Twenty-two Laughs

It took Tom Dreesen six months, but in October 1975, he finally convinced *The Tonight Show*'s Craig Tennis to come see him at the Comedy Store. Tennis arranged a so-called showcase audition for Dreesen and two other acts, a comedy team called Bauman & Estin and a new kid in town by the name of Billy Crystal. It was set for Tuesday night, the early show, when normally only about twenty people would be in the audience. Dreesen was a little worried because he knew that the bigger the crowd, the bigger the laughs, but when he pulled up to the club in his old VW, he saw at least 150 people milling around outside the club. "Fucking great," he said as he drove up the ramp to the parking lot behind the Hyatt House. It got fucking greater when he reached the entrance and saw that the crowd included Norman Lear and Carl Reiner, two of the biggest names in television comedy. "Holy shit," Dreesen said as he bounded inside, where a few audience members were already seated. He counted eighteen, including Tennis, as he paced nervously and waited for the rest to be let in. But before they had, Tennis told him it was time to go on.

"What do you mean?" Dreesen asked. "What about all those people outside? Aren't they going to let them in?"

"No," said Tennis. "They are here to see Billy Crystal, and his managers don't want them to see anyone else. That's the way it's done."

Dreesen did twenty minutes and made all eighteen people laugh heartily. When he finished, Tennis said to him, "Come to my office Tuesday." Passing through the Crystal crowd on the way out, Dreesen thought, Well, at least he didn't reject me. (Billy Crystal passed his audition, too, winning a spot on *The Tonight Show* and a recurring role on Norman Lear's hit show *Mary Hartman, Mary Hartman*. Bauman & Estin didn't make the cut.)

On Tuesday, Tennis got right down to it: "Tell me what material you'd do on *The Tonight Show*."

Dreesen started going through the bits he'd done at the Comedy Store audition.

"No, take that one out," Tennis would cut in. "Yeah, that's good. Keep that one."

At the end of the session, Tennis smiled and said matter-of-factly, "You got the show. You're on next week."

Dreesen left with his brain doing cartwheels. "I got *The Tonight Show*," he shouted as he ran down Sunset Boulevard to find a pay phone to call his wife and everyone else he ever knew. "I got the fucking *Tonight Show*."

Then he was hit by a wave of fear. Oh shit! he thought. What if it doesn't work? What if I bomb, with every agent, manager, studio and network executive in the world watching? He spent the next week working out at the Comedy Store and the Improv, doing all three shows every night.

Dreesen knew that Johnny Carson had a very strict view of what worked on *The Tonight Show* and what didn't. Johnny expected comics to deliver a fast-paced, joke-filled, laugh-packed set no shorter than five minutes and no longer than six. No long setups: You needed quick payoffs—a punch line every thirty seconds. For a stand-up comic, a minute on TV without a laugh was death. And Carson was adamant about the formula. He had recently stopped by the Improv to see Jay Leno and Andy Kaufman perform and had pronounced both of them "not ready," telling Budd Friedman, "They're funny, but they don't have six minutes."

By Dreesen's calculation, his six minutes contained twenty-two laughs. On the appointed day, October 21, he went to the NBC studios in beautiful downtown Burbank all by himself. He needed to focus. He tried not to think about the fact that everyone he knew inside the business and out would be watching, that this could be the biggest break of his career or the end of it. Some comics who were good enough to get on *The Tonight Show* still avoided it out of fear that the slightest stumble would put them out of the business. Dreesen sat nervously in the green room through most of the then ninety-minute show. Comics were always the last to go on. The minutes ticked away, and then time ran out. The interviews with Eydie Gorme, Vincent Price, and Buddy Hackett had run long, and he'd been bumped. He would have to come back another night. He drove home feeling equal parts disappointed and relieved. At least he got paid—a grand total of $212.

Over the next few weeks, the scene repeated itself as Dreesen was bumped on October 28, when time was eaten up by actor Robert Blake, and on December 2, when Lucille Ball and Johnny Mathis exceeded their allotted minutes. His hometown newspapers in Chicago picked up on his ordeal. "Waiting (and Waiting and Waiting) for Tom," read one of the headlines. The groundswell of interest only served to heighten his anxiety. On December 9, he was sitting in the makeup chair for the fourth time when *Tonight Show* executive producer Fred DeCordova walked in and said, "I have some bad news for you." DeCordova paused for a beat before delivering the punch line. "You're going on."

In his head Dreesen saw a scene from his days in the navy—on a ship, running for battle stations, with the sound of a horn and a voice coming through the loudspeakers: "This is not a drill. I repeat. This is not a drill."

Then began an age-old *Tonight Show* ritual. He was walked down a long hallway to a designated station just behind the curtain. As he passed among them, all the stagehands turned their backs or looked away so as not to make him more nervous than he was. He could hear them whispering, "It's his first time."

At the end of the hall, he was left standing alone facing the stage curtain that separated him from 10 million TV viewers. "You're fine. You're fine. You're okay," he kept telling himself. He was hyperventilating. Coming out of the last commercial break, Doc Severson and the band were playing. Then the music stopped, along with his heart. He heard Johnny saying the words he would remember the rest of his life.

"We're back now, and I'm glad you're in such a good mood because my next guest is making his first appearance on *The Tonight Show*. Please welcome . . . *Tom Dreesen!*"

Like hundreds before him, Dreesen stepped into the blinding light of *The Tonight Show* arena. It was nothing like a nightclub, more like an operating room. The audience was hidden in shadows beyond the lights and cameras; he couldn't see faces. He stepped to the *T* marker taped to the floor and looked straight at the red light on the center camera. This was it.

"I grew up in a suburb on the south side of Chicago called Harvey, Illinois," he began, and the audience applauded, presumably for Chicago. "It was what you'd call a 'changing' neighborhood."

He told of attending "St. Rocky Graziano grade school" and of all the black guys who apparently thought he was some Chinese kid named Sayfoo "because every time I walked by they'd call out 'Say, foo'!"

The line got a big laugh, and he was off to the races. He described what happened after one black classmate taught him the art of "woofing," which was (much like a dog barking) bluffing an opponent by acting braver than you really are: "One day, one of the nuns reached into her drawer for a ruler to rap me on the knuckles, and I said to her, 'I'm thinking you better be pullin' a gun outta there.'"

After counting eleven applause breaks, he closed with an endearing appeal to the crowd. "You've been a wonderful audience," he said. "And because this is my first appearance here and show business is such a tough life, I'd just like to say this to you: If you liked me and you are a Protestant, then say a prayer for me. If you are a Catholic, then light a candle. And if you are Jewish, then someone in your family owns a nightclub, so please tell them about me. Thank you very much. Good night."

He'd killed, and he knew it. He turned and walked back through the stage curtain, where Craig Tennis grabbed him by the arm and propelled him back toward the stage. "No, no, no," he said. "Johnny wants you back out there to take a bow."

The audience was still applauding wildly as he stepped back into the lights, waved, and bowed. Over to the right he could see Carson smiling broadly, nodding approval, and giving him the big okay sign. He thought he might pop. He had never experienced such a sense of exhilaration.

Back at the Comedy Store, David Letterman, George Miller, and Johnny Dark were gathered around the little black-and-white TV in the kitchen, watching their friend's triumph with a mixture of pride and envy. He was the first of their class to make it. As Dreesen walked on rubber legs past the stagehands on his way out that night, they all turned toward him and applauded.

The next day, a William Morris agent named Herb Karp got a call from CBS development executive Lee Curlin, who said, "I saw this kid on Carson last night. His name is Tom Dreesen. Do you have him under contract?"

"Why, are you interested in him?" Karp replied, not answering the question.

"Yes, we are."

"Deal interested?"

"Yes, deal interested."

"I know Dreesen," Karp said. "I've played softball with him. I'll give him a call."

Karp told a surprised Dreesen that he'd like to take him on as a client. "I won't lie to you," he said. "There's a deal waiting for you."

So, within twenty-four hours of his first *Tonight Show* appearance, Tom Dreesen had signed with the biggest talent agency in Hollywood and had a $25,000 development deal with a major TV network. That was enough to pay for his food and rent for an entire year.

He would never again pick up an unemployment check.

# The Boys' Club

When Elayne Boosler arrived in Los Angeles in the spring of 1976, she already had a rep. She was, after all, the only female regular at the New York Improv and a headliner to boot. It didn't hurt that she'd been Andy Kaufman's girlfriend and protégé for two years—he was the newest big sensation on the comedy scene. And unlike most of the young comics on the West Coast, she was making a living. She'd toured as an opening act for the Pointer Sisters, had performed on an NBC comedy show called *Saturday Night* (hosted by sportscaster Howard Cosell), and was booked to appear on a summer replacement TV series starring Monty Hall, the longtime host of the game show *Let's Make a Deal*.

The word among her fellow comics was that Boosler had balls. At the New York Improv, she would beg Budd Friedman to let her go on after Freddie Prinze, a slot her male counterparts preferred to avoid because Freddie was the proverbial tough act to follow. (Andy Kaufman was the toughest because he closed his set by leading the audience in a Conga line out of the club and into the street.) But Boosler's attitude was, "I'm as good as any of the boys. Don't make it easy on me because I'm a girl."

No one made it easy on her, that's for sure. "Hey, baby, you wanna fuck?" was a common heckle she heard from the crowd in the early days. She handled the abuse with such aplomb that Richard Lewis dubbed her "the Jackie Robinson of stand-up comedy." She preferred to describe herself as "the first young, unmarried, dressed-up-for-a-date female stand-up comic."

Boosler's material sprang from a female perspective, but it stopped short of being stridently feminist. "They never want you to think the pictures are posed," she said of the then dominant *Playboy* magazine. "'We just happened to catch Cathy typing—nude on top of a Volvo in a field this morning.' Maybe I'm sheltered, but I don't know anybody who takes a shower in a baseball cap and knee socks." On the subject of prostitution, she quipped, "Why would any woman sleep with a total stranger without having had dinner and a movie first?"

It was originally expected that Boosler would be among the headliners at the new Los Angeles Improv. But before leaving New York, she had a falling out with Budd Friedman, who'd paid her only $78 a week as a hostess for two and a half years, and she vowed that she would never again work in a club he had anything to do with.

Boosler auditioned for Mitzi Shore on a Monday night at the new Westwood Comedy Store. She had no problem breaking into the regular lineup or gaining admittance to the West Coast boys' club of comics. Richard Lewis and Jay Leno, of course, were old pals from the Improv, and she was soon a fixture at Tom Dreesen's nightly after-hours gatherings at Theodore's and Canter's Deli, where she met Johnny Dark, George Miller, and David Letterman. Boosler thought the guys were a godsend, especially Dreesen and Dark because they were older and married, with kids and homes you could always go to on the holidays. It was like the best version of a family that she would have designed for herself, comprised entirely of quirky, funny people on a shared mission and completely supportive of one another.

Working the Westwood Store, she got to know an entirely different group of comics: Michael Keaton, who was edgy and sexy and did a hysterical routine as a driving-school instructor with a flip chart; Charlie Hill, a Native American comic who drew constant titters from the crowd by holding a tom-tom in his hand throughout his entire set without ever acknowledging its presence; the comedy team of Rick Granat and Jim Carozzo, who became heroes to poor and hungry comics—and the butt of many Jay Leno jokes—for discovering that every Tuesday night, the Ralph's supermarket on Wilshire Boulevard in West Los Angeles tossed a veritable truckload of slightly spoiled, but still very edible produce in its dumpster; and Mitch Walters, a chronically broke, inveterate gambler whose day job selling lightbulbs in a telephone sales call center provided him with emergency material he used whenever his act bogged down on stage. He'd urge people in the audience to shout out where they were from, then dazzle them with his encyclopedic knowledge of U.S. area codes: "Atlanta? Hey, 404. Lansing? 517. Sierra Madre? What, are you kidding me? 818." Boosler was amazed that the bit rarely failed to save his butt from bombing.

On nights Boosler wasn't with her fellow comics, she would hang at the Tropicana coffee shop on Santa Monica Boulevard in West Hollywood with a group of musicians that included Tom Waits and Chuck E. Weiss. Her regular routine was to have dinner with friends until around 10:00 p.m., head back to her apartment to do her hair and makeup, hit the Comedy Store for her set at 11:00 or 12:00, then hang out with the guys until dawn. Being one of the few females running with a pack of randy young men meant that she didn't lack for male attention. After breaking up with Andy Kaufman (they remained close friends until his death from a rare form of lung cancer in 1984), she had brief, friendly flings with both Letterman and Leno, then a more serious romance with Robin Williams that ended in heartbreak when she learned that he was simultaneously engaged to dancer Valerie Velardi, whom he eventually married. Boosler's liaisons with four of the fastest-rising young comics only added to her reputation in the comedy community. As Tom Dreesen joked, "Maybe we should *all* start dating Elayne."

Boosler worked as hard as she played. As a client of Jimmie Walker's Ebony Genius Management, along with Leno and Letterman, she booked any paying gig she could get, from country club lunches to movie studio promotional parties. When *Grease* opened, Paramount threw a huge party on the lot with little pockets of entertainment scattered around the grounds for the strolling guests. Boosler sat on a stool at her assigned station and launched into her act whenever people passed by. "I feel kind of like a mental patient on the street," she cracked.

She was hired several times as a secret backup for young female guest stars in sitcoms who'd landed the parts for reasons other than their acting ability. She was paid to sit in a room near the soundstage and watch rehearsals on closed-circuit TV. If the actress in question didn't cut it, Boosler was expected to step into the role for the run-through with the rest of the cast. She never had to, but that was okay because she got paid anyway. Everything is an adventure, she told herself. Nothing is bad because it's all going somewhere.

Though she was hardly a household name, Boosler was quickly becoming a role model to a growing number of young female stand-ups. They were trickling into Los Angeles from around the country at a ratio of about one to twenty of their male counterparts. They saw her success as proof that they didn't have to be Phyllis Diller or Joan Rivers, that maybe there could be a female Mort Sahl, that there was more to women's comedy than vacuum cleaners and visits to the gynecologist.

Dottie Archibald was a thirty-year-old housewife living in Ojai, California, an artsy little community in the Santa Monica Mountains between Los Angeles and Santa Barbara. One night after watching David Brenner on *The Tonight Show*, she announced to her startled husband, "I'm going to become a stand-up comic." She wrote up a five-minute act about being a housewife in Ojai and invited all the doctors, lawyers, and neighbors she knew in Ojai to come see her try out on a Monday night at the Comedy Store.

Onstage for the first time in her life, she rushed through her five minutes of material in about a minute and a half and didn't get a single laugh, not even an embarrassed giggle. The crowd applauded politely when she was done, and her husband jumped up from his seat to present her with a bouquet of roses, but she knew that she'd bombed beyond hideously and thought it would be a mercy to die right then and there.

Instead, she went back twelve more Monday nights and suffered through the same stony silence from the crowd. On her thirteenth try, she broke down and started crying, and someone laughed. The seeds of an act were sown.

Marsha Warfield spent two years working for free at Tom Dreesen's Monday night comedy showcase in Chicago before she decided to follow him west. "I can be broke anywhere," she told her friends. "I might as well be broke where it's warm." She flew to Los Angeles the day after her twenty-first birthday with $100 in her pocketbook, a return ticket paid for by her mother, and no intention of ever going home. She checked into the Continental Hyatt House, then walked straight next door to the Comedy Store and waited for it to open. She watched every night for the next two weeks until she got up the nerve to go onstage at a Monday tryout in Westwood. Letterman and Leno were sitting in the back and came up to her afterward offering encouragement. "They kind of adopted me as a little sister mascot," she recalled years later. "I wouldn't go away, so they accepted me."

Besides Boosler, Warfield and Archibald were the only two women welcomed into the late-night male-bonding rituals at Canter's and Theodore's. Archibald had to pester comic Michael

Rapport for weeks, begging, "Can I please go to Canter's with you
tonight?" before he finally agreed to take her. She found the
scene as instructive as watching the guys onstage.

Typically, there were at least twenty comics on hand, divided
up among three or four tables. The atmosphere was brutally competitive, but in a good-natured way, as they tried to top one another's stories. The one-liners and the laughter came like bursts
of machine-gun fire, and you could cut the testosterone in the air
with a machete.

Jay Leno was a human joke machine—put in a quarter and out
they came, one after another, a seemingly inexhaustible supply.
Letterman was his polar opposite, never taking center stage at
one of the larger tables, preferring to sit a little apart at a deuce or
four-top, talking with Dreesen or George Miller. Dreesen played
paterfamilias, moving from table to table, telling tales of growing
up poor and working the Playboy circuit. Johnny Dark entertained the entire restaurant with his wildly physical impressions,
such as John Wayne trying to coax his horse up to Letterman's
table, urging, "C'mon boy, c'mon, that's it," then hollering
"Whoa, whoa, whoa," as the frightened invisible animal reared,
wheeled around, and galloped about round the room with the
Duke bug-eyed and hanging on for dear life. Dark's peers considered him the world's greatest "table comic." The only one who
could compete with Johnny was Robin Williams, who'd come in
still throbbing from a performance, put his head between two
pieces of bread, jump up on a table, and emit sounds like he was
speaking in tongues.

Everyone got their moment in the spotlight. One night, comic
Mark Goldstein arrived fresh from working a private party at a
Beverly Hills mansion, where the owner had paid him a whopping
$200 to entertain one hundred people gathered for his wife's sixty-
fifth birthday. As recounted by Goldstein in his morose, loser
stage manner, the evening had not gone well. He performed his

act in the middle of the living room under a huge chandelier and could not get a laugh to save his life. "So I went abusive on them," he confessed, ticking off the insults he hurled at the stunned guests sitting around on the expensive sofas. When he was finished, the wife got up, walked over to him, looked him straight in the eye, and said sadly, "You ruined my birthday." Then, she turned, ran up the stairs, and disappeared. Goldstein's monotone, deadpan delivery made Dottie Archibald laugh so hard she slid off her seat and ended up lying under the table, gasping for breath.

For Archibald and Warfield, the most impressive aspect of these sessions was that amid all the boyish showboating, Elayne Boosler more than held her own, proving that contrary to the conventional wisdom of the time, women *could* compete with men in the comedy arena. That was the reason Boosler's prime-time weekend sets at the Comedy Store were "must see" performances for the female comics who were just starting to break into the lineup at the club. She was their dog in the fight, their gladiator in the Coliseum.

All handpicked by Mitzi Shore, they ranged in sensibility from Robin Tyler, a militant feminist lesbian given to snarling at male hecklers, "You can be replaced by a tampon," to waiflike Lotus Weinstock, a classically trained musician and former student at the Philadelphia Dance Academy, who was once engaged to Lenny Bruce and dropped bon mots like "Angels can fly because they take themselves lightly." Jo Anne Astrow was a young mother who had fled from a suffocating marriage to the son of a wealthy Manhattan dress manufacturer, fallen in love with an actor named Mark Lonow, and joined him in the comedy improv trio they called Off the Wall—a series of decisions her Brooklyn family likened to running off and joining the circus. Off the Wall was performing regularly at the New York Improv when Lonow landed a role in a TV series called *Husbands, Wives and Lovers*, which was produced in Los Angeles. So the trio joined the westward migration. Once in

LA, Astrow was encouraged by her old pal from Brooklyn, Elayne Boosler, to give stand-up a try. Emily Levine was an honors graduate from Radcliff who was teaching emotionally disturbed children before she moved to Los Angeles as part of a comedy troupe named the New York Stickball Team. The club's growing female roster also included Shirley Hemphill, Lois Bromfield, Roberta Kent, Anne Kellogg, Diane Nichols, Hilda Vincent, Susan Sweetzer, Maureen Murphy, and a caustic part-time manicurist named Sandra Bernhard.

Despite Shore's patronage and the preeminence of the Comedy Store, they all faced an uphill battle, Boosler included, because Johnny Carson thought that, with the exception of Joan Rivers, women weren't particularly good at stand-up comedy. As he explained in an infamous *Rolling Stone* interview at the time,

> A woman is feminine, a woman is not abrasive, a woman is not a hustler. So when you see a gal who does "stand-up" one-liners, she has to overcome that built-in identification as a retiring, meek woman. I mean, if a woman comes out and starts firing one-liners, those little abrasive things, you can take that from a man. The ones that try sometimes are a little aggressive for my taste. I'll take it from a guy, but from women, sometimes, it just doesn't fit too well.

The women comics didn't need Carson to tell them what they already knew from watching the show and dealing with the talent coordinators: Johnny preferred breathy and busty to ballsy, zany to brainy. To make the cut, a female performer had to project a non-threatening "golly-jeepers-oh-Johnny" quality, like Carol Wayne. She had to appeal to older male viewers who liked to go to Vegas. If she wasn't a bimbo, she at least had to be willing to play one on TV.

By those criteria, Elayne Boosler didn't have a prayer. Word kept coming back to her from *The Tonight Show* talent coordinators that she was "too tough."

The Comedy Store women knew that Carson's prejudice threatened their livelihood. Without a presence on *The Tonight Show*, they had a tougher time landing other TV gigs. Their lack of exposure to a national audience made it harder to convince club owners to hire them. And without more chances to perform live, they couldn't develop their acts. It was a vicious cycle.

Fortunately, they thought, they had the backing of the most powerful woman in comedy, and Mitzi had a plan for breaking the log jam. In the belly of the Comedy Store, she was going to build them a room of their own.

# Guns, Drugs,
# and Westwood

For the comedy community, 1977 started out with a bang, liter-ally. In the early morning hours of January 28, Freddie Prinze, stoned on cocaine and quaaludes, put a .32 caliber pistol to his temple and fired a bullet into his brain. He lingered on life support for thirty-three hours and died on January 29. He was twenty-two.

Prinze's peers were stunned. For the past three years, they had measured their success against his. Freddie's career path was their road map—Comedy Store, Carson, Hollywood, the world. He'd performed at President Jimmy Carter's inaugural ball just the week before, and he'd dropped by the Westwood Store several times in the past month. Nothing seemed amiss; he was the same old Freddie. Sure, everybody knew he had some problems. His wife of two years, Kathy, was divorcing him and had obtained a restraining order against him. And he'd been arrested in November for driving under the influence of methaqualone, his favorite drug, which had been prescribed by his shrink. But drugs were an old story with Fred-die, dating back to his days at the New York Improv. Everyone knew he liked to wash down his 'ludes with cognac and do some blow to stay on his feet. Freddie was ahead of the curve when it came to the harder drugs. He could afford them, whereas most of his friends had to settle for pot. Freddie got sloppy, slurred his words, and sometimes had to be supported by his female companion(s), but he was always sweet and amiable, never angry or belligerent. You'd never meet a nicer or more charming guy. And even though his success seemed out of proportion to his talent, no one resented him for it.

In the aftermath of Prinze's death, a more disturbing picture began to emerge. News footage from the Carter inaugural showed Freddie looking pretty wired, with his eyes darting all around. Comic Alan Bursky, one of Prinze's closest friends, told people he went to Freddy's apartment at the Beverly Comstock after the shooting and found "a mayonnaise jar full of coke." That was a lot of blow even by Freddie's standards. There were stories of bizarre gunplay going back a couple of years. Jay Leno recalled the time Freddie stayed at his apartment in Boston and fired so many bullets into the living room wall that it made a hole "the size of a small window" into his bedroom. Others told of Freddie's shooting his gun (the rumor was that Bursky had given it to him) out the window of his apartment on Wilshire Boulevard in Beverly Hills and of his scaring people by pretending to play Russian roulette, spinning the cylinder then pointing the barrel at his head and pulling the trigger, not telling them that the gun was empty. His cruelest joke was on a female assistant who heard the gun go off in the next room and ran in to find Freddie sprawled on the floor. After she screamed, he raised his head and grinned, "Fooled you, didn't I?" It was as if he'd been rehearsing his final act.

The Los Angeles coroner ruled the death a suicide based on a statement from his manager, who was present at the time of the shooting and claimed he tried to grab the gun, and on a series of phone calls Prinze made and a note he left behind that repeated the line, "I can't go on."

Prinze was buried in Forest Lawn Memorial Park in Burbank after a celebrity-studded funeral. Writing in his autobiography twenty-five years later, Leno still seemed miffed that Prinze's manager arranged front-row seating for Freddie's new "big-name" friends Tony Orlando, Sammy Davis Jr., and *Chico and the Man* costar Jack Albertson, while his old pals from the Improv and the Comedy Store practically had to crash the event. He also noted the irony that above the door of the Forest Lawn chapel, an engraving commemorated the first skirmish of the Revolutionary War: "The shot heard 'round the world."

In the end, the media chalked the tragedy up as a case of too much too soon: Prinze just couldn't handle his success. Prinze's comedian friends drew a narrower lesson: Freddie just couldn't handle his drugs.

Within days of Prinze's death, comedians were hit with another calamity: The Comedy Store on Sunset Boulevard was forced to close because Mitzi Shore lost her lease, which was all the more shocking because she owned the building. She had purchased the property on July 5, 1976, the day after the nation's two hundredth birthday, and immediately marked it as her own by painting the exterior black to match the inside. She'd never seen an entirely black building before and thought perhaps it was the only one in existence. In any case, she was sure it would make a statement and be noticed.

Even though Shore owned the property, she didn't control all of it. The building came with a tenant grandfathered in by the previous landlord, Frank Sennes, who'd owned the building since it housed Ciro's nightclub in the 1940s and 1950s. The tenant was Art Laboe, a longtime Los Angeles disc jockey who'd coined the phrase "oldies but goodies." Laboe produced his KRLA radio show from the first floor of the building in the space next to the Comedy Store. Shore coveted Laboe's space, which was larger than hers. She dreamed of turning it into a Vegas-style showroom for established comedians like Jackie Mason, Shecky Green, Buddy Hackett, and Rodney Dangerfield, performers she'd hung out with during her years with Sammy.

Laboe still had a year to go on his lease, but Shore hatched a plan to get him out sooner. No one had used the offices above

Laboe's studio, which were part of his lease, for years, and they were trashed. Shore had her lawyers take pictures of the mess and then filed a lawsuit seeking to evict Laboe on the grounds that he wasn't taking proper care of the building and was creating a fire hazard. Problem was, Laboe's lease also included the space that housed the Comedy Store, which Shore subleased from him. And it just so happened that Shore's lease was up. So Laboe counter-sued to have her evicted, and he won.

Shore moved her entire operation to the Westwood Comedy Store, and the comics banded together in support, agreeing to cut their sets to ten minutes so that no one lost any stage time. As if to rub salt in the wound, Laboe opened his own comedy room in the Sunset building. Called the Funny Farm and featuring come-dian Leonard Barr, an old crony of Dean Martin, it played as a poor impersonation of the Comedy Store and was doomed from the start. None of Shore's comics would work there. After a few months, Shore ended the pissing match by paying Laboe $50,000 to relinquish his lease on the Sunset building, and everything re-turned to normal on the Los Angeles comedy scene. The one change was that the months of exile had firmly established the Westwood club as a major entertainment venue in its own right, not just the poor stepsister of the Sunset Store.

From the start, the Westwood Store had a different vibe from Sunset. It was formerly Leadbetter's, a coffeehouse named after folk blues legend Huddie Leadbetter, known as Leadbelly, and owned by Randy Sparks, founder of the New Christy Minstrels, the perky and very popular folk-music troupe of the 1960s. The room was larger than Sunset—220 seats—with a bar accessible to customers and brick walls that bounced the laughter all over the place. With UCLA a short walk away, the club catered to the college crowd with a $2 cover charge and $3 pitchers of beer. It also featured a limited menu of inexpensive entrees so that patrons under twenty-one could be admitted legally. That drew students from Beverly Hills and Taft and El Camino high schools in the San Fernando

Valley. As a result, the Westwood audience was younger and whiter than the Sunset crowd. Sunset had a hip, New York kind of feel, which was why many of the East Coast comics preferred it. Westwood was all-American.

Shore tailored her Westwood lineup to reflect the audience. Comic Argus Hamilton described the core group, of which he was a member, as "Mitzi's little Anglo Saxon Triple A ball club." Hamilton was the son, grandson, and great grandson of southern Methodist ministers. His grandfather, Argus Hamilton III, was a lifelong friend of Will Rogers; their fathers had fought together in the Confederate army. His father, Argus IV, delivered Roger's eulogy on NBC Radio. Argus V decided to become a comic one night when he was lounging around the ATO fraternity house at the University of Oklahoma and caught Freddie Prinze's debut on *The Tonight Show*. After graduating in 1976, Hamilton drove straight to Los Angeles in his new MG Midget, a gift from his "very indulgent parents." He quickly became a Mitzi Shore favorite and a devoted employee, drawing three salaries as emcee, doorman, and Shore's personal "runner."

Another Westwood regular, Mike Binder, was younger than almost anyone in the audience—just seventeen and fresh out of high school when he arrived at the Sunset Strip club only to find it closed due to the lease dispute.

"Where do the comedians go?" he asked a guy who was sweeping up in front.

"They don't anymore," he was told. Binder had driven from his hometown of Detroit in four days, having told his father, a well-to-do home builder, that he had a job waiting for him. Fortunately, he found his way to Westwood and killed in his first Monday night audition. Shore put him in the lineup, gave him a part-time job as a doorman, and sort of adopted him as a member of her family.

Shore's other white-bread regulars at Westwood included Ollie Joe Prater from Michigan, Nebraskan Skip Stephenson, Bill Kirchenbauer from St. Petersberg, and San Diegans Biff Maynard and Tim Thomerson. She added color to the lineup with Jimmie Walker, who worked the first and second shows every Friday night, John Witherspoon, Brad Sanders, and Marsha Warfield, as well as with Native Americans Charlie Hill and Gary Muledeer.

The Westwood comics were a hard-partying crew. At closing time, they'd pull aside the most attractive women, turn on the beer taps, turn up the Eagles tunes, fire up a few joints, lock the doors, and carry on until 4:00 a.m. Occasionally someone would score some coke, which meant they could drink longer. Sometimes they'd party until the sun came up at Fort Bursky or Argus Hamilton's Beverly Hills apartment, nicknamed "the Crosby Ranch" because of Argus's penchant for breaking into an impression of Bing Crosby doing his famous Minute Maid orange juice commercials: "Here at the Crosby Ranch, we like to pick our oranges. It's a shame we can't pick our children" (two of Crosby's older sons had recently accused him of being a physically abusive father).

The Westwood clique was younger than the Canter's crowd by a couple of years. Born deeper into the baby boom, they were less affected by the Vietnam War and the draft, and their material tended to be less political. "We're just as funny but not as afraid," Hamilton joked. They were more likely to employ props in their acts and engage in outright silliness on stage. Leno and George Miller, in particular, disdained prop comedy. "Props are the enemy of wit," Leno liked to say. But the two groups mixed easily and shared a communal sensibility left over from the 1960s. When Hamilton competed as a contestant on *Hollywood Squares* and won six hundred steaks (complete with a freezer to store them) from Cattleman's in Omaha, he immediately threw a party at the Crosby Ranch and split the spoils with twenty other comics. Everybody went home with a stack of steaks.

It was a time of no comic left behind. Nobody ever went without a beer, a joint, or a ride to the club. It was Camelot. And it wouldn't last.

# Comedy University

The Sunset Strip Comedy Store had one thing that no other comedy club had: Richard Pryor.

Beginning with the preparations for his 1974 breakthrough album *That Nigger's Crazy*, Pryor used the Sunset Store almost exclusively as his incubator, trying out the material that would fill his best-selling, Grammy-winning follow-up albums: *Is It Something I Said?* (1975), *Bicentennial Nigger* (1976), and *Wanted: Richard Pryor Live in Concert* (1978). At the Sunset Store, Pryor completed his transformation from Bill Cosby clone to comedy revolutionary, perfecting the dangerously funny stage persona that Argus Hamilton described as "Dark Twain."

For Mitzi Shore, Pryor was the goose that laid the golden egg. His name on the marquee guaranteed sold-out shows every night. So, whenever Pryor wanted to work out some new material, all he had to do was let her know, and she'd clear the decks for as many nights or weeks as he wanted. He usually did a show of at least ninety minutes that included two other comics he hand-picked to precede him. He favored frequent collaborator Paul Mooney, Marsha Warfield, and David Letterman.

When Pryor worked at the Store, it cost other comics their time slots, but this was the only time none of them cared. They each had their personal heroes and major influences—for Jay Leno it was Robert Klein, for Robin Williams it was Jonathan Winters, for many it was Johnny Carson—but collectively they recognized that Pryor was the closest thing their peculiar profession had to a genius on the scale of a Beethoven or Van Gogh. Pryor was the cutting edge of their art form—a black man taking stand-up comedy to a place that even the persecuted and prosecuted Lenny Bruce had not. Pryor's use of ghetto slang and profanity on stage made George Carlin's "Seven Words You Can Never Say on Television" routine seem almost like a graduate lesson in linguistics. What were a few lost time slots compared to the chance of studying the master at work? When Pryor took the stage at the Comedy Store, nearly every local comic who wasn't on stage somewhere else was on hand to watch and learn.

A Pryor appearance on Sunset Strip had the frenzied feel of a heavyweight title fight in Vegas, with lines stretching around the block as tourists and celebrities jostled for the fewer than two hundred seats per show, which, amazingly, Shore kept priced under $5. The gap between supply and demand proved a boon to the club's senior doorman, Harris Peet, whose primary job was to escort patrons to their seats. Shore paid Peet $16 a night and apparently didn't mind if he augmented his income at the expense of the paying customers. Peet unabashedly gave seating preference to patrons who were willing to grease his palm, to the point where he even handed out his home phone number to favored customers so they could call him well in advance to let him know how many seats they needed held. Thus, Pryor made it possible for Peet to buy his first color TV and stereo system.

Pryor's drawing power also helped make it possible for Mitzi Shore to expand her comedy empire rapidly. She spent $50,000 turning Art Laboe's former space into a 450-seat showroom, which she christened "the Main Room." Much of the work was done by her in-house labor force of comics. While some scraped and hammered and painted, Argus Hamilton and several other runners were dispatched to fetch supplies from merchants all over town, armed with Shore's credit card and her driver's license for verification. As a safeguard, she blacked out her birth date on the license, saying, "It's none of their business how old I am." Hamilton risked immolation by carting lumber and painting materials from the hardware store in Shore's Ford Pinto.

Shore opened a Comedy Store branch in the Pacific Beach neighborhood of San Diego and purchased three beachfront condos nearby, one for herself and two for the comedians who would be performing at the club. And she pushed her brand beyond California by launching a college concert tour called "A Night at the Comedy Store," featuring three comics. (Shore later moved the club from Pacific Beach to the far more upscale community of La Jolla).

When Shore surveyed her thriving operation, she saw not a nightclub business but a kind of college of comedy with a curriculum that allowed young comedians to develop their art in graduated stages—from potluck nights, to the regular lineup at Westwood and the Original Room, to headliner status in the Main Room. She saw the San Diego club as a paid vacation for comics who had done particularly well. They earned $300 for the Tuesday-through-Sunday gig and were sometimes driven down to La Jolla by limousine on Monday night. She thought of the college concert tour, which paid $100 per show, as on-the-job training for their eventual careers as opening acts on the road. In this view, she was the founder of Comedy U, its head of faculty and dean of students. And Professor Pryor was the school's comedian emeritus, her genius in residence.

Everywhere she looked in the spring of 1977, Shore saw signs that her grand vision was producing results for her comics.

Jay Leno made his first appearance on *The Tonight Show* on March 2, nearly three years after he moved to Los Angeles. Robin Williams and Mike Binder accompanied him to the taping.

He stumbled out of the box when his first two bits fell flat. Then, in a rare *Tonight Show* moment, a man in the studio audience heckled him. Leno paused for just the right fraction of a second, then turned slightly toward Carson and said, "This is the same guy who talks to the TV at home: 'Look out, Kojak! Behind you!' 'Oh, thank you, Mr. Viewer.'" He'd used that comeback on hecklers dozens of times during his years playing small clubs, but he never got a bigger laugh than the one he got from Carson.

Having righted himself, he sailed through the rest of his autobiographically inspired six minutes, which included a supposedly typical dinner-table discussion with his father:

"Dad, could you pass the salt?"

"Salt? We didn't have salt when we were kids. We had to live without it. We didn't have underwear or potatoes. We ate dirt every day of the week. Your mother and I hunted wild dogs for food. We had nothing when we were your age."

All in all, it was a solid debut. But Johnny didn't invite him over to chat on the couch, and Leno went to bed that night deeply bummed. But he bounced back with five more appearances that year.

Elayne Boosler finally got on *The Tonight Show* on August 9, no thanks to Carson. Boosler owed her big break to guest host Helen ("I Am Woman, Hear Me Roar") Reddy. She did well enough to be booked again on September 15, with Tim Conway and Johnny Mathis as guests and Carson hosting. But Johnny proved true to his bias. He never booked Boosler again.

George Miller made six *Tonight Show* appearances in 1977. He finally broke through when Craig Tennis, who didn't think he was very funny, left the show and was replaced by Jim McCawley, who did.

After knee surgery that kept him from performing for nearly a year, Richard Lewis made a triumphant return to *The Tonight*

*Show* in June 1977 and logged three more appearances before year's end.

David Letterman made his national TV debut in the summer of 1977 as a regular on the musical variety series *The Starland Vocal Band*.

Robin Williams and Argus Hamilton were cast as regulars in a new version of *Laugh In* that aired over the summer.

After scoring big ratings in the spring with a one-hour NBC TV special, Richard Pryor was signed by the network to do a comedy variety series, *The Richard Pryor Show*, beginning in the fall. Pryor showed his loyalty to the Comedy Store by hiring a cast comprised almost entirely of the club's young performers: Robin Williams, Argus Hamilton, Marsha Warfield, Sandra Bernhard, Paul Mooney, Tim Reid, John Witherspoon, and Charles Fleisher.

Robin Williams's rise had been meteoric. The product of a privileged upbringing in affluent Marin County, across the Golden Gate Bridge from San Francisco, he'd attended the Julliard School of Drama on scholarship and performed at San Francisco's Holy City Zoo before migrating to Los Angeles in September 1976. In the comedy capital of America, he had caused an instant sensation. Mitzi Shore was so knocked out by his first Monday night audition at the Sunset Strip Comedy Store that she immediately called the Westwood club and told Argus Hamilton, "I'm coming over right now with this new comic so he can do there what he just did here." Williams walked onto the Westwood stage barefoot and dressed in a T-shirt and overalls, placed his hands on his hips just so, and said with a spot-on prissy gayness, "Now a reading from *Two Gentlemen of Santa Monica*, also known as *As You Lick It*." Then he broke into full Shakespearean profundity: "Hark, the moon, like a testicle, hangs low in the sky." The audience exploded with laughter.

Shore wasted no time in giving Williams the best time slots at both clubs and putting out the word in the business that there was a new kid in town whose act had to be seen to be believed. Soon the lines to see Williams were long, and the buzz was palpable.

But it was Tom Dreesen who outdid all his Comedy Store pals in 1977. Following his first *Tonight Show* appearance the previous December, Dreesen appeared in quick succession on every TV show that booked comics: *The Merv Griffin Show*, *The Dinah Shore Show*, *The Mike Douglas Show*, *American Bandstand*, *Midnight Special*, *Don Kirschner's Rock Concert*, *Soul Train*, *Match Game*, and *Hollywood Squares*. A guest appearance on the talk show *Sammy and Company* moved host Sammy Davis Jr. to announce, "Man, I'm taking you on the road with me." Dreesen spent the rest of the year opening alternately for Davis and Tony Orlando in the biggest showrooms in Vegas, Tahoe, Reno, and Atlantic City. He also logged eight more appearances on *The Tonight Show* (for a total of fifteen since his debut). Two years before, he'd been broke and worried about paying rent. Now, his annual income was approaching $300,000, and he was able to buy a house in Sherman Oaks with a bedroom for each of his three kids. Thank you, Johnny.

But the biggest thrill of the year for Dreesen was when he went back home to Harvey, Illinois, where the city fathers proclaimed "Tom Dreesen Day" in honor of his three sold-out nights in the 1,000-seat ballroom of the Harvey Holiday Inn. People paid $25 each to see the local boy who'd made good, netting Dreesen a nifty payday of $58,000. At the close of each hour-plus performance, he turned serious.

"Normally, wherever I go I end the show with my biggest laugh and then walk off," he said. "But this isn't just any audience in any town. This is my home. And it's a very emotional night for me because when I look out at you, I see the faces of people whose golf bags I carried in the hot sun, for nickels and dimes. I see people who I sold newspapers to on the street corner, for nickels and dimes, and people whose shoes I shined on my hands and knees, for nickels and dimes. And as I stand here now, I can't help thinking. . . . Boy, I really got you bastards back tonight."

# Richard's Baroness,
# Steve's Movie

No one took more advantage of the era's prevailing sexual promiscuity than Richard Lewis. One of the reasons he preferred performing at the Improv to working at the Comedy Store was that the bar at Budd Friedman's place was a much better scene for meeting beautiful women.

One night, he managed to get picked up by a pair of them, but when they got him to their apartment, he passed out on the bed from drinking while they were taking their clothes off. Later, he dimly remembered them, naked and irritated, trying to get him to perform, to no avail. The next thing he remembered was being dumped out of their car a few blocks from the Improv. Such misadventures became grist for his act, entries in the sex manual he told audiences he was writing, titled *Ow! You're on My Hair*.

There were serious relationships as well. Lewis had a whirlwind romance with actress Debra Winger, a former cocktail waitress at the Improv who'd become an overnight sensation for her performance in *Urban Cowboy*. Unfortunately for him, Winger was just taking flight and not interested in limiting herself to the exclusive sort of relationship he envisioned. After a few months, she left him nursing a badly broken heart.

He bounced back quickly, however. One night that spring, he'd just finished a terrific set and was huddled with a handful of comics in the Improv bar when he spotted the most beautiful woman he'd ever laid eyes on. She was looking right at him and smiling, so he assumed she'd just watched the show. Suddenly he realized he knew who she was: Nina van Pallandt, the Danish actress and baroness who'd starred with Elliott Gould in Robert Altman's *The Long Goodbye*. She'd been on the cover of *Life* magazine.

"I'm going to go over and talk to her," he said to his friends.

"Get the fuck outta here," was their response. "She's a princess or something."

"I don't care," he shot back. "I'm a regular at the Improv."

He walked across the room, figuring he had nothing to lose and maybe twenty seconds to make an impression. He introduced himself and dropped one of the greatest pickup lines in the history of male-female relations: "I'll take you out for a tuna fish sandwich anywhere in the city." She laughed. The next night they went for a long walk on the beach in Santa Monica. He was twenty-nine and she was forty-three with three teenage children, but none of that mattered. They fell madly in love.

Lewis spent the summer of 1977 on the road opening for Sonny and Cher. The duo's reunion TV series had fizzled, but they remained a big draw on the concert circuit. Lewis was paid about $500 a week (they got as much as $175,000 a night), and his job was basically to keep the crowds occupied for half an hour or so while the stars put on their makeup. In the stand-up comedy trade, it's known as "custodial work."

The tour was stressful for Lewis because he missed Nina, and the only thing he could count on was the fact that no one in the crowd had paid to see him or even knew who he was. At the state fair in Harrisburg, Pennsylvania, he had to perform outdoors at 4:00 p.m. with a roller coaster running full bore behind him and circus animals being paraded around a race track between him and the audience. He was supposed to do thirty minutes, but the distractions were so extreme that he raced through his routine and bolted from the stage after ten minutes, sure that it meant the end of his career. He was consoled by a grizzled patron who told him, "Trust me, kid. Bill Cosby was here last week, and he only did fifteen minutes."

In Hartford, Connecticut, they played the 15,000-seat Hartford Civic Center. Before the show, Lewis had dinner in the center's glassed-in VIP restaurant. From where he sat, he could barely see the stage; it had to be a quarter of a mile away. He looked around at all the people drinking and eating steaks and lobster and realized that in a little while he was going to be playing to them, competing with the booze and the butter sauce for their attention. That's when the fear set it, and he started drinking. By showtime he was slurring his words. It was not a good performance, even if the folks in the restaurant were too far away to tell.

The next day, Sonny Bono chided him. "Were you a little loaded last night? You seemed kind of off." Lewis told him what had happened at the restaurant. "Well, you really should try to cool it," Bono said gently.

Lewis didn't know Cher—she always showed up just before the couple went on stage—but he considered Sonny a friend. They'd hung out together after shows. And Sonny had given him his big break in show business after all. Lewis was determined to make up for letting Sonny down in Hartford. Later in the tour, they were playing the Montreal Forum, home of the Canadiens hockey team. As Lewis walked onto the stage, he decided that for Sonny he was willing to sell out his own beloved hockey team. "The New York Rangers suck," were the first words out of his mouth. The crowd was instantly on its feet cheering. He never lost them after that.

When the tour moved to Wisconsin, they played another outdoor venue, with 15,000 people spread out on picnic blankets.

Lewis's show was at 7:30 p.m. when it was still light out. Bono knew that was a bad situation for a stand-up comic, so he surprised Lewis by showing up just before he went on stage. "I just came to see the fear in your eyes," he said with a smile. That triggered something in Lewis that moved him to deliver his best set of the entire tour. He didn't just kill—he destroyed. Walking back to his hotel at dusk, he looked back over his shoulder at the huge banks of ballpark lights illuminating moths the size of Rodan, and he heard the announcer say over the loudspeaker, "Ladies and gentlemen, please welcome Sonny and Cher." He felt a surge of pride. All by himself, he'd made 15,000 people laugh in broad daylight. He had nothing more to prove to anyone. When this tour was over, he was never going to be an opening act again.

Between touring with Sonny and Cher and falling in love with Nina, Lewis had little time to hang out with Steve Lubetkin. But from their frequent phone conversations, he gathered that Steve's career was not rising with the comedy tide. *Dante Shocko* apparently was a bust. After spending eighteen months getting the film shot and edited, Steve couldn't get anyone to distribute it. Richard had attended one of the two industry screenings that Steve set up at the Encore Theater on Melrose Avenue, along with one hundred plus agents, managers, distribution executives, fellow comics, friends, and friends of friends. Steve's brother, Barry, even flew in from New York to see the movie. Mitzi Shore came, too.

Lewis knew he wasn't the most objective judge of Steve's work, but he thought the movie was funny, rough in places, sure, with some jokes that fell flat, but with lots of energy and Steve-ness. Mostly, he was impressed that Steve had pulled it off, down to getting all those people to show up for the screening. He didn't know any other young comic who'd written, produced, and starred in his own movie.

As usual, Lubetkin put on a brave face for his best friend. He was disappointed about the movie but not discouraged, he said.

He still thought *Dante* would be released eventually, and it would be a success. The problem, he said, was that all "the biggies" running the movie companies just didn't know what funny was.

Steve told Richard that he and Susan Evans were now working together as a stand-up team, billed as Lubetkin & Evans. He was writing the material for them, and they were gigging at small clubs around LA in preparation for taking the act to the Comedy Store stage.

Richard didn't say it, but he was concerned that Steve was letting another career setback send him spinning off in an entirely different direction, just as he'd done when *The Tonight Show* rejection caused him to quit stand-up and turn filmmaker. He worried that Steve was far more upset about the fate of his movie than he was letting on.

In fact, Steve was devastated, in no small part because most of the money spent to make *Dante Shocko* had come from his father. Jack Lubetkin lent him more than $15,000, which was a lot of money for a man of his means to lose. Barry kicked in a few thousand, too. Both men had been reluctant to invest in the movie, but Steve lobbied hard, peppering them with phone calls and letters that played up the project's "can't-miss" qualities. "The director thinks *Dante* will be a giant hit."

They weren't persuaded by his rosy predictions of huge profits; they put up the money because they feared he'd take their failure to do so as lack of faith in his talent. The movie was so important to him—he had so much of his ego invested in it—that they felt they needed to back him to whatever extent they could.

The long production and editing process had put a strain on family relations, as Jack Lubetkin fretted that the first-time director Steve had hooked up with, William Larrabure, was more interested in taking the money than making the movie. Steve defended Larrabure's slow pace by saying he was "a perfectionist and a meticulous editor whose wife had a miscarriage, which took him out of action for a period." Later, he revealed that "Bill is leaving his wife and has been living under intense stress" and that the director "simultaneously had to work on another project."

The tension between father and son got to the point where Steve began communicating only with Barry. "If you call me on my birthday please give me a birthday present by sparing me the doubts, accusations and second guesses that help nothing and just give me physical pain," he wrote in a letter.

"I'll tell you, living as I do (poor) and with the expectations I have (justified and big) it's a wonder I haven't had a nervous breakdown already. Barry, in a short while you and daddy will be very, very proud of me, not only because of the movie I've created but because of the hell I've lived through in waiting for it.

"The film is going to stun you," he wrote. "*Believe me.*"

Jack and Barry Lubetkin wanted to believe in Steve's dream, but the demise of *Dante Shocko* made it exponentially more difficult. They'd watched him ride the comedy roller coaster for six years—rising and falling, veering one way and then the next, from Budd Friedman to Mitzi Shore to Johnny Carson to *Dante Shocko*—and now they feared he was careening toward a crash.

It was Steve's idea to form Lubetkin & Evans; Susan had reservations. For one thing, in an effort to work her into the act, he was writing skits that involved putting on wigs and hats and changing characters, and she didn't think the material went over as well as when he was just going one-on-one with the audience. That's where he excelled—in working off the cuff, responding to heckles. But Steve was certain that the new act would work. As he wrote in a two-page manifesto aimed at girding them for the task ahead, "If we stick it out, we'll make it. If we follow these rules, we'll stick it out. Therefore, if we follow these rules and read them, we will make it." The "rules" included

- We're the only male-female comedy team. That's the kind of selling point that speaks to people. Stick it out.

- The more we do it, the more we can make a living from it.
- Everyone endures failure, hecklers, noise. . . . Just brush it off, hang in, and make it.
- Totally disregard embarrassment, criticism, etc.
- The rewards for sticking it out are the biggest of any business.
- The heckles and put-downs are just like the occasional rejection you get in any business.
- Worst thing just a temporary pain.
- We could experience one of the greatest joys imaginable—shared joy as it happens.
- We could help people we like, if we make it. . . . Stick it out.

# The Funniest Year Ever

In the annals of American entertainment, 1978 will be remembered as the Year of Comedy. The Fiftieth Annual Academy Awards ceremony kicked it off on April 3 when Woody Allen's *Annie Hall* won an unprecedented (for a comedy) four Oscars—Best Picture, Best Actress (Diane Keaton), Best Director, and Best Original Screenplay (both to Allen).

Faster than you could say, "I'd like to thank my agent," the major Hollywood studios had multiple picture deals in place with Steve Martin, Mel Brooks, Gene Wilder, Richard Pryor, Lily Tomlin, David Steinberg, Martin Mull, Marty Feldman, Chevy Chase, Cheech and Chong, and the writing staff of the *National Lampoon*. A number of them got what was becoming known in the business as "the Woody Allen deal." Steve Martin's contract, for example, called for him to receive $500,000 to write and star in his first movie, *The Jerk*, which he could also direct if he wanted to (he didn't). In addition, Universal Pictures agreed to give Martin and his company, Aspen Film Society, the final cut, the last word on the movie's marketing campaign, and 50 percent of the profits.

Martin quickly set a new standard for stand-up success. On April 22, he promoted his upcoming national concert tour with his fifth appearance as the host of *Saturday Night Live*. His musical guests that night were John Belushi and Dan Aykroyd in their debut as the Blues Brothers. *SNL* was just hitting its creative peak in 1978, becoming the highest-rated late-night show in TV history and forging what was being hailed as "the best demographic in television," an audience dominated by eighteen- to thirty-four-year-olds, the big spending, record-buying, and movie- and concertgoing public.

Martin went on to play sixty sold-out one-nighters (at a minimum fee of $75,000), packing concert halls and stadiums with as many as 20,000 near-hysterical fans who came not so much to laugh as to cheer their favorite Martin routines—his greatest hits—not waiting for punch lines, breaking into applause at the first hint of "happy feet."

"It's kind of like being Jesus or Hitler," Martin told the *Los Angeles Times*, referring to the phenomenon that his fellow comics dubbed "rock 'n' roll comedy."

Indeed, Martin's first album, *Let's Get Small*, went multiplatinum during the tour, and he scored a No. 1 single with *King Tut*, which was born as a musical comedy sketch on *SNL*. (*King Tut* was featured on his follow-up album, *A Wild and Crazy Guy*, which was named after another *SNL* sketch. Together Martin's two albums sold more than 5 million copies.)

Meanwhile, based on their *SNL* appearance with Martin, Blues Brothers Aykroyd and Belushi landed a million-dollar contract of their own with Atlantic Records. On September 18, they opened for Martin at the Universal Amphitheater in what was regarded as the concert of the year in Los Angeles. Atlantic recorded the Brothers' performance and released it as an album titled *Briefcase Full of Blues* during the first week of December. Naturally, it shot to No. 1 on the pop charts on its way to selling 2 million copies. At the same time, Belushi's first movie, *Animal House*, was setting a box office record for a comedy, racking more than $100 million in U.S. ticket sales. Executives at Universal Pictures, which produced and distributed *Animal House*, fell all over themselves to sign Belushi and Aykroyd to write and star in *The Blues Brothers Movie*. By the time *SNL's* fourth season got underway in the fall, most of its cast had movie and/or record deals in the offing. "They've become the Beatles of comedy," said talent manager Bernie Brillstein, who numbered Aykroyd, Belushi, Gilda Radner, and *SNL* producer Lorne Michaels among his clients.

Any showbiz suit could see that America was in a mood to laugh. And that put Mitzi Shore and Budd Friedman and their stables of stand-up comics at the vortex. The atmosphere inside the Comedy Store and the Improv was positively charged as an army of agents, managers, talent scouts, network executives, and show producers prowled the showrooms, hallways, bars, and parking lots, looking for new talent to feed the public's appetite for humor. In the days before twenty-four-hour cable TV and videotapes that could be sent around to serve as auditions, if you wanted to see comedians, you had to go see them perform live.

A quartet of TV heavyweights stopped by the Sunset Comedy Store on February 23 to check out Andy Kaufman's performance in the Main Room. James L. Brooks, Ed. Weinberger, Stan Daniel, and Dave Davis were the writing-producing team responsible for one of the most successful sitcoms in TV history, *The Mary Tyler Moore Show*, and they wanted to see if Kaufman's "Foreign Man" character would fit into their follow-up sitcom, which was to be set in a New York cab company.

Kaufman was about the last young comic you'd expect to take a regular role on a sitcom. A veteran of seven appearances on *SNL* and four on *The Tonight Show*, he was enjoying a thriving business on the college concert circuit and was booked to play such upscale venues as the Huntington Hartford Theater in Los Angeles and Town Hall in New York. Kaufman's envelope-pushing act— featuring Conga lines, bikini-clad female wrestlers, and audience sing-alongs of "The Cow Goes Moo"—seemed the antithesis of prime-time network fare. And he had a reputation among his peers (no matter how weird they thought he was personally) as a true and fearless artist. It would be like Belushi taking a role on *Three's Company*.

But the historical imperatives were compelling. Freddie Prinze had proved to TV executives that it was time for baby boom comics to take over the American sitcom (*Chico and the Man* didn't survive Prinze's death by much), so the networks were offering bags of money and making unusual creative concessions to young comic talent. To everyone's surprise, including his own, Kaufman agreed to join the cast of *Taxi*, playing the gibberish-spouting mechanic Latka Gravis. His pay was $10,000 per episode. He assuaged any guilt he may have had by agreeing to appear in only eight episodes in the first season.

The same month, two other unlikely candidates for sitcom stardom, Richard Lewis and Robin Williams, sat side by side in a Paramount casting office waiting to audition for a guest-starring role in an episode of the hit sitcom *Happy Days*. The episode was titled "My Favorite Orkan," and the role was that of an alien named Mork from the planet Ork. Lewis knew he didn't have a chance in hell because you were supposed to deliver the lines in what you imagined was the voice of a space alien. Lewis didn't do voices. The best he could manage was a pathetic imitation of his girlfriend Nina's accent. Williams, on the other hand, couldn't stop doing voices. "Man, this is practically written for you," Lewis said. "If you don't get this part, it's a joke."

Lewis was called into the audition room first. He started reading as if he were a Danish alien but then stopped. "You know, Robin Williams is next," he told the casting director and his assistants. "He *is* Mork, and if he doesn't get this, then you are all crazy. I don't want to waste any more of your time," he said, walking to the door and opening it. "Mork is waiting outside, and I'd like to bring him in right now. So would you all please welcome . . . *Robin Williams!*"

Williams bounded into the room and blew the doors off the place. He got the part "because he was the only alien who showed up for the audition," executive producer Gary Marshall was quoted as saying later. When the "My Favorite Orkan" episode aired a few weeks later, Williams's performance as Mork generated the most viewer mail in the show's history, and he was offered his own spin-off series, *Mork & Mindy*, beginning in the fall. The contract that Paramount put on the table was for $15,000 an episode, or $3 million over five years. Williams quickly worked into his club act a mock-Shakespearean soliloquy about the decision he faced:

> TV or not TV; that is the question. Whether 'tis nobler to do stupid shit at 8 o'clock, aye to take the money and run and yet buy a condominium, this all vexes me thus. Yon video will take your mind and turn it to Jell-O, but yet whether 'tis nobler to take arms against the God Nielsen or to stay here and be in small clubs. . . .

In the end he took the money but passed on the condo in favor of a house in Topanga Canyon near the beach.

*Mork & Mindy* premiered September 1 on ABC and quickly became the No. 1 show on television. Williams was featured in *Time* magazine and *Newsweek*. *US* magazine and *People* both put him on the cover, the latter proclaiming him "the lunatic spark of TV's newest smash." The *Los Angeles Times* called him "comedy's newest phenomenon . . . an immediate contender for the sort of massive appeal that Steve Martin commands." Actually, Williams was more than a contender. With about 57 million viewers tuning in to see him each week, he clearly held the title as America's favorite funnyman. And all the media attention focused on him served to shine the spotlight more brightly on the Comedy Store and his fellow comics.

Mike Binder was working as the doorman at Sunset one night when *All in the Family* producer Norman Lear walked up to him and said, "Call me tomorrow." Binder did, and Lear cast him as a regular on his new sitcom, *Apple Pie*, guaranteeing the eighteen-year-old an income of at least $100,000.

Jay Leno was standing outside the club when a noted Czech film director named Ivan Passer handed him a card and asked if he wanted to be in a movie. Leno didn't recognize the name and thought it was a joke at first, but several weeks later he was on location in Switzerland, making a movie called *The Silver Bears* with Michael Caine and Cybil Shepherd.

At times, it seemed as if there were more Hollywood talent hunters, entertainment reporters, and celebrities in the audience than there were paying customers. At Westwood one night, the comics were unnerved to find themselves facing an audience that included Johnny Carson, Steve Martin, Paul McCartney, and Ringo Starr. At Sunset, Burt Reynolds and his then girlfriend Sally Field, Willie Nelson, and Sugar Ray Leonard came to see Richard Pryor, and after the show, they all sat at a table in the main room while Nelson played guitar and performed a private concert until 5 a.m.

Ringo Starr made a memorable solo appearance at Sunset one night, arriving so intoxicated that Mike Binder, who was working the door, had to help him to a seat in back. Starr was seated just as David Letterman took the stage, and the former Beatle immediately began heckling him, which attracted the attention of every comic within earshot. Letterman had a reputation for eviscerating hecklers, and as word spread along the back hallway, other comics started filing into the room to watch the impending bloodshed.

It wasn't a fair fight. In the spotlight, Letterman couldn't see who the heckler was, so he showed no mercy, and Starr was too drunk to appreciate how badly Letterman was beating him up. Finally, one of the comics took pity and called out, "Hey, Dave, it's Ringo."

"Oh, that makes sense," Letterman shot back in the direction of Starr. "You ruined your career, and now you've come here to ruin mine." George Miller almost fell off his stool laughing.

Letterman's TV career was starting to heat up. With the help of his new management company, Rollins-Joffe, he was cast, along with Michael Keaton, as a regular on *Mary*, CBS's new Mary Tyler Moore musical variety show. The series's show-within-a-show conceit had him playing the part of a behind-the-scenes staff member helping put together Mary's weekly TV variety program. Almost the only things the critics liked about *Mary* were Letterman and Keaton. Viewers avoided the show, and the network pulled the plug after only two months, but not before it dragooned Letterman into appearing as a member of "Team CBS" on *Battle of the Network Stars V*.

He was still smarting from that indignity when he finally got the break he'd been waiting for. Talent scouts from *The Tonight Show* had checked him out at the Comedy Store three or four times, and each time they'd come away saying he was "not quite ready." But on the strength of his performance on *Mary*, Rollins-Joffe went over the heads of the talent coordinators and arranged a meeting with the NBC development department, which was eager to have Letterman in its talent stable. With Carson's approval, NBC agreed to an unprecedented package of three *Tonight Show* appearances with a guarantee that Letterman would be invited over to sit on the panel with Johnny on his debut night.

Letterman was elated with the deal, but discomfited as well because it seemed as if he was being given an exemption that the other guys didn't get. Traditionally, you had to earn that invitation to sit on the couch; there was suspense. But thanks to his high-powered managers, he knew the outcome in advance. As he sheepishly admitted to Tom Dreesen, "It feels like a fixed fight."

Even so, Letterman was nervous and distracted on the day of his first appearance. Dreesen went with him to the taping, and while they were sitting in the green room waiting for the call to go on, Dave turned to him and said, "Well, this is it. Tomorrow I'll be back in Indianapolis."

Letterman's jitters evaporated the instant he stepped through the curtain. He could hear and feel the audience out there in the blackness beyond the camera lights, but the pressure wasn't the same as when he stood on a nightclub stage facing an expectant crowd of people who had hired babysitters, driven miles, parked their cars, and paid good money. The fear of letting the audience down was muted. He'd been practicing the lines for years, and they flowed flawlessly: "Yeah, Dave, this is Earl down at the garage. . . . "

After the show, Letterman said no to Dreesen's suggestion that they celebrate his triumph by watching the show with the gang at the Comedy Store. Dave wanted to be alone that night because, as usual, he didn't think he'd done very well.

Johnny Carson disagreed. The next day, *The Tonight Show* opened discussions with Rollins-Joffe about having Dave appear not as a guest but rather as a guest host. That was a breathtaking leap of fortune, on a par with Freddie Prinze's rocket ride out of obscurity. Just a few weeks earlier, Letterman had been unable to persuade Chris Albrecht, the manager of the New York Improv, to cash a $10 check. Now the world was being very nice to him. Nothing had changed except everything.

Jay Leno was not among those who got scooped up by network TV in 1978. He believed it was because the programming executives were afraid that his prodigious chin would scare away viewers, not because he was a lousy actor. He was a fierce competitor, but he didn't waste time brooding about the rejection because that summer he attained a longtime career goal by landing a two-week engagement opening for singer Tom Jones at Caesar's Palace in Las Vegas. When he was growing up and hoping to become a comedian, Caesar's was as good as it got, signaling that you'd made it to the big time. So the way he saw it, he didn't need TV; he was a stand-up comic, not a sitcom performer.

For Steve Lubetkin, 1978 turned out to be another disappointing year. After six months of occasional appearances at small clubs and a handful of late-night spots at the Westwood Comedy Store, the comedy team of Lubetkin & Evans called it quits, agreeing that she was happier as an actress, and he was better as a solo act. Susan knew it was hard for him to see everyone else catching breaks and succeeding, even though he was genuinely happy for them. He accompanied Richard to a live interview on *The Paul Wallich Show* on KIEV radio and recorded it for posterity on his portable cassette recorder. It meant so much to him when Richard gave him a shout-out on the air that he put the tape away with his keepsakes, writing on the label, "Lewis on Wallich, August 18, 1978; mentions my name."

Susan was supporting them with an office job, and Steve's dad contributed regularly. On a trip to LA, ostensibly to meet Susan, Jack Lubetkin bought Steve a car, a 1963 Buick Skylark. Susan and Jack hit it off immediately, and she could see that he adored Steve. On an outing to the Santa Monica pier, the two played off one another constantly, doing what they called "schticklacht," making it obvious where Steve got his offbeat sense of humor. But even in the most lighthearted of moments, she would see a worried look flicker across on Jack's face as he contemplated his son. He was proud of Steve's ability to make people laugh but doubtful that, given the economics of the club scene, it would lead to happiness for him. "Stevie," he would say, "maybe this just isn't for you."

Susan knew that deep down Steve wanted to be like his dad, a mensch who took care of his family and loved ones. But she also saw that Steve couldn't conceive of making a living in a practical way. He'd worked for a while as a file clerk at Paramount, where he contributed a comedy column to the company newsletter and played Santa Claus at the office Christmas party. But Steve had a resistance to what he called "straight jobs," believing that any time he spent in them subtracted from his chance of making it as a comic. His usual routine was to write in the morning, rehearse in the afternoon, and perform at night, working out the material in tiny venues like the Natural Fudge and Vegetarian Restaurant until he thought it was ready for the Westwood Comedy Store. Susan believed in Steve and his talent. She'd been in the audience at Westwood on nights when he was so "on" that people had tears of laughter in their eyes. The high of those moments, coupled with the success he saw happening all around him, kept Steve's comedy dreams alive. As he wrote in a motivational message to himself titled "Why I Should Never Get Uptight About Stand-up,"

- It's the thing I do best.
- It's the only thing I can do well that I can make big money with.
- I need to show success to Dad and Bar.
- I could advocate for good if I was famous—for decency, national health insurance, candidates I like.
- It's the only way I can achieve fame.

# Roommates

Mitzi Shore had reason to feel proud. Not quite five years after her ex-husband asked her to tend to his troubled business while he was out of town, she sat at the center of the biggest boom in show business. Yes, she'd been lucky to be in the right place at the right moment, but she had made that moment her own. The networks' prime-time schedule read like a roster of young comics whose careers she'd fostered: Jimmie Walker, Andy Kaufman, Robin Williams, David Letterman, Jay Leno, Michael Keaton, Mike Binder, Billy Crystal (now a regular on the sitcom *Mary Hartman, Mary Hartman*), and Steve Landesberg (a regular on the sitcom *Barney Miller*). Of course, Budd Friedman could—and did—claim the same influence over many of their careers ("According to Budd, Magellan got his start there," Letterman once quipped). But Shore got more ink, partly because she was a female in the traditionally male role of club owner and partly because she was so odd that she made for a better story than Budd, what with her unforgettable voice, stringy beatnik hair, and dark, rococo office lit only by Tiffany lamps that made the room look, in the words of one comic, "like a brothel designed by Disney." This, after all, was a woman who named her daughter Sandi Cee Shore.

Shore no longer held a monopoly. There was now a third major showcase club in New York, the Comic Strip, and two more paying clubs in the Los Angeles area, the Comedy and Magic Club in Hermosa Beach and the Laff Stop in Newport Beach. Clubs that used to feature comics as entertainment one night a week were adding nights, and more clubs were being planned. But the Comedy Store was more than a nightclub. Under her tutelage, it had become an institution. And Shore was more than a club owner. ABC made that official by signing her to a contract as a consultant, charged with seeking out young comic talent for the network's shows. As 1978 drew to a close, Mitzi Shore was the undisputed queen bee of comedy, and her hive was humming.

Shore chose that moment to reveal her latest plan for expansion. She called a meeting of all her female comics and told them that she was going to convert an empty space next to her office on the second floor of the Sunset building into a showroom for women only. It would be called the Belly Room, in honor of the belly dancers who had performed there back in the days of Ciro's. She liked the name because it also called to mind the womb and the best kind of laughter. So it had a triple meaning.

"This will be your own space where you can develop your own style of comedy," she said. It would be a supportive atmosphere, where they could be their feminine selves, free from the testosterone-fueled competition and male dominance of the other rooms.

"Women are not like men," she explained. "You can't do the same kind of comedy they do. Now Totie Fields, God rest her soul, she could because she had a very masculine delivery, but most women can't."

The twenty or so women gathered in the Original Room to hear Shore ranged from thirty-six-year-old Lotus Weinstock to fifteen-year-old Alison Arngrim. So Shore's words fell upon ears separated by a generation. Weinstock loved the idea so much that some of the others suspected she had planted it with Mitzi. Robin Tyler, too, was all for it. Of course, as a militant feminist lesbian, she was pretty much for anything that excluded men. Some of the younger women were ambivalent. They were happy to hear that Mitzi understood their plight as women comics and wanted to do something about it. And they could sure use the additional time slots. But they wondered if this was the best way to gain parity with the men in the marketplace. To be assigned to a special room? Sent to special school? They worried about being marginalized, ghettoized.

Elayne Boosler dismissed the whole idea as ridiculous. There was no need to separate the sexes, she thought. People laughed at what was funny. No one ever sat there and said, "Gee, that was funny. Too bad you're a girl." Marsha Warfield was offended, "just like I would be if someone was proposing a 'Negro Night.'" Neither woman had any intention of ever performing in the Belly Room. No way.

The youngest in the room, Alison Arngrim, was appalled by what she heard but not completely surprised. She'd experienced a side of Mitzi that few, if any, of the others had seen.

Arngrim was not a typical teenager. For one thing, she was already famous. America knew her as Nellie Olson, the mean little girl on *Little House on the Prairie*. Arngrim had grown up in Los Angeles, the product of a show business family. She'd been around performers, agents, managers, producers, and impresarios all her life. But she thought she'd never met anyone more cunningly manipulative than Mitzi Shore.

After passing a Monday night audition, Arngrim had started performing at Sunset, mostly in the wee hours on weeknights. By law, she couldn't even be inside the club unless she was performing. So, she waited out in the parking lot until someone signaled through the front window that it was time for her to go on. Then, she'd run into the building and up onto the stage and launch into an act that played off her precocity: "Hi, I just came from the Roman Polanksi Day Care Center."

The fact that a young actress on a hit TV show still aspired to be a stand-up comic indicated the respect the profession was accorded at that moment. And for all her Hollywood worldliness, Arngrim still retained some vestige of teenage girlhood. She had a secret crush on Jay Leno and thought he had a really cute butt.

Arngrim had been performing for a few months when Shore called her and said she wanted to meet with her in her office. "No one else, just you alone," she said. As a fifteen-year-old, Arngrim wasn't allowed to go anywhere unescorted. Someone always accompanied her to auditions and engagements. Her agent thought Shore's request was weird but decided it was okay for Arngrim to go because Shore was a woman—"and what could she possibly do to you."

In the course of the meeting, Arngrim concluded that Shore wanted to control her, dictate what kind of material she did, become her mother. Shore launched into a spiel about "what was appropriate for a young lady," as if she found the very idea of a fifteen-year-old female comic distasteful. After a few minutes, Arngrim cut her off with her own spiel.

"Look, if you don't like my act and don't think I'm funny, then don't give me any times," she said. "If I come in and perform and people don't laugh, then don't book me. And if you don't think that any of the tourists in the audience watch *Little House* and sometimes come here because they heard the girl from *Little House* is performing here, then okay."

Shore wasn't used to being talked to that way. She was seething when Arngrim left, and Arngrim felt like she'd just done battle with Cruella De Vil. Shore kept booking her, but not at Sunset, only at Westwood, which suited Arngrim just fine because she thought the Sunset building had a kind of dark, spooky energy.

As she listened to Shore sharing her vision of the Belly Room several months later, Arngrim realized that the previous encounter really hadn't been about her at all. Shore was just the product of another time. She was channeling her Jewish mother and grandmother from whom she'd inherited the mind-set that women had certain roles to play. It was like in the 1950s when young women were told what courses to take in college to attract a good husband. "My home ec teacher wouldn't give this speech," Arngrim thought to herself. "Any minute she's going to start telling us what kind of material we should do to be better wives and mothers."

Shore didn't hear any of the women's concerns about the Belly Room, however. No one said anything to her that day for fear of upsetting her. She may have been wrongheaded, but she still owned the club. Most of the women adopted a wait-and-see attitude.

As far as Shore was concerned, the main problem she faced at the Comedy Store had to do with the Main Room—it wasn't working out as planned. Hoping to rekindle the glamorous spirit of Ciro's by offering a taste of the Las Vegas strip on Sunset Strip, she had opened the venue with considerable fanfare in the fall of 1977, with Jackie Mason headlining a four-night stand. After Mason came similar multiple-night runs by Mort Sahl, Shelley Berman, Dick Gregory, and Andy Kaufman. But booking acts with names big enough to sell tickets became more difficult as 1978 wore on because the Vegas headliners Shore had been counting on—the Don Rickles and Shecky Greens of the world, her old buddies—couldn't be convinced to appear there. Even with her offer of half the door—amounting to an easy five grand for 90 minutes of in-town work—they worried about the financial impact on their careers. They earned their biggest paychecks in Vegas and feared that if people could see them in Los Angeles—just a six-hour drive or one-hour plane flight away—then it would siphon off their customers in the casinos, causing their prices to drop. They sympathized, but it just wasn't worth the risk, they told her. As a result, Shore was reduced to booking such marginal acts as Tiny Tim, who drew barely a handful of people one Saturday night. After she'd spent a small fortune redecorating it, the Main Room sat empty most of the time.

She was discussing the problem one day with two of her most loyal employees, Argus Hamilton and Biff Maynard, when Hamilton hit on a possible solution. Why not put her most popular performers in there, say, a package of five, doing twenty-minute sets? Imagine the marquee: "Tonight: Robin Williams, Jay Leno, David Letterman, Elayne Boosler, and Tom Dreesen." Who wouldn't pay $5 or $10 a pop to see that? Call it "The Best of the Comedy Store." It had a young, rock 'n' roll ring to it, like "The Comedy Store's Greatest Hits." It could be a record album.

Shore thought it was brilliant, a no-brainer: more time slots for the comics, more customers for the Store. Win-win. It never occurred to her that it would spark a rebellion, with the women at the forefront.

# The New Year's Resolution

At 3:00 a.m. on New Year's Day 1979, the tables at Canter's Deli were groaning with comics just coming down from the high of their New Year's Eve performances at the Comedy Store. Both the Sunset and Westwood clubs had been filled to capacity, and the crowds ringing out the Year of Comedy had been promiscuous with their laughter. To hear the comics tell it, there'd been so much killing, destroying, and massacring from the stage that it was a miracle anyone in the audience got out alive.

At Tom Dreesen's table, Michael Rapport was rhapsodizing about his set at Westwood, telling the others, "It was the best I ever did. I mean, every bit worked. I've never experienced anything like it." A few minutes later, he turned to Dreesen and said, sotto voce, "Hey, Tommy, can you lend me five bucks for breakfast?"

"Sure, man," Dreesen whispered, digging a bill out of his wallet and passing it under the table. Dottie Archibald caught the exchange and quickly turned away so as not to embarrass Rapport. Like Dreesen, she was known as a soft touch and had been hit up for a fiver numerous times. It always made her feel sad; there were so many broke comics.

Dreesen usually didn't stop to ponder the underlying inequity of working comics having to borrow money to eat. He figured it was part of the deal that they'd all signed onto. But on this night, the deal seemed more unfair than usual because Mitzi Shore had charged $20 a head at the door. He did the math in his head: $20 times approximately four hundred seats times three shows equaled $24,000, not a penny of which went to the comics. It seemed all the more unfair a little later when one of the Comedy Store waitresses stopped in at Canter's and mentioned that she had made $214 that night.

Two Saturday nights later, Dreesen arrived at the Comedy Store for his 9 p.m. set and was informed by one of Mitzi's assistants that instead of performing in the Original Room, he would be appearing in the Main Room, along with four other comics.

"No shit?" he said, pleased at his apparent promotion. He'd been on the road and hadn't heard about Mitzi's new plan for making the Main Room profitable. This was debut night for "The Best of the Comedy Store," and the others on the bill were Robin Williams, Jay Leno, David Letterman, and Elayne Boosler.

None of them had played the Main Room before. It was considerably larger than the Original Room, with nearly four times the seats, a higher ceiling, a wider stage, and more sophisticated lighting. It was much more a professional showroom than a showcase club, and it definitely didn't feel like a workshop. The experience reminded Dreesen of performing in Tahoe or Vegas.

At Canter's after the show, Jay Leno got right down to it. "Does anyone think this system is fair anymore?" he asked rhetorically. "I mean, that place was fuckin' packed tonight. It took five of us to do it, but it was still packed, at $15 a head with a two-drink minimum. Shouldn't we get something for that? When Rodney [Dangerfield] and Richard [Pryor] play that room, Mitzi gives them the door. Shouldn't we get, like, I don't know, half the door?"

He got no argument from anyone at the table. They could calculate the cut as easily as he could: Half the door came to a little more than $800 per person. Leno didn't need the money. Like Dreesen, he was making a good living on the nightclub showroom circuit. Letterman's managers were negotiating a so-called holding deal with NBC that would pay him $250,000 to sit tight while the network figured out what to do with him. Robin Williams was a newly minted millionaire. Of the five who'd performed in the Main Room that night, only Boosler wasn't in a high tax bracket.

Dreesen kept thinking about Michael Rapport having to borrow five bucks for breakfast on New Year's morning after performing in one of the most prestigious entertainment venues in the country. And plenty of other Comedy Store regulars in Canter's that night were in the same boat. Eight hundred bucks would make their month, covering rent, food, and transportation. Some of them were in fairly desperate circumstances, practically subsisting on the two free beers they got for performing and on the condiments at the bar—the cocktail cherries, olives, and lemon wedges that they only half-jokingly referred to as "the buffet."

There was no end to the survival stories. Marsha Warfield was often so broke that she was reduced to stealing restaurant crackers, which she took home to the apartment she shared with comics Brad Sanders and Jimmy Cook and turned into fried cornmeal. Cook was the only one of the three who had a car, so on nights when there was no money for gas or Cook couldn't pick her up, Warfield walked home from the Comedy Store at 2:00 a.m., a one-hour trek to the corner of Santa Monica Boulevard and Tamarind Street through an area being terrorized by a sadistic serial killer known as the Hillside Strangler.

Acting on a tip from comic Johnny Witherspoon, Warfield and Sanders sometimes went to the Comedy Store in the morning and crawled around on the floor in search of change dropped by the previous night's customers. One day, they came up with just enough to buy some Rice-A-Roni at the Ranch Market on Vine Street. Hoping to stretch the meal a little further, Sanders slipped a package of ground beef down the front of his pants, but an old security guard spotted him and confronted the pair with a can of mace. "I'm not going to call the police because I can tell you're hungry," he said, "but you have to put it back and leave."

Warfield even panhandled for food on occasion, but always in true stand-up comic style. She'd walk up to women on the street and ask, "How are you doing today? Do you have any food in your purse?" She learned that a surprisingly high percentage of them did, about one in ten. And the percentage only dropped slightly when she specified, "You got any chicken?"

The experiences were hilarious in the retelling, but they'd been humiliating in the moment. The talk at the table quickly turned from getting a cut of the door in the Main Room to getting paid in the Original Room and at Westwood, too—the ultimate heresy.

Why shouldn't they get paid in all the rooms? A lot had changed in four years. The Store wasn't a small struggling club anymore. It was a massive, cash-generating laugh factory. And Mitzi was no longer a brand-new divorcee worrying about how to keep the business afloat and feed the four kids. She was driving a silver Jag and having an affair with Steve Landesberg. Rents had risen, and gas had just gone to $1 a gallon. About the only thing that hadn't changed was Mitzi's policy of not paying them.

For Leno, it was a matter of principle. "The sense is that our time and effort and talents aren't worth anything," he said.

"Jay's right. This isn't fair anymore," Boosler said. "We gotta have a meeting."

She and Dottie Archibald worked the phones the following week. It was a little like herding cats, but they managed to corral about twenty comics, including Leno, Letterman, Dreesen, Robin Williams, George Miller, Gallagher, and most of the headliners who were being asked to appear in the Main Room.

They met at Boosler's apartment on Sweetzer Avenue in West Hollywood, about half a mile from the Comedy Store. It was her third apartment in three years, and Leno had helped her move into each one. The last one, on Larabee Street, they nicknamed "the thirty-nine steps" because they had to haul all her belongings up several flights of stairs. At the end of the day, he pleaded, "Promise me you'll never buy a couch."

She had one now, plus a dining room table and chairs and a real bed—all signs of her burgeoning career. But she still had two wooden salad bowls in her cupboard that she'd "borrowed" from the Comedy Store in the early days, when they were all she had. Most of the comics had swiped dinnerware from the Store. They saw it as a kind of payback for not being paid, an unauthorized perk.

Despite the supposedly serious intent of the gathering, the conversation quickly took on the cadence of a session at Canter's, with people talking over one another and lobbing good-natured insults at anyone trying to make a point. Comics just can't help themselves; it's their nature. Life's a roast.

As host, Boosler tried to focus the group's attention on the subject at hand: getting paid for performing in the Main Room. "All of a sudden there are rules," she said. "We're not allowed to break in new material. We have to do what Mitzi calls 'a Vegas act.' We're supposed to dress up, no jeans and sneakers like in the Original Room. We're not allowed to 'experiment.' Does that sound like a workshop to you? What the hell. Why aren't we being paid?"

Once again, there was little disagreement. All present thought they should be paid some portion of the door. After all, Mitzi was already splitting the take with the older performers, so there was a precedent. All they had to do was ask her. They'd never done that before. Surely she'd realize that it was only fair and reasonable. Leno was so convinced she'd go along that he volunteered to be the go-between. After about an hour, the meeting appeared to be heading toward an easy resolution when Boosler asked a question that few of them expected. "What about the Original Room?"

Her question hung in the air unanswered as they pondered its import. The Original Room *was* the Comedy Store, its heart and its soul. For most of them, the Original Room had served as a womb, where they were nurtured in their fetal stage of funny. Professionally speaking, they were born in the Original Room. To propose any kind of change seemed like blasphemy. "No payment" was a founding premise of the place. To ask for money in exchange for performing there was like proposing that the "all men are created equal" line be removed from the Declaration of Independence. At least that was how Mitzi was likely to see it.

A psychologist would have had a field day with their conflicting feelings toward Shore. She was by turns their boss, their friend, their surrogate mother, their harshest critic, and their biggest fan. They flattered her to her face, made fun of her behind her back, craved her approval, and resented her dominion over their lives. They admired her and thought she was wacko. But none of them disliked her, and all felt a measure of gratitude for her patronage. Was this any way to show it?

Dreesen finally broke the silence. "The thing is, us getting paid for working the Main Room doesn't help the majority of our fellow comics who *aren't* working the Main Room and who really need the money," he said. "I don't think anyone here has had to borrow five bucks for breakfast recently."

There was no easy consensus this time. Some thought it was wrong to expect to be paid in the Original Room because most of the comics performing there weren't at a professional level yet. The workshop atmosphere allowed anyone with talent to rise at their own pace, they said. And weren't they all proof that the system worked? Why turn it into a professional room and run the risk of fucking everything up?

Others argued that it was a professional room already because there was so much media and industry presence on any given night that some comics had stopped trying out new material for fear of, as Robin Williams put it, "going down *el tubo* in front of the man from *Time* magazine."

Leno and Boosler floated a compromise idea borrowed from the New York Improv, where the new owners—Budd Friedman's ex-wife Silver and her partner Chris Albrecht—were giving comics $5 to cover cab fare between clubs so they could do sets at several places a night. Mitzi could give the comics $5 a night, too, they said, but call it "gas money" instead. That way she could preserve her no-payment policy and the comics still would be able to buy breakfast. Dreesen, Miller, and Letterman were among those who liked the idea and thought Mitzi might go for it. Leno again volunteered to be the messenger. But after more discussion, they decided they didn't feel comfortable speaking for the entire comedy community. By their own estimate, as many as two hundred performers worked the local club scene, with more hopefuls arriving every week. Shouldn't they have a say in this, too?

It was partly the optimism of the age and partly their sense of community that led them to believe they could get that many comics into a room to debate a common cause. It had never been done before. There'd never been a need. But now there was a growing feeling among them that the time had come to take some control of their futures. They'd been going to comedy college long enough. It was time to graduate.

They left Boosler's apartment that evening with a promise to call every comic they knew and use their status as Comedy Store headliners to convince their colleagues to show up at a time and place to be determined. It was a nutty notion—a convocation of comedians? Woodstock for clowns?—and a haphazard plan. But the stage was set for a historic confrontation.

# Drugs and Theft

Mike Binder felt like he'd died and gone to heaven. Among his earliest memories of growing up in Detroit was riding by Baker's Keyboard Lounge down the street from his house and seeing Lenny Bruce's name on the marquee. It was one of the first things he was able to read. He remembered watching Woody Allen on *The Ed Sullivan Show* and practically wearing out his George Carlin and Robert Klein albums. From age thirteen on, all he wanted to be was a comedian.

Now he was. More than that, he stood at the epicenter of comedy in America, a regular at the Comedy Store, where he might run into Carlin any night. And if that happened, he'd likely say, as casually as he could, "Hey, George," and shake his hand. And Carlin would say, "Hey," back and maybe even know who he was.

It was heady stuff for someone six months shy of his nineteenth birthday. Headier still was the feeling Binder had that he belonged there. He'd come to Los Angeles two years earlier clutching a copy of Phil Berger's book *The Last Laugh: The World of Stand-up Comics*, which chronicled the New York comedy scene of the late 1960s and early 1970s. Within days of his arrival, Binder was rubbing elbows with some of the guys in the book: Richard Lewis, Jay

Leno, Michael Preminger. The first money he earned in show business was $25 that George Miller paid him for a joke he wrote: "When I was in high school, I did a lot of drugs. Yeah, it was high High." It was a stupid joke, but filtered through George's persona, it was funny as hell. The night George used it on *The Tonight Show*, Binder called his father in Detroit to tell him to be sure to stay awake all the way to the stand-up comic near the end. "The guy's a friend of mine, Dad. And I wrote the fifth joke in." In the Comedy Store kitchen later that night, they all gathered around the TV to watch, and Binder's joke got a big laugh from both audiences.

Binder reveled in the camaraderie, loving the hanging out nearly as much as the performing. He was closest to Leno, who was ten years his senior and had slipped easily into the role of watchful big brother. One night, when Binder was deathly ill with an intestinal virus, bleeding from his butt and scared out of his mind, Leno literally carried him to the hospital and then phoned his father in Detroit to tell him what was happening and assure him that everything would be okay.

On a more typical night, Leno would pick Binder up in his mammoth '58 Buick Roadmaster—"Mr. Buick," as Jay called it— and they'd motor to the Store, where Binder would do an early spot and then wait around for Leno to perform in prime time. He never tired of seeing Leno rock a room. Afterwards, they'd hit Canter's and then head over to Jay's place to play the board game Risk for hours or watch tapes of other comics on *The Tonight Show*. For all his good fellowship, Leno had a latent cruel streak. He taped every comic on Carson and loved nothing better than to invite people over to watch particularly bad performances. "Hey, you wanna watch [so-and-so] bomb?"

Some weeknights they'd go to the Posh Bagel on Santa Monica Boulevard in West Hollywood to see Andy Kaufman perform, not as a comic but as a busboy. One or two nights a week, the breakout star of a hit network sitcom worked for minimum wage and went unrecognized for the most part, which is why he did it and why his comedian friends would show up to participate in his peculiar brand of performance art. They'd sit at a table like normal patrons, pretending not to know him. He'd ignore them and go about his busboy business. Then, something would happen: He'd drop or spill something, or they would. An argument would break out; shouting would ensue. Chairs might be knocked over, bagels thrown. Kaufman's pals would bolt for the parking lot before dissolving into laughter, and he'd resume bussing tables for the stunned customers without ever breaking character.

Kaufman had time to moonlight because, thanks in part to Binder, he didn't have to work very hard at his day job on *Taxi*. Kaufman hated the rehearsal process, believing it detracted from real performance. So, to keep him happy, Paramount agreed that he didn't have to rehearse all week with the rest of the cast just so long as he showed up fully prepared for the Saturday taping. The studio hired Binder to run Kaufman's lines with costars Judd Hirsh, Danny DeVito, Marilu Henner, Tony Danza, and Jeff Conaway—a move that didn't endear Andy to the others. Binder then would meet Kaufman on Friday night with a copy of the script and a diagram of the set—"Okay, they are doing this bit here, and Latka is over here by the car"—and Kaufman would go in the next morning and usually nail it in one take.

The gig was a great deal for Binder. He got $1,000 a week out of Kaufman's salary and daily access to some of the best writers, producers, and directors in the TV business. But he didn't take advantage of it. He really only wanted to be a nightclub comic and stay out until 5:00 a.m. with other nightclub comics. So, he constantly showed up half an hour late and dog tired for his 10:00 a.m. call on the *Taxi* set, irritating the cast and crew, who couldn't believe they had to wait "for a fucking stand-in." It pissed them off all the more at Kaufman.

When Binder wasn't hanging out with Leno, he gravitated to the hard-partying crowd. No teenager ever had easier access to controlled substances. Among comics, alcohol and pot were givens. You couldn't stand in the Comedy Store parking lot for five minutes without someone passing you a joint. Jay Leno, David Letterman, Tom Dreesen, and Andy Kaufman were in the small minority that didn't indulge. George Miller indulged more than anyone. His consumption of various and sundry downers began to worry his best buddies, Letterman and Dreesen, to the point that one afternoon they drove deep into the San Fernando Valley to check out a drug-rehabilitation facility. They explained to the woman in charge that they were interested in getting treatment for a friend. As they talked, she kept smiling at them oddly and glancing out the window. Finally, she admitted that she recognized them from *The Tonight Show* and asked if this was some sort of comedy bit they were doing. Was there a camera truck outside?

A few days later, Tom and Dave took George for a drive. "We need to talk to you," Dreesen said. "We're really concerned about your drug use. It seems to be getting out of hand."

"Oh, come *on*," George protested. "It's just recreational. I'm fine; don't worry about it." He was adamant that he would not go to rehab and said if they took him there, he would not get out of the car. Letterman looked at Dreesen and shrugged, "Well, we tried."

In the late 1970s, Hollywood was having a honeymoon with cocaine. The drug seemed tailor-made for the show business lifestyle—perfect for production crews working fourteen-hour shifts and six-day weeks on movie sets, just the thing for actors suddenly called to action after hours of sitting around waiting, a godsend for musicians dragging their tired asses off the tour bus for yet another two-hour show in yet another two-horse town.

Coke made its way into the comedy community, not surprisingly, around the time more and more people started getting paying gigs. Someone would come in off the road and walk into the

Westwood or Sunset club with a little extra swagger, and you could tell he was carrying. Having a little blow meant you could stay up drinking and partying a few hours longer. But coke was not like pot, a communal drug that could be passed around openly. You couldn't share your coke with a group because you couldn't afford to. The best you could do was pick a friend or two to do "bumps" with in the bathroom. Either that or hang with others who likewise were gainfully enough employed to have their own. In that way, coke was a separator, a barrier between the haves and have-nots. In a line that always got a big laugh, particularly at the Sunset Store, Robin Williams observed, "Cocaine is God's way of telling you that you're making too much money."

He would know. In the months since he had become a household name, Williams had turned into a party animal nonpareil. Despite the rigors of a weekly TV show that was built around him, he was out on the town nearly every night, making the scene at Westwood and Sunset, at the Improv, at the Off the Wall studio in Hollywood. If there was a stage, he got on it. "Live performing, that's my drug," he told one interviewer. "I really do feel like a junky, not just for the laughs but the energy."

Some of Williams's fellow comics knew that his energy was fueled increasingly by cocaine. He was part of a group that regularly ended up back at Mitzi Shore's house after the clubs closed on the weekend, drinking and snorting coke until near dawn. In addition to Williams, the gathering usually included Argus Hamilton, Biff Maynard, Ollie Joe Prater, Mike Binder, Richard Pryor, and Shore herself.

Pryor was the main attraction to the young comics. For them, to sit at the feet of the master while he told hilarious, wildly animated stories about his life in comedy was a near-religious experience. The blow just made it last longer.

Word of the after-hours get-togethers quickly got around and created bad feelings toward Mitzi's "pets." The uninvited resented the special access to Shore, to Pryor, and to the coke.

Straight-arrow Leno was upset for another reason. He thought the drugs and drinking were taking a toll on his two pals, Binder and Williams. He felt personally responsible for Mike because he'd told Burt Binder that his son was doing great out in Hollywood and promised to look out for him.

"You're going over to Mitzi's tonight, aren't you," Leno would say whenever Binder declined his invitation to come to his house after the show. "What are you doing that for? Why are you hanging out with those guys doing drugs? Don't you see that you are wasting your talent. You should stay home and work on your act."

But neither Binder nor any of the others heeded Leno's warning, and the results eventually proved disastrous for all of them.

Williams was causing concern among his fellow comics for another reason in early 1979. Of the group that emigrated to Los Angeles in the mid-1970s, he was the first to hit it big. And no one had ever hit it bigger, not Freddie Prinze, not even Steve Martin. With *Mork & Mindy* atop the TV ratings, Williams's fame was such that he wasn't merely recognized in public—he was mobbed. Even at the usually too-hip Comedy Store, newcomer fans began hollering out Mork's Orkan greeting, "Na-noo, na-noo," when he took the stage. Williams was embarrassed by such outbursts and uncomfortable being treated like a celebrity. But he didn't exactly hide from the spotlight. He seemed to turn up on every talk show and at every celebrity event; camera crews and reporters trailed him wherever he went. His face was unavoidable. *Time* magazine was about to put him on its cover, accompanied by the headline, "Chaos in Television, and What It Takes to Be No. 1."

In Williams's case, it took a lot of material. Much of what came out of Mork's mouth came straight from Williams's brain. The show's writers left him plenty of room to improvise by salting the script with stage directions like "Robin goes *off* here" in place of written dialog. The combination of *Mork & Mindy*, his club performances, extracurricular TV appearances, and constant media interviews put extreme pressure on Williams to be "on" during every waking moment. And it was that pressure, some of his pals said, that led him to commit the cardinal sin of comedy: borrowing other comics' material.

In a *People* magazine profile, Williams was depicted in full improvisational mode, suddenly interrupting the interview to answer a pretend telephone: "Suicide hotline. Hold please." It was a funny bit, but, as Williams's colleagues knew, it belonged to Gary Muledeer. He'd delivered the line many times at the Comedy Store with Williams in the crowd. In another instance, Williams uttered the vaguely druggie line "Reality, what a concept" so often that it became synonymous with him (and later the title of his first comedy album) instead of comedian Charles Fleisher, who had been saying it for years.

Williams attended a Gallagher show at the Ice House in Pasadena one night when the watermelon-smashing comic joked from the stage, "You know, I think marijuana is great for old people because it slows down time. I gave my grandmother a kilo of Columbian and a ton of yarn, and I got back an Afghan big enough to cover a garage."

A few nights later, Gallagher saw Williams on a talk show riffing about marijuana being good for old folks "because it makes time go so slow."

"That little fuckhead sucked up the essence of my joke," Gallagher was still complaining decades later.

Bill Kirchenbauer had a routine about playing Superman as a kid. He'd pull a towel out of his prop bag, tie it around his neck like a cape, run in a semicircle around the stage, then leap and land on a stool balanced on his stomach with his legs straight out in Superman flying position. It always got a great reaction from the crowd, in part because it was such an unexpectedly agile move for a man of Kirchenbauer's ample size.

Kirchenbauer was watching Williams onstage at the Comedy Store one night when Robin suddenly hopped onto the stool on his back, imitating the Man of Steel flying upside down. "Superman on drugs," he said.

Everybody laughed except Kirchenbauer, who confronted Williams afterwards and lit into him. "I'm sorry, man, it just popped into my head right then," Williams said by way of explanation, "my mind gets going so fast."

Tom Dreesen had a talk with Williams after he heard a line of his come out of Mork's mouth in the show's closing voice-over, when the lovable alien always reported his earthly observations back to his home planet. Williams was so apologetic and seemed so genuinely distraught over the "mistake," that Dreesen believed it truly had been inadvertent. He knew that Robin absorbed influences like a sponge, and given his wild performing style, it seemed entirely plausible that when he got on a roll and was literally spinning onstage, he really didn't know what he was going to say next. Richard Lewis, who had a similarly frantic, off-the-top-of-his-head style, had stopped watching other comics perform for fear of unconsciously doing the same thing.

Bill Kirchenbauer and others didn't buy it. These were no accidents, they argued. A comic knew when he was treading on another comic's idea. They'd all seen one another's act so many times that they knew every bit by heart. And everyone knew the rules: Whoever said it or did it first, owned it.

Before long, others were exaggerating the Dreesen-Williams conversation as an angry confrontation in which Dreesen had thrown Williams against the wall and threatened to punch him. "Why do you think they call him *Robin*," was one joke going around. "Did you hear that Canter's now has a Robin Williams sandwich?" went another. "Yeah, they give you the bun, but you have to steal the meat."

There was a measure of envy in the meanness. Williams had everything, all the talent, success, and money the others dreamed of. So, the idea that he would stoop to steal material on top of all that made people's blood boil. It wasn't like he was Ollie Joe

Prater, who stole material all the time but wasn't very good, so no-body gave a shit. Ollie Joe didn't have a snowball's chance in hell of getting on *The Tonight Show*. But what if Robin blurted out one of your bits while yukking it up on Johnny's couch? Accident or not, that material would be gone forever: You could never use it again or audiences would think you stole it from him. That's why Kirchenbauer, Gallagher, and a few others decided they would no longer perform in front of Williams. If he was in the room, they wouldn't go on.

The unpleasantness marked the first tear in the tightly knit fabric of the LA comedy community. Soon there would be others.

Richard Lewis with New York pals at a going-away party thrown for him the week he moved to Los Angeles to appear as a regular in an ill-fated Sonny and Cher TV variety series. From left to right: Louis Hall, Larry David (of *Curb Your Enthusiasm* fame), Lewis, and Mickey Appleman.

Portrait of a young comic: Richard Lewis on the author's back porch in Westwood, CA, May 1979.
PHOTO BY WILLIAM KNOEDELSEDER.

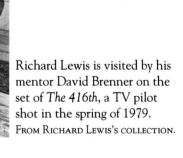

Richard Lewis is visited by his mentor David Brenner on the set of *The 416th*, a TV pilot shot in the spring of 1979.
FROM RICHARD LEWIS'S COLLECTION.

Steve Lubetkin. COURTESY OF BARRY LUBETKIN.

Steve Lubetkin and Susan Evans on a weekend trip to Las Vegas in 1978, a gift from Steve's brother Barry. COURTESY OF SUSAN EVANS.

The comedy team Lubetkin and Evans, 1978. COURTESY OF SUSAN EVANS.

Tom Dreesen as a young father in Harvey, Illinois, in 1968 before he became a stand-up comic.

"The world's fastest Caucasian"; Dreesen performs with Tim Reid in the early 1970s as part of the first and only black-and-white stand-up comedy team.

A photo taken from Dreesen's first appearance on *The Tonight Show*, December 9, 1975. The inscription is to Jeanne and Willie Franks, the husband-and-wife owners of the Junction Lounge in his old neighborhood in Harvey, where Dreesen was the only white patron. COURTESY OF THE FRANKS FAMILY.

Now a *Tonight Show* veteran, Dreesen gets to sit with Johnny.

Mitzi Shore in the spring of 1979, just days before the strike that changed everything. PHOTO BY WILLIAM KNOEDELSEDER.

Shore's favorite photo of herself—young and sexy in a see-through blouse—which she displayed on her desk and handed out to young male comics. COURTESY OF LUE DECK.

Budd Friedman perched proudly in front of his West Hollywood club in January 1980, after the comics helped him rebuild from an arson fire that almost put him out of business. PHOTO BY WILLIAM KNOEDELSEDER.

Best friends forever Tom Dreesen, George Miller, and David Letterman hanging out between shows at the Icehouse in Pasadena, circa 1977. FROM PERSONAL COLLECTION OF TOM DREESEN.

Tom Dreesen with Letterman on April 9, 1979, the night Dave made his first guest-host appearance on *The Tonight Show*. Immediately after the show, Dave made his first appearance on the picket line, breaking Mitzi Shore's heart in the process.

David Letterman sits for one of his first major newspaper interviews dressed in a YMCA T-shirt, May 1979. PHOTO BY WILLIAM KNOEDELSEDER.

Jay Leno, circa 1976, with his ever-present pipe and hip 1970s attire. COURTESY OF BUDD FRIEDMAN.

Jay Leno, with pipe in hand, surveys the packed front room of the West Hollywood Improv, circa 1976. In foreground, actor Peter Riegert.

Jay Leno on the street outside his West Hollywood apartment in May 1979. PHOTO BY WILLIAM KNOEDELSEDER.

The Comedy Store "Bombers" basketball team, 1979. COURTESY OF LUE DECK.

Dave Letterman, power forward and gum chewer. COURTESY OF LUE DECK.

Tim and Tom (Reid and Dreesen) broke up their historic black-and-white stage act but remained teammates on the Bombers. COURTESY OF LUE DECK.

Andy Kaufman performs at the West Hollywood Improv as club owner Budd Friedman (far right in rear) looks on. Photo courtesy of Budd Friedman.

Andy Kaufman doing his famous Elvis impersonation complete with sequined leather jacket and sneer, November 1978. Photo by William Knoedelseder.

Andy Kaufman getting ready to wrestle on the author's patio, November 1978.

Elayne Boosler, relaxing in her West Hollywood apartment in May 1979.
PHOTO BY WILLIAM KNOEDELSEDER.

Robin Williams mugs for Budd Friedman (with his trademark monocle).
COURTESY OF BUDD FRIEDMAN.

Robin Williams, photographed in his street clothes just prior to the debut of *Mork and Mindy*.
PHOTO BY WILLIAM KNOEDELSEDER.

Dottie Archibald, housewife turned standup comic turned strike organizer. She served as the model for Sally Field's character in the 1988 movie *Punchline* (with Tom Hanks), which was written by David Seltzer, her former neighbor in Ojai, California.

Little girl on the picket line: Teenage TV star Alison Arngrim (*Little House on the Prairie*) joins her fellow strikers outside the Comedy Store. Courtesy of Alison Arngrim.

Putting it all on the line, April 1979: Jo Anne Astrow (kneeling, second from left); Steve Lubetkin (kneeling far right, holding the "Yuk Stops Here" sign); Mark Lonow (second row, second from left, leaning); Dottie Archibald (second row, in white tunic, holding the "I said I wanna be a star" sign); Tom Dreesen (third row, far left, wearing Chicago Cubs jacket); and Ollie Joe Prater (back row, far left, in plaid shirt). Photo by Rick Bursky.

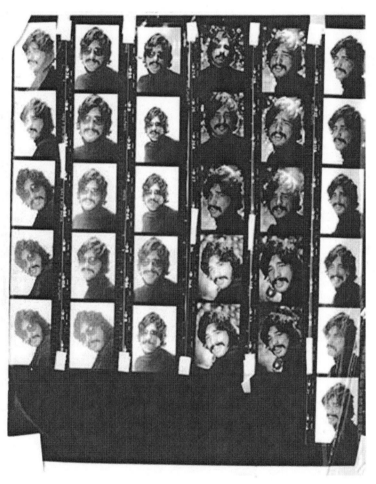

Contact sheet for Steve Lubetkin's professional head shots, circa 1976.
Courtesy of Barry Lubetkin.

# Order, Please

The late-night coke sessions at Mitzi Shore's house did more than separate the haves from the have-nots, the pets from the peons. They served to further distance the men from the women since Shore was the only female who attended.

The women comics weren't bothered so much about not being invited—coke was mostly a guy thing back then—as they were about the fact that Mitzi participated. In the winter of 1979, the so-called women's movement was in full roar. All across the country, supporters were pushing hard for states to ratify an equal rights amendment to the U.S. Constitution. And yet, here was a woman in a unique position of power, supposedly the champion of female stand-up comedy, having affairs and sharing drugs with her male employees, one of whom, Mike Binder, wasn't even old enough to drink legally. These weren't the sort of equal rights they had in mind. If Mitzi were a man, they'd want her arrested.

What's more, Shore's grand plan for providing female comics with a level playing field in the form of the "ladies-only" Belly Room wasn't working out as originally envisioned.

With seating for about fifty and its own entrance from the parking, the Belly Room looked pretty much like the rest of the

Comedy Store—black on black on black—with the exception of a red satin heart that Shore affixed to one wall. When the heart disappeared one day, Shore posted a notice on the Comedy Store bulletin board announcing that it had been stolen by her daughter, Sandi. "And I want it returned," she wrote. "So if anyone sees her, tell her to put it back."

There were about twenty women who worked the Belly Room regularly. Elayne Boosler and Marsha Warfield, the two women with the most polished acts, kept their vows not to perform there. For some of the others, the Belly Room proved to be pretty much what Mitzi had promised: a space removed from the rat-a-tat-tat, rim-shot rhythm of the Original Room, where they could find a distinctly female voice and develop a unique style at a comfortable pace. It was a room where they could be bad, fall down, and fail without fear of wrecking their careers. In fact, Judy Carter did fall down onstage one night, twisting her ankle so badly that she had trouble getting up. In pain, she called out to the audience for help but people just sat there smiling, waiting to see how the bit was going to pay off. The Belly Room was more free-form than the Original Room, more experimental.

"It was a jazzy atmosphere," Sandra Bernhard told writer Lawrence Christon years later. "The great thing about that space is that people looked for the unusual. It gave me the opportunity to explore and express myself."

Bernhard and Lotus Weinstock were the two performers who used the Belly Room to the best advantage. As the eldest comic in residence, Weinstock functioned as the room's soulful den mother, sometimes emceeing in her bathrobe. Bernhard was her onstage opposite, the brash (to say the least) young newcomer whose intentionally obnoxious persona had often caused walkouts when she performed in the Original Room. The opposites eventually attracted, and the two teamed up to produce some memorable moments in the Belly Room.

"I've spent fifteen years transcending my anger, and dealing with you it all comes back in one night," Weinstock would say as they launched into a ferocious onstage cat fight—grabbing onto one another, pulling hair, yowling, wrestling to the floor, and rolling around on the stage. Then, Bernhard would suddenly leap to her feet and say breathlessly, "I feel so *close* to you."

Shore loved the two of them, especially Bernhard, whom she thought was destined for stardom because she was so different from anyone else, and she let them have as much stage time as they wanted. On weekends, they often did an hour-long set, which didn't sit well with their comedy sisters because it meant fewer time slots to go around, and most of the women hadn't been given any spots in either the Original Room or at Westwood since the Belly Room opened. Only Elayne Boosler, Marsha Warfield, Shirley Hemphill, and Lois Bromfield, another Mitzi favorite, were getting spots in the bigger rooms, which males now dominated even more than before. The Belly Room was functioning as an overflow space. When the other rooms were full, the doormen directed people up the back stairs to be entertained by the females until the next show of male comics began. Many of the women thought they were being treated as a third-rate attraction (at least the belly dancers of yesteryear got paid). Intentionally or not, in the name of equality, they were being discriminated against.

The growing disenchantment among the women about opportunity dovetailed with that of the men over the issue of pay. And it all came together in a series of unexpected phone calls that invariably went something like this:

"There's going to be a meeting of all the comics on Thursday at the union hall [International Alliance of Theater and Stage Employees] on Sunset."

"*All* the comics? What for?"

"As many as we can get. We're gonna talk about getting paid for our performances at the Store."

"Wow! What time Thursday?"

"Two o'clock."

(Pause)

"Is that a.m. or p.m.?"

About seventy-five comics, including nearly all the women, showed up that Thursday afternoon for what may have been the largest-ever gathering of stand-ups outside of a Friars Club roast. Alison Arngrim cut her afternoon classes at Hollywood High to attend. She figured that a meeting of comedians trying to get organized about anything was bound to be hilarious, like spending the afternoon in a great big fuckup class. Her comrades didn't disappoint her. Chaos reigned at the outset, with everyone shouting and trying to talk at the same time. When someone called out, "Order please," half a dozen voices from around the room hollered back in unison, "Cheeseburger, fries, and a coke."

Jay Leno tried to frame the discussion but couldn't keep from telling jokes or refrain from responding to heckles. It was a repeat of what happened at Boosler's apartment, but much worse, cacophony cubed. Finally, Tom Dreesen couldn't take it any more. He got up from his seat and walked to where Leno stood in the front of the room. Raising his hand for attention, he started talking above the din.

"Guys, *guys*, I know it's a lot of fun being all together like this, but we really have some important things to talk about today, and it would be better and more effective if we got a little organized about it and spoke one at a time," he said.

Knowing the basics of Roberts Rules of Order, he tried to apply them to get the crowd quieted down and focused. "Okay, the chair recognizes Jay Leno. Jay, you have the floor; make your point. Gallagher, please sit down and be quiet."

Dreesen's stature as the most experienced comic in the room and his reputation as a mensch helped overcome the fact that Leno stood behind him throughout the meeting, miming his every word and gesture as if signing for the deaf. The meeting was ostensibly about money, but the discussion turned mostly on Mitzi, with opinion quickly dividing into two camps. The she-owes-us group argued, "She's making millions and should share some of it with us." The we-owe-her faction countered with, "We should just be grateful that she lets us perform at the Store."

After a couple of hours and several motions along the lines of "I move you go fuck yourself," money won out over gratitude when a majority voted to send a delegation to Shore to broach the idea of getting paid a modest amount, as little as $5 a set. It was moved, seconded, and carried that Dreesen would head the delegation and pick the others to go with him.

Dreesen wondered what he'd gotten himself into. He hadn't figured on becoming a spokesman for the group. Looking out over the room, he couldn't help thinking he was the keynote speaker at an ADD convention. Still, it would be a short booking, he thought, maybe even a one-nighter. Like nearly everyone else, he was sure that Mitzi would see the reasonableness of their position. Sure, she'd probably get all weepy and do the Jewish (or Catholic) mother trip—after all I've done for you kids, *this* is the thanks I get?—but in the end she'd go along with it.

Just to be sure, he picked his fellow delegates carefully. He wanted people whom Mitzi liked personally and professionally, people she felt comfortable with, who had no animosity toward her and wouldn't antagonize her. She loved Jay, of course, but Jay always wanted to be the center of attention, and he couldn't be serious for more than a few minutes at a time. Robin Williams couldn't be serious even that long, and besides, he hadn't come to the meeting. Mitzi also loved Dave Letterman, but Dave would never do it; he wouldn't feel comfortable being that involved. Elayne Boosler was a leader among the women, but Dreesen didn't know if Mitzi respected her or, for that matter, any of the women.

He decided on Paul Mooney, who was part of Richard Pryor's inner circle; Tim Thomerson, a handsome budding actor who had invented the "surfer dude" character on the Comedy Store stage; and George Miller, the only comic that Dreesen had ever seen make Mitzi laugh at herself. On stage one night, with Mitzi in the audience, George launched into an impersonation of her, saying, "That Tom Dreesen! He called me the other day while I was in the kitchen scrubbing out the sink . . . with my hair." The only person who laughed harder than Mitzi was Marsha Warfield, who appeared to pass the better part of a drink through her nose.

All four men genuinely liked Shore, were grateful for the break she'd given them, and felt they were in her debt. Dreesen figured if they just approached her with respect and affection, she'd agree to their proposal. How could she not?

# Diary of a Young Comic

Richard Lewis didn't attend the comics meeting, but he had a good excuse. He was caught up in the biggest break of his career.

It came about in the usual way, which was almost a cliché at that point. He had just finished his set at the Improv and was having a drink at the bar one night when a stranger walked up and introduced himself. "Hi, my name is Bennett Tramer. I'm a big fan of yours. I'm writing a show for NBC and producer Lorne Michaels, and I think you'd be great for the lead part."

"Oh, good, I thought you were a bill collector," Lewis quipped.

Tramer explained that he was writing the screenplay for a feature film called *Poison Ivy* to be directed by Gary Weis, a young director who'd made a name for himself with his short films on *Saturday Night Live*. Weis also had a deal with Michaels and NBC to make ninety-minute specials that would air periodically in *SNL*'s time slot, and he wanted to do a film about a young comic from New York trying to make it in Los Angeles. "Your act would fit into it," Tramer said. "We could include a lot of your performance and shoot it right here."

Tramer brought Weis to the Improv the following night, and Lewis made their presence part of his act. "There's a little pressure on me tonight," he told the audience as he paced back and forth across the stage, running his hands nervously through his long hair. "There are people here to see me, but I don't want you to worry about it. I'm going to come through for you. I'm going to come through for myself." Then, he went into a rant about his grandpa Yikva who, he explained, "was named for a Jewish expression that means 'killed by an avalanche.'"

Afterwards, Weis told him, "You remind me of Woody Allen," and offered him the starring role. Lewis agreed to do it if he could be part of the writing process as well. Done.

Lewis and Tramer crafted a loosely autobiographical script, titled *Diary of a Young Comic*, in which the hero, Billy Gondola, leaves his Jewish family (including Grandpa Yikva) in New York to try for stardom in LA. "We gotta write a scene for my friend Steve," Lewis told Tramer. "It'll be a favor but he'll earn it." They wrote a scene in which Steve Lubetkin and Susan Evans were to be part of an acting class that Billy attends, and they gave them both lines. Finally, Lewis thought, he could pay Steve back for his help in those early days when they swore a blood oath on a street corner in Greenwich Village.

But hard luck hit Lubetkin once again. Two weeks before filming was to begin, director Weis and the NBC production executives decided they had to cut some scenes from the script to conform to the ninety-minute format, and the acting class scene was among those that had to go. Lewis pleaded for it to be left in, but they had a fifteen-day shoot with a $230,000 budget, the acting class scene was peripheral to the storyline, and none of the people in it (with the exception of Billy) were in any other scene. So, it was the easiest and most logical thing to cut. This was a production decision pure and simple, and Lewis was powerless to do anything about it.

He was sick at heart that his good fortune was going to cause his friend more pain. Here was the double-edged sword of making it in Hollywood, today's entry in the *real* diary of a young comic.

He was going to have to tell Steve that he wasn't invited to the party after all.

They met for coffee at a little restaurant across the alley from Steve's apartment where they often got together. Not five seconds after they sat down, Lewis blurted out, "I'm so fucking disappointed, man, but they had to make edits when they were finalizing the shooting schedule, they saw how long it was, and they had to make cuts, and they are taking out your scene, and I can't get them to put it back in."

Whatever disappointment he felt, Lubetkin didn't show it. "That's cool," he said. "I know you did the best you could. Don't worry about it." He told Lewis that he was working on his solo stand-up act again and was getting good feedback from Mitzi Shore and good time slots at Westwood. He had some great new bits he was doing, including a Jewish pimp wearing a fedora festooned with bagels and shuffling around the stage muttering in an *alter kocker* voice, "Hustle, hustle," and a "quick impression" of a Polish pope giving the papal blessing by holding his arm in place while moving his body in the sign of the cross. In fact, Mitzi had booked him to play the San Diego Store, and Susan was going down with him to stay for a few days, he said. So things were looking up.

*Diary* was shot at a handful of locations around Los Angeles. A cheap motel in the shade of the Santa Monica freeway recalled the hooker haven next door to Lewis's first LA apartment, down to the detail of the "used" condoms from the prop department lying around on the ground. A health food store was the setting for Billy to pick up Nina van Pallandt. And the Improv was the scene of Billy's triumph, complete with Budd Friedman bounding onto the stage just as he did after Lewis's first performance at the New York club, proclaiming to the audience, "We've found the rookie of the year."

As if to prove he had no bad feelings, Steve came to the set several times during the shoot. He was there for the filming at the

Improv and seemed fine. He chatted up Bennett Tramer, who thought he was a really sweet, funny guy. Apparently, there'd been no harm done. At least, that's what Richard wanted to believe. But in his heart he knew better. Steve always kept his fears and frustrations hidden. On stage he walked with a swagger, exuding confidence, a man's man, but inside he was still a scared little boy who missed his mom and desperately wanted to impress his dad.

As the air date for *Diary* neared, Lewis was swept up in the network's promotional push. NBC's publicity department set up a score of interviews for him, ranging from *Daily Variety* to the *Washington Post* to *The Today Show*. They even booked him on *The Tonight Show*, where he killed. Maybe it was the fact that Johnny Carson wasn't sitting there judging him (Gabe Kaplan was guest hosting that night), or maybe he was just on a sustained roll with all the hoopla surrounding *Diary*, but it was his best *Tonight Show* appearance ever. The audience was still applauding as he sat down on the couch next to ABC sportscaster Dick Schapp, who leaned over and said to him, "That's the hardest I've laughed since the last time I saw my old friend Lenny Bruce playing in Greenwich Village." Lewis would have been hard-pressed to conjure a higher compliment.

NBC flew him to New York first class for his appearance on *The Today Show* and put him up at the Plaza Hotel. On the ride from the airport, his limo driver suggested that he stop at a particular men's clothing store and charge whatever he wanted to the network's account, indicating that others before him had done so, and nobody knew the difference. Lewis declined, but he felt great later when he took his mother and her boyfriend to dinner at the Plaza's famous Oak Room and with a flourish signed the check to his room.

On *The Today Show* the next morning, he chatted with co-hosts Tom Brokaw and Jane Pauley and introduced a clip from *Diary* in which Billy Gondola's sister Shirley joins a weird cult that reduces everything, including language, to its essence, so that Shirley becomes simply "Shi" and her boyfriend, Fred, is called "Fre." The bit went over so well on the studio set that at the end of the broadcast, the cohosts cracked Lewis up by signing off as "Tom Bro" and "Jane Pau."

*Diary of a Young Comic* received generally good reviews. Even the critics who noted its production shortcomings and occasionally flat moments lauded its originality and sense of fun. The *Washington Post*'s Tom Shales pronounced it "a pretty darn funny movie" and listed among its highlights a scene in which Billy Gondola goes to a celebrity shrink who has eight-by-ten photos of his famous patients on the wall with black tape over their eyes to disguise their identities. Still, Billy is able to recognize one patient. "Isn't that Flipper?"

*Diary* got nothing but raves from Lewis's fellow comics, many of whom watched it crowded around the TV sets at the Comedy Store and the Improv. Lewis was well-liked in both the Los Angeles and New York comedy communities, and his success gave everyone a psychological boost. Not even Robin Williams or Andy Kaufman had yet to star in a movie that he had cowritten. Lewis had pulled off a Woody Allen, and he'd done it with the story of their lives.

At Canter's Deli the night *Diary* aired, a particularly large gathering of comics greeted Lewis as conquering hero. He was glad Nina was there to share it with him. Robin Williams brought his wife, Valerie, and when they walked over to congratulate Richard, Robin suddenly leaped up onto the table and kicked into an inspired, improvised performance that stopped all other activity in the room. The sight of Mork taking flight on a tabletop caused quite a few forks and jaws to drop in the restaurant. Some of the comics saw it as Williams trying to steal Lewis's thunder, but Lewis felt anything but upstaged. In his view, Robin was just overcome with happiness for him and was celebrating the best way he knew how—by devouring an audience.

As laughter rolled around the room, Lewis smiled at the sight of Robin's right foot bouncing up and down just inches from his corn beef sandwich, and the thought occurred to him that he'd probably remember this moment for the rest of his life.

In all the hilarity and camaraderie, he didn't even notice that Steve wasn't there.

# The Gauntlet

On Sunday, March 11, 1979, Tom Dreesen pulled his silver Cadillac Eldorado into the Comedy Store parking lot just before 10:00 p.m. The car was as new as his money, and he'd taken a lot of ribbing about it from the boys, especially Jay Leno. He knew it was flashy and that some of the comics probably thought he was being a self-aggrandizing asshole. But he didn't care what they thought. They hadn't grown up in Harvey, Illinois; they'd never lived out of an abandoned car in an alley. He drove the Eldo for the same reason he stood in the shower every morning until the hot water started to run out. It reminded him of how far he'd come.

In front of the club, George Miller, Paul Mooney, and Tim Thomerson were waiting for him. Tonight was their meeting with Mitzi Shore to talk about getting paid. She was waiting for them at her house about a mile away, so the other three piled into the car for the five-minute drive. On the way, they went over their strategy, such as it was.

The important thing, they agreed, was to be cool and remain calm no matter what happened. Mitzi could be volatile and dramatic, and they didn't want to do anything to set her off or make her feel threatened. They were four to her one, after all, and with his bad-ass black-dude persona, Mooney was intimidating enough all by himself. So, they planned to keep it light and keep the dialog going until she saw the rightness of their position, as she eventually would, they thought, because at her core Mitzi loved the comics and wanted what was best for them.

At the house, one of Shore's female assistants answered the door and ushered them to the large family room on the first floor where Mitzi always entertained. It was a room they all knew, Mooney better than the others because he was often present for the all-night coke sessions with his pal Richard Pryor. They gravitated naturally to the bar and pulled up stools. Mitzi didn't keep them waiting long, and within a few minutes, they were all chatting about happenings in and around the Store. It fell to Dreesen to bring the conversation to ground.

"Mitzi, you know what we're here to talk about," he began. She nodded and waited for him to make his pitch. He started by assuring her that they hadn't come for themselves; they were all fine, making a good living and grateful as all get-out for all she'd done for them. They were there on behalf of scores of other comics, he said, the ones who hadn't gotten their big breaks yet but were nonetheless entertaining people from her stage and contributing to the success of the Store. He told her there was a growing feeling among the comics that maybe it was time for the Store to start paying them for performing.

"We're not talking about a salary," he hurried to add. "We're talking about a small stipend really, a token amount acknowledging that they are professionals. Believe it or not, for some of these kids, $20 or $30 a week would make all the difference. It would mean they didn't have to take that second shitty job working in a restaurant or parking cars, and they could spend that time writing and coming up with new material. The Store would be the beneficiary of that. They'd develop faster and contribute even more to the success of the club."

Shore listened calmly, patiently, letting him finish before saying anything. When he paused long enough to let her know he was done, she said, "You know, Tommy, when I was married to Sammy, I saw how comics were treated. As Rodney would say, they didn't get any respect."

Dreesen and the others knew this story by heart because they'd heard her tell it so many times.

"They always had to open for a singer," she went on, "as if what they did wasn't as important. They were treated like second-class citizens, like comedians weren't good enough or entertaining enough to merit their own audience. I didn't think that was right."

When she got to the part about how she had the interior of the Store painted black so that all attention would focus on the comic on stage, Dreesen wanted to interrupt with "Yes, Mitzi, we know, because we did the painting, remember?" But he held his tongue, and she continued painting her picture of the Store as a comedy utopia, part college and part artist colony, where funny young people from all over the world could come to drink the water and then, when their time came, burst into bloom like rain forest flowers.

As visions go, it was a bit overblown, but the four young comics listening couldn't fault her for that. Without the club she'd created, they couldn't imagine where they would be or what their lives would be like. There was no doubt they owed her. But by the same token, didn't she owe them? Where would the Store be without the likes of Jimmie Walker, Robin Williams, and so many others? Mitzi seemed impervious to that viewpoint. She could say in all seriousness, "You know, Richard Pryor got *Lady Sings the Blues* [his first feature film role] after an appearance in the Main Room," as if Pryor's talent would have gone unrecognized by Hollywood if not for her and the Store.

After Dreesen and Shore completed their opening statements, the three other comics took turns trying to bring Mitzi around, each arguing from a different angle. They brought up a number of formulas for paying that the headliners' group had kicked around, ranging from the $5-per-set "gas money" program practiced in New York to 50 percent of the cover charges divided up among the comedians performing each night. Shore would not budge. The Store was not a nightclub, she said again and again. It was a training ground, a workshop, a college. The comics were learning their craft. They were not professionals yet. They did not deserve to be paid.

The tenor of the conversation remained friendly throughout—no one got mad; no voices were raised. George Miller did his best to keep things light with one-liners, the best of which he delivered when Mitzi excused herself to go to the bathroom. "Mitzi and Steve Landesberg are making love and Mitzi moans, 'Oh, Steve, hurt me, hurt me.' So, Steve whispers in her ear, 'Pay the comics, pay the comics.'"

After several hours, Dreesen noticed that only he and Mitzi were left standing. The other three were asleep—Thomerson on the couch, Miller in a chair, and Mooney with his head resting on his arm on the bar. Dreesen was astonished by Mitzi's stamina. She'd exhausted three men twenty years her junior.

He tried again, reminding her of the time he was doing a series of radio interviews in Chicago and brought her along with him to promote the Store on a 50,000-watt station, something she never would have had the courage to do on her own. She remembered but didn't see his point.

He told her about Michael Rapport not having $5 for breakfast on New Year's morning after appearing on her stage before a sold-out crowd. "Then he should get a goddamn job," she said.

"He has a job, Mitzi," he said. "He works for you."

She disagreed. Rapport did not work for her. He worked for himself, and she just gave him a place to do it, a stage where he might be seen and become a star. She was his patron, not his employer.

"I just don't get it, Mitzi," Dreesen said, finally exasperated. "You pay your waitresses. You pay your bartenders. You pay the guy who cleans the toilets. Why would you *not* pay the comics who are bringing people into the club?"

"People don't come to see the comics," she said. "They come to see the Store. It's famous."

"Well, who made it famous if not the comics?"

"People come for the ambience."

"Then don't put on any comics one night and see how long they stay."

She just looked at him—composed, impenetrable, a brick wall. Drained by the endless chicken-or-the-egg go-around, he woke the others, and Mitzi walked them the door. "This isn't personal, Mitzi," he said in parting. "We think the world of you. The comics aren't asking for a piece of the Store. They just want to get paid something, that's all."

When he dropped the other three off at Sunset, it was after closing time, and no one was around. He was too tired to go to Canter's, and he didn't know what to tell people if he did. All he knew was that he'd failed in his mission. Piloting his Eldorado through Laurel Canyon to the valley and home, he felt numb and sad. This is no joke, he said to himself. We are in for a real fight here.

# Comedians for Compensation

Tom Dreesen was rousted out of bed the next morning by calls from comics telling him that Mitzi Shore was convening her own meeting at the Sunset club that afternoon. Her minions were phoning people already, telling them to be in the Original Room at 4:00 p.m. And get this, he was told: Everyone was invited *except* the headliners.

Dreesen stood in the shower for a full fifteen minutes that morning trying to glean Mitzi's strategy and plot the comics' next play. Obviously, she was going to try to divide and conquer, pit the rank and file against the headliners. She was moving quickly to determine if they really had broad support and attempt to turn it around if they did. She wanted to talk to all the comics before he and the other three had a chance to report on their meeting with her. She didn't want them speaking for her because that would give them power. It was a smart move on her part, he thought. It wouldn't surprise him if she made an offer at the meeting, proposing one of the solutions they put forward last night as if it were her own idea.

All day long his phone kept ringing, and fellow comics kept asking, "What are we going to do?" All he could think of was,

"Wait. Let's see what she says first." He was fairly certain that a majority of comics would come down on the side of getting paid. Then again, he'd been certain that Mitzi would capitulate last night. So, he was worried. If she made enough people feel guilty about going against her, then she could make this very difficult. It would only work if the comics stuck together; he was sure of that.

With Mitzi apparently going on the offensive, Dreesen figured it was time to line up a lawyer for the comics. He knew just the guy to call. Ken Browning was David Letterman's attorney, recommended to him by none other than Johnny Carson. Ken was a junior partner at Bushkin, Koppelson, Gaims, and Gaines, whose founder, Henry Bushkin, was Carson's longtime attorney. The Bushkin firm was built around Carson, who'd made his feisty lawyer something of a household name with frequent on-air quips about "the Bombastic Bushkin," which never failed to break up Ed McMahon. Letterman had introduced Dreesen to Browning at the Comedy Store one night a few months back, and Dreesen had run into Ken at the Store and the Improv several times since then. He liked Ken. More important, he thought Browning's connection to Carson would stand the comics in good stead in any negotiations with Mitzi. She might not respect the comics, but she sure as hell respected Johnny, so if it appeared that Johnny was on their side, well. . . .

Browning was happy to get the call from Dreesen. Of all the young comics he'd met in his forays into the club scene, Dreesen was the most established in his career, and he seemed particularly well-grounded, focused, and sober, a real grown-up in the land of the maturity challenged. Browning had noticed that the other comics—David Letterman, Jay Leno, George Miller—seemed to look to Dreesen for advice and counsel, as if he were a trusted big brother—all of which would make him an ideal client. Browning was trying to build his own practice, after all, and even though he was working with Carson in the comedian's purchase of a Las Vegas TV station, he knew that Johnny would always be Bushkin's client, not his. He wanted to represent the *next* Johnny, and if that wasn't Dreesen, then it was likely someone Dreesen could introduce him to.

"Ken, we're finally trying to do something to get the kids paid," Dreesen said, adding, "and we may need your help at some point." Browning didn't need to hear much more. He remembered Dreesen telling him the first time they met at the Comedy Store that the comics didn't get paid for working there, and his reaction had been, "You're kidding!" Dreesen went on to say that, in fact, some of the younger comics who performed that night were so poor they were living out of their cars. Browning had been appalled. He was twenty-nine and had come to Los Angeles straight out of Cornell Law School in 1974, right around the time the great migration began. He identified with the comics and loved being in their company. It wasn't just the laughs that attracted him; it was the feeling of being at the center of a generational, even epochal, change in American culture. And now, on the phone, Dreesen was offering him a chance to play an important role that not only challenged his lawyering skills but also fired his idealism.

Their conversation was short, but before they hung up, Browning uttered the two words Dreesen was hoping to hear: pro bono.

It was a different Mitzi Shore who showed up in the Main Room that evening. The impenetrable brick wall that Dreesen, Miller, Paul Mooney, and Tim Thomerson had run into the night before was replaced by a trembling, wounded bird of a woman who seemed in desperate need of protection. She sat on a chair on the stage with comedian Dave Tyree beside her, sometimes patting her hand, sometimes handing her a tissue to dab away tears. She told the audience of about one hundred comics that representatives of the headliners—whom she referred to derisively as "the fourteen 10 percenters" for reasons that were unclear (they all had agents?)—had come to her "demanding that you all be paid." She delivered this news in a tone that assumed the crowd would be just as shocked and offended as she was by the idea. Then she launched into her I-have-a-vision speech. "This is a college," she said. "I started this for you."

For anyone who hadn't heard it more than once or twice before—and there were many of those in the room—it could be an inspiring oration, offering understanding and support, promising a safer passage through the jungle that was show business. "I have such great plans for you," she said poignantly.

Not even the most cynical among them doubted her sincerity. This was no act. It was pure Mitzi, behaving exactly like a doting parent who'd been wounded by the ingratitude of her rebellious children. The hurt was real. And so was the anger. When Severin Darden, an improvisational actor from Second City, lightened the mood by sweeping into the room wrapped in a cape and calling out dramatically for "sanctuary," Shore shot him a withering look and said sharply, "Sit down and shut up!"

Argus Hamilton arrived in the middle of the meeting as well. He came straight from the airport, carrying his luggage after three weeks on the Comedy Store college concert tour. He'd heard nothing about the payment controversy and was stunned to find Mitzi defending her policy in front of a not entirely friendly audience. In Hamilton's mind, Mitzi could do no wrong. He thought she was an artistic genius, a visionary, a gutsy businesswoman, and a gifted nurturer of comedic talent. The way he saw it, no one had a better understanding of the often tortured psyches of stand-up comics, and no one was better at getting them to perform their best for the audience and for themselves. Yes, of course, she was eccentric and sometimes difficult to deal with. But was she any weirder than the average comic? Hardly. And if she was blunt in assessing someone's prospects for success, it was only because she thought it was cruel to foster false hope. She had a placard on her desk, placed so that only she could see it, that read, "It's a sin to encourage mediocre talent." Mitzi didn't bullshit, which was a rare and admirable attribute in show business.

Truth be told, Argus Hamilton was more than a little in love with Mitzi Shore, and the sight of his fellow comics in open conflict with her turned his world upside down. He was heartsick as he watched a question-and-answer session turn contentious.

"Why couldn't you pay the comics $5 per night like some of the New York clubs are doing?" Jeff Altman asked Shore.

"I would never disgrace the profession by paying a comedian $5 for a performance," she responded. "The Original Room and Westwood are showcases. And I'm standing by this. They are not nightclubs. They are places for you to learn your craft and work out new material."

"Mitzi, I'm sorry," Kip Addotta cut in, "but I'll break in new material at Caesar's Palace before I will the Comedy Store, because you never know who's going to be in the audience. It could be the end of your career."

At that, Shore's paramour, Steve Landesberg, stood up and shouted, "Career? What career? If you're still working here, then you don't have a career yet."

Before the day was done, Shore had issued a statement to the *Los Angeles Times*: "The Comedy Store is a workshop type club. If the 40 or more comedians working nightly in the workshop were paid, the workshop simply would not exist." The Comedy Store's publicist, Estelle Endler, added that Shore would not comment further until the dispute was settled.

Tom Dreesen's phone would not stop ringing following the meeting. Jay Leno called. George Miller called. Elayne Boosler called. The *Los Angeles Times* called. Everyone wanted to know what the dissidents were going to do next. So did Dreesen. He volunteered to host a meeting at his house in Sherman Oaks the next afternoon, but he stopped short of issuing a call for everyone to attend. They needed to organize a plan of action, and he didn't think one hundred agitated comics would help that process.

That night at Sunset and Westwood, at the Improv and at Canter's, the comics talked—or argued—about one thing: to be paid or not to be paid. Emotions ran high, especially on the pro-Mitzi side, but it appeared that sentiment was running about two to one in favor of being paid.

About thirty comics showed up out at Dreesen's the next day, including Leno, Miller, Mooney, and Boosler, as well as Marsha Warfield, Dottie Archibald, and Jo Anne Astrow. Dreesen was surprised at the percentage of women who turned out. Astrow brought her husband, Mark Lonow. Ken Browning also attended, introduced by Dreesen as "our lawyer." He handed out business cards to everyone.

The first order of business was to get a clearer picture of their support in the comedy community. "We need to see how strong we are," Dreesen said. "We need a list of every comic who works in this town, and we need to call them and ask, 'Are you for us or against us? Yes or no? Do you think comics should get paid?'" From his years with the Jaycees, he knew the organization had to form committees, put people in charge of them, and let them do their work. Jo Anne Astrow volunteered to head the membership committee. She was to enlist a handful of others to canvas the comics to see where they stood. She was also tasked with finding a place for the next general meeting, the sooner the better, and letting everyone know the date and time.

Steve Bluestein volunteered to chair the media committee. The press was already onto the story. Not only was the *Los Angeles Times* calling, but the *Hollywood Reporter* had run a small item that morning headlined "Comics to Picket Comedy Stores." The item reported erroneously that both Sunset and Westwood "will be struck at 6 p.m. today by comedians who play those clubs," attributing the information to "a spokesperson." The fact that there'd been no talk of picketing and that there was no spokesperson for their group pointed up the need to control the information that went out. Everyone agreed that Dreesen should be the spokesman. Which immediately raised the question, spokesman for what? They didn't have a name for themselves. For whom would he be speaking? After many suggestions and much debate, they settled on the name Comedians for Compensation (CFC), which stated clearly what they were about and avoided making them sound like a labor union.

Since no one present thought they shouldn't get paid, most of the meeting was taken up with discussion about what would constitute fair and acceptable payment. In the Sunday night meeting with Dreesen's delegation, Mitzi had rejected two proposals for payment in the Original Room—$5 per set and 50 percent of the door—as well as the idea of splitting the door in the Main Room. But she didn't mention the Main Room in her big meeting Monday, which might indicate that she was open to negotiating. Some people thought they should take a fifty-fifty split in the Main Room if they could get her to agree. Perhaps they could then divide that money up among all the comics. Others were adamantly opposed to accepting payment in the Main Room only. "A cover charge is meant to *cover* the cost of entertainment," Marsha Warfield argued, "so Mitzi should pay us in any room where she charges a cover."

Through it all, Leno maintained that Mitzi could still be reasoned with and offered to approach her. Ultimately, it was decided that the newly named CFC spokesman was the more appropriate person to conduct any negotiations. The general feeling was that Jay would be too willing to compromise to make peace. Dreesen agreed to talk to Mitzi. As Warfield described it later, "It's like your mother told you she wasn't going to feed you anymore. You can't quite believe it, so you go back and ask again."

Toward the end of the meeting, Mark Lonow finally spoke up. "You know, at some point you are going to have to decide how far you are willing to go with this," he said. "If you keep asking, and she keeps saying no, then either you agree that you'll never get paid, or you go on strike and throw up a picket line around the place. Unless that is one of your options—unless she believes it's one of your options—she has no reason to change the way she's been doing business."

A startled hush settled on the room. Despite the *Hollywood Reporter* item that morning, no one had given a serious thought to actually going on strike. At first blush, it seemed like a ridiculous notion: comedians' strike? Wasn't that an oxymoron or something?

The idea of a strike came naturally to Lonow. He'd been raised in Brighton Beach, Long Island, by his paternal grandparents, Minnie and Davin Lonow, Russian immigrants who were card-carrying Communist labor agitators. A so-called red diaper baby, Mark had been bounced on Paul Robeson's knee as a child and grew up in a home steeped in revolution, where talk of union organizing, staging strikes, and manipulating public opinion in favor of the workers was served up nightly with dinner. He was sent for two weeks every summer to a Zionist sleepaway camp in New Jersey where, in the spirit of the Boy Scouts, Jewish children were trained as guerilla fighters. During the first week, half the campers would occupy a house, and the other half would try to take it over; then, they'd switch for the second week.

It might have given Mitzi Shore pause to learn that one of her rebellious Belly Room comediennes was married to the grand-nephew of Eli Swerdloff, the first president of the Soviet Union and the man who, according to Lonow family lore, not only signed the death warrants but also physically carried out the execution of Czar Nicholas II and his family in the basement of the Romanoff summer palace in 1918. Mark remembered his grandmother tut-tutting on more than one occasion, "They shouldn't have shot the children."

Dreesen knew that Lonow's observation about their willingness to strike was true. He'd been a member of the Teamsters in the years between his navy stint and his stand-up career. But he didn't want to think about a strike just yet, and he certainly didn't want to be pegged as some sort of Jimmy Hoffa union heavy. For now, he just wanted to keep the dispute inside the comedy family and prove to Mitzi that the community overwhelmingly supported the comics.

After the meeting, as Jo Anne Astrow and her membership committee began phoning up the rank and file, Dreesen went after a couple of big names. First, he drove to the home of Jimmie Walker, whose name on the Comedy Store marquee during the height of the "dy-no-mite" craziness had been invaluable. Only Richard Pryor had contributed more to the club's prestige. Dreesen figured that eliciting Walker's support for the CFC would go a long way toward persuading Mitzi to negotiate.

Walker was torn. He not only loved Mitzi but had also been a good friend of Steve Landesberg since their days together at the New York Improv. Dreesen lobbied hard, playing up the comics' shared experience, recalling all those late nights when they made a roomful of drunks laugh their asses off and still didn't have five bucks to buy breakfast.

Walker agreed that it was wrong to make comedians work for free in a club as successful as the Comedy Store. He didn't want to go against Mitzi and the Store, but in the end he agreed not to go against the comics, whatever they decided to do. If it came to picketing, he wouldn't cross the line. That was good enough for Dreesen.

The next stop was Robin Williams, who had the same concerns as Walker and gave Dreesen the same commitment: He wouldn't go against Mitzi, but neither would he go against the comics. If a picket line went up, he would honor it. He hoped it wouldn't come to that.

That was two down and one to go. Richard Pryor, the most sacred of Mitzi's sacred cows, was at his home on Maui, and Paul Mooney had agreed to approach him. Dreesen reasoned that if Pryor needed persuading, then Mooney was the man for the job. Few people outside the comedy community knew that Mooney had been a major influence in Pryor's transformation from lovable, middle-of-the-road comedian to incendiary social commentator. Mooney was the éminence grise behind Dark Twain. Pryor trusted his instincts and listened to him.

Back at CFC Central, the news from the membership committee was all good. For starters, they'd obtained the Comedy Store's master phone list of all the comics who worked the clubs. A friendly employee in the front office just gave it to them. More surprisingly, they'd requested and received permission to hold the next CFC meeting on Monday evening in the Original Room. And, best of all, they were finding overwhelming support among the comics, easily 90 percent. In the aftermath of Mitzi's meeting, people were calling *them*, volunteering to help in any way they could. Her gambit appeared to have backfired.

With all that in his hip pocket, Dreesen put in a call to Shore. She was a little frosty, but the conversation was polite. She said that after considerable thought, she'd decided that she would be willing to give performers 50 percent of the door in the Main Room Thursday through Saturday. That was a major concession on her part, and it would have sufficed a few weeks before. Now, however, the offer stood little chance of being accepted. Not forty-eight hours before she'd tried to pit the rank and file against the headliners; now she was putting forward a plan that would only pay the headliners. What was she thinking?

Dreesen explained as gently as he could that the CFC had widespread support, including that of Robin Williams and Jimmie Walker, and that the issue had moved beyond the Main Room. If she didn't offer some sort of payment for performances in the Original Room and at Westwood, then he was afraid the situation would become more inflamed.

After half an hour of back-and-forth, they arrived at a compromise. She would offer to donate all the Saturday night cover charges once a month to a fund to be distributed equally among all the comics working the three locations. It would cost her less than the $5-per-set proposal that she'd already rejected, and it would preserve the notion of the Comedy Store as a workshop since donating to a fund was not the same as paying for performances. Dreesen thought it just might fly. He told her he would put it up for a vote at the meeting on Monday. He hung up feeling hopeful. They might just pull this thing off.

On Wednesday, Steve Bluestein arranged for both Dreesen and Mooney to talk to the *Los Angeles Times* about the dispute, and he set up interviews with *Variety* and the *Hollywood Reporter* as well. Dreesen was impressed at how quickly the CFC had coalesced from a ragtag band of malcontent clowns into a focused and effective band of malcontent clowns. It made sense when he thought about it. They were, after all, college-educated, highly intelligent products of 1960s social activism. While he was unloading trucks on the Chicago docks, they were demonstrating against the war in Vietnam, marching for civil rights, and protesting the proliferation of male chauvinist piggishness. The women seemed particularly passionate about the principle involved, more offended by the unfairness of the system. As a result, they were more willing than their male counterparts to show up, make the calls, and perform the drudgery of organizing.

On Thursday, March 15, the *Los Angeles Times* published the first major media story about the dispute between Mitzi Shore and her comics. Headlined "Comedy Store Picket Threat," the article cast the controversy as a classic clash of labor and management with national implications:

A dissident group of stand-up comedians calling themselves Comedians for Compensation (CFC) threatened to throw a picket line around the Comedy Store Tuesday unless management granted a pay hike, from nothing to something.

"We are serving notice to clubs across the country that we will no longer work for free to make them rich," said comedian Tom Dreesen, a CFC spokesman.

According to Dreesen, a CFC "steering committee" has agreed tentatively to accept Shore's compromise offer, but the matter will be taken before the "general membership" Monday for a deciding vote.

Although the comics strike had been averted temporarily, and the CFC was claiming "total victory," the dispute appeared far from over.

Despite the fact that there had been no real threat to picket or strike, the *Times* article presented the CFC as a credible organization with "elected representatives," a "steering committee," and a "general membership." It went on to note that the CFC represented "less than a quarter of the comic workforce in Los Angeles" and reported that some of the lesser known were rallying around Shore. "We should strike the headliners," the newspaper quoted one unidentified comic as saying. "They have a lot of nerve saying they represent me." The quoted comic was described as "one who doesn't think he should be paid for his performances."

The article concluded by stating that the dispute "could have far-reaching effect," which it backed up with quotes from Dreesen and Paul Mooney. "It's not just the Comedy Store," Mooney said. "It's this whole atmosphere of working for free around the country. Showcasing is catching on because it's good for club owners. We just felt it had to end." Dreesen added, "We don't want to form a union, but the CFC is asking comedians in other cities to join us by doing in their cities what we are doing in LA."

In sum, the *Times* article created the perception that the CFC was a force to be reckoned with. In Hollywood, of course, perception *is* reality, as evidenced by the telegram Dreesen received that evening:

Dear Tom,
　So glad you've arrived. Have cue cards man who does great picket signs.
　Congratulations, and go get 'em.

It was from Bob Hope.

# Choosing Up Sides

All weekend the shows went on as usual. Audiences at the Comedy Stores and the Improv didn't notice any difference, but the molecules of the comedy world had been moved around.

In the parking lot at Sunset and the bar at Melrose, the conversation among comics went beyond the usual themes of getting jobs and getting laid. Wherever they gathered in clumps, you could hear the same words rise above the murmur: "Headliners . . . picket line . . . strike . . . vote . . . CFC."

Everyone had gotten a call and everyone had an opinion. Jay Leno was still confident that Mitzi Shore would come around and everything would be fine. Elayne Boosler was ready to storm the Bastille. David Letterman thought the idea of comics walking a picket line was silly, but he'd support whatever Tom Dreesen and George Miller chose to do. Johnny Dark was horrified at the thought of having to choose between Mitzi and his best friends—Dreesen, Letterman, Miller, and Boosler.

"Sure, I want to get paid, Tommy," he said to Dreesen. "But you gotta remember that when Johnny and Susie Dark came out here, we had nothing. I was selling oven ware. And Mitzi believed in me and put me on and validated my act. Everything that ever happened for me happened at the Comedy Store. You're looking at a guy who owes her."

"I know, Johnny," Dreesen replied. "We all owe her to one degree or another. But if you're ever going to get paid, you've got to be strong and stand with us on this."

Emotionally, Steve Lubetkin was in the same boat as Dark. He worshipped Mitzi. She had been his champion when he first arrived in town, made him part of her family, and invited him to her house for dinner. Now, after the disappointments of *Dante Shocko* and Lubetkin & Evans, she was giving him good spots again. He'd been working at Westwood three or four nights a week, including New Year's Eve. He had recently played the La Jolla club for the first time, earning $250 for eleven performances over five nights. In addition, he'd recently earned $175 for eleven performances at the Laff Stop in Newport Beach. So that came to $425 in a single month, which was a pretty big deal to him, given that he'd earned less than $1,000 in the previous twelve months. Maybe, at long last, something was going to break for him. He'd seen it happen before. Guys he knew had gone from where he was right now to stardom in the span of a few weeks. He was excited by the reawakened promise—and frightened, too. If the break came next week, would he be ready? He sat down and wrote a long letter home:

Dear Dad and Barry,

   I am sending one copy of this to each of you. It is important.

   One of the worst offshoots of the *Dante Shocko* affair was that it gave both of you a negative experience in the area of investing in my word (predictions), my comedy and my assurances.

   What the whole thing came down to is I was right. *Dante Shocko* was funny and made people laugh. But I was wrong. In an industry controlled by a few big distributors, the only things that interest them are films that look like big, big moneymakers, with big stars and often big special effects.

My crazy little low-budget film might have made money in New York in the 1960s and early 1970s, but it just wasn't to be, especially now, with millions of dollars in Hollywood hype to compete with.

Anyway, as I've told you both, the only way I can see the film making money is if I get hot as a performer. And that is starting to happen. I'm getting great spots at the Comedy Store on a regular basis while experienced friends of mine call in and get a lone spot every two weeks. It becomes quite evident that I'm hot and getting hotter.

But it's still no easy road. I'm still in trouble economically. Yes, I can barely take care of food and rent, but I'm so close to making it that it kills me to think of the vital things I can't afford.

Including:

1. At least two good suits (one casual, one a little more formal) for auditions, meeting people, important gigs and TV: Right now my best outfit for stage is Richard Lewis's hand-me-down jeans (frayed at the bottom) and a slightly wrinkled (and out-of-date) jeans jacket. Sometimes it's downright embarrassing.

2. Boots: My boots are cracking, the heels are run down and they are best described as embarrassing. I need new boots.

3. My other shoes are a pair of run-down sneakers that are peeling. I need new sneakers.

4. I need at least another pair of regular shoes for stage.

5. A few pairs of jeans: Most of mine are too tight, have a faded crotch or just look crummy (remember, it's not like 20 hippies looking at me at Folk City. It's 150 hip people at the Comedy Store and 80 rich, hip people at the Laff Stop, looking me over thoroughly). I really need to look better on stage.

6. Shirts: I keep wearing the few good ones I have over and over. It's ridiculous. I need three or four new ones. Critical!

7. Pictures taken and printed: I'm the only comic who doesn't have an 8 × 10 (without a moustache, the way I look now). I need money to get them taken and printed. At the Laff Stop, everyone had a picture on the outside billboard. For me, they had a yellow piece of paper with my name written across it. In this highly competitive business, image is very important. Any sign of being a poor, unsuccessful loser can actually undo the good my comedy talent creates. It's very frustrating.

8. Have my two front teeth filed down: A quick simple procedure that will take away an unprofessional jaggedness when I smile. (Has to be done before pictures.)

9. Acting lessons: Between Richard Lewis getting his own pilot and a trend toward hiring stand-ups in sitcoms (mainly because we can hype their shows when we do Carson, Griffin, Dinah and Douglas, which helps their ratings). Because of this I will soon be going to read for acting jobs. Only one problem. I haven't had the slightest bit of training. I have no doubt that the verbal adeptness and stage presence that have made me a good comic will be useful as far as becoming a competent actor. But I still need actual acting work and I need it now. Susan is in Victor French's acting class (he's the star of the ABC series *Carter Country* and one of the best teachers in Hollywood). Susan could actually get me into class. It's $50 a month (four Saturdays) but more than worth it.

10. Haircuts: I have to be able to look neat in this image-conscious town. I can't ever go to something looking sloppy 'cause I couldn't afford a haircut. Finally I've got my foot in the door and I hate to have it slammed shut because of stupid things.

11. Dining: Although I never do, and would never eat dinner out for pleasure on borrowed money, it's important to be able to afford an emergency meal if it's "good for business." Even late-night snacks at Canter's sometimes create deeper friendships and new "ins" to do other gigs.

12. Singing lessons: I do some singing (half-joking) in my act. But I've been told I don't have a bad voice. I'm sure singing lessons could help and possibly bring out a real and useful talent.

13. Car insurance: To prevent a big liability disaster that can cripple me for life. (I also need AAA for emergencies.)

14. Car repairs: Not many, but I have to be prepared for the occasional new tire or other little screw-up.

15. Improvisation classes: Without any training I'm one of the best natural improvisers around. If I had some training I could do improvs on stage and just boost my worth even more.

16. Money to legally change my name when appropriate.

17. Tape record cassettes, food, rent, vital expenses for these next critical months.

Now, if you are saying, "Why doesn't he get a job?" Well, here's why: I have a job. Stand-up comedy. It's a job important enough for 780 people (three shows) to stand in line in the cold out at Newport Beach and pay $9 to see me. Two other comics and me is what beautiful rich people are fighting for tickets to see.

He didn't say anything about the pay dispute or the CFC. He'd been trying not to think about all that, as if to acknowledge it would give it life. A strike at the Store was about the worst thing he could imagine. Despite his loyalty to Mitzi, he could never cross a picket line. He was predisposed by heredity to support the masses against the Man. But where would he perform if the Store were cordoned off by picketers? He couldn't play the Improv at will like Lewis and Leno. He wasn't on Budd Friedman's A list (or B or C list, for that matter). TV talent scouts didn't drive down to the Laff Stop in Newport Beach to check out acts. And even if they did, stage time would be at such a premium in a strike that the Laff Stop's owner, Michael Callie, could pick and choose among the headliners whose TV appearances drew customers. If the comics struck the Store, it would stop his recent career progress in its tracks and mark the return of Bad Luck Lubetkin. He put the letter to his father and brother in a drawer.

Richard Lewis was working on a network TV pilot he had landed in the wake of *Diary of a Young Comic.* Called *The 416th,* it was a sitcom about a dysfunctional National Guard unit, sort of a countercultural remake of the old *Sgt. Bilko* series. The day job had prevented him from attending any of the comics' meetings, but he'd heard all about the issues during after-hours gatherings at Canter's.

The truth was, Lewis was ambivalent about the labor dispute. "Of course the comedians deserve payment for making the club owners so successful for so many years," he said. "There's no legitimate rationale for them not paying. Without us, they'd have an empty shell with cockroaches. There's no movie without a script, and there is no comedy club without comics."

At the same time, he thought that Lubetkin and a lot of other comics gave the club owners too much power by focusing on them. "I'm not working for Mitzi or Budd," he said. "I'm working for me and the audience. I'm using their clubs for my purposes."

He wasn't sure that a picket line or a boycott would accomplish anything constructive. "I don't want their $5 or $10 or $15," he said. "I want their stage. I don't want that price tag put on my set. I'm better than that. Yes, it's humiliating to work for nothing. But is it any less humiliating to work for *almost* nothing? Would I feel better using their stage to get ahead or having my work priced at $15?"

Argus Hamilton felt no such ambivalence. He was among a group of about a dozen hard-core loyalists who quickly formed a protective circle around Shore. Shore was clearly shaken by the events of the previous week, stunned by both the number and names of the comics apparently allied with the CFC. Jay Leno? David Letterman? She couldn't believe they would turn on her after all she had done for them. My God, Dave was set to guest-host *The Tonight Show* in a few weeks after only two previous appearances on the show! Wasn't that proof enough that her concept worked? Couldn't he see that the Store was the light?

Hamilton had never seen Mitzi so agitated and unsure of herself. He took on the role of Dreesen's counterpart, lobbying other comics to support her in her time of trial, rallying everyone he could around the queen. And no one could talk up Mitzi better than Argus. In describing her particular genius, he would work himself into flights of pure Southern oratory. "She plays each one of us like a different instrument," he'd say, "and has an incredible capacity for knowing just how to tune each one, especially those of us she has developed from scratch. The comics are her palette, and each night she uses the colors to paint a different beautiful picture that is the Comedy Store." It moved some people nearly to tears and made others want to puke, but everyone knew it came from his heart, and they respected him.

That wasn't the case with Ollie Joe Prater, who assumed a less admirable role in Mitzi's defense, that of spy or snitch. Pretending to be sympathetic to the CFC, he eavesdropped on conversations and reported back to Mitzi on what he heard. That's how she knew about Letterman's leanings. Of course, everyone knew what Prater was doing because he was as subtle as an anvil. He might as well have cupped his hand to his ear.

The CFC had its own spies in Shore's camp. A waitress named Robin called Dreesen to say that she had eavesdropped on an early evening meeting between Shore and her supporters in the Original Room and had overheard something she thought he should know about. Dreesen arranged to meet her at the coffee shop of the Continental Hyatt House. Robin told him that in the meeting Mitzi had expressed concern that the comics might boycott the Store in favor of the Improv. Argus and others said they doubted that would happen because, first and foremost, comics needed stage time, and the Improv only put on ten comics a night to the Comedy Store's forty. The CFC would never get a majority to go along with eliminating that many time slots. But Mitzi wasn't convinced. Then someone in the back of the room, maybe Ollie Joe or Biff Maynard—Robin said she couldn't tell because it was dark—shouted out, "What if there were no Improv?"

Dreesen didn't attach any significance to the comment. He was just glad to know that Mitzi was worried that they might go on strike. He thanked Robin and told her to keep her eyes and ears open.

Shore was absent from the Sunset club that Monday night when the CFC held its meeting to vote on her payment offer. More than one hundred comics showed up, including the Mitzi loyalists and the headliners. Once again, Dreesen chaired the meeting, and once again Leno played class clown to a whole class of clowns. This time, however, there was an underlying soberness in the room that wasn't there when they gathered at the union hall back in February. Dreesen saw determined faces looking back at him. They weren't there to fuck around; they were there to get something done.

The first thing they did was officially elect him chairman of the CFC. He was both moved and unnerved by the vote. Did he really want to put himself in this position? Did he want to be responsible for all these inordinately needy people? Was he out of his mind?

For the first order of business, he yielded the floor to Paul Mooney, who had received a telegram earlier in the day that he wanted to read aloud. Mooney held his hand up for quiet, and when the crowd settled down, he started in:

> To the comics of the newly formed comedy union I write these words of support because I believe your cause to be just and wholly within the concept of management and labor. It is not only immoral to work for nothing, it is also illegal. Slavery was banned with the signing of the emancipation proclamation over one century ago. I believe it is within the artist's rights and

privileges to receive proper compensation for his or her efforts.
I want you to know I would honor your picket lines if need be. I
am sure that most fair-minded artists in the community would
be supportive of you also.

Sincerely,

Richard Pryor

A collective whoop of surprise went up as people jumped to
their feet and applauded wildly, while Mitzi loyalists sat in slack-
jawed silence. Dreesen followed Mooney by reading his telegram
from Bob Hope. Again, there was a combination of applause and
glum looks. Hope wasn't anywhere near as popular with this crowd
as Pryor, but no one missed the significance of the two statements:
The CFC had support across the broad spectrum of established comedians, from Hope to Pryor.

Thus emboldened, the assemblage quickly voted down Mitzi's
offer by a wide margin. "If she charges a cover, then she has to
pay" had become a battle cry. They weren't going to accept any
proposal that didn't include payment for performances in the
Original Room and at Westwood. Before they adjourned, several
shouting matches broke out between dissidents and Shore stal-
warts, causing some to wonder whether they were witnessing the
first shots fired in a civil war.

Dreesen was troubled by the evening's events. He'd been hoping the membership would accept Shore's offer and everything
could return to how it was before. He was surprised at how strong
and united they'd become. He felt some pride about that, but he
also worried that they were about to pass the point of no return. If
Mitzi didn't come back with a better offer, then what was their op-
tion other than, as Mark Lonow had said, to throw up a picket line
and shut the place down? And where would that put him? At the
front of a pack of placard-carrying clowns demanding to be treated
like longshoremen? Holy shit! How in the fuck did he get here?

In the middle of a fitful sleep that night, he sat bolt upright in bed. He had it! An idea that would solve everything! He marched right into Shore's office the next day.

"Mitzi, I think I have a way for everybody to get what they want. It hit me last night; you just raise the cover charge by a dollar, from $4.50 to $5.50, and give that dollar to the comics. They get paid and it doesn't cost you a dime. It so simple I can't believe we didn't think of it before."

She looked at him as if he were a tiresome child and began shaking her head.

"No, Tommy. Like I keep telling you, the Store is a workshop and in that environment the comics don't deserve to get paid."

He sat there for a few moments saying nothing, running her statement through his head: They don't deserve to get paid. So, it was never about money, he thought; it was always about power and control. And she was never going to pay them unless she was forced to. Holy shit, indeed.

As he got up to go, she said, "I don't want you here anymore." She was talking about the CFC meetings, but he knew that she meant him, too.

# Fire!

However much Budd Friedman may have secretly been enjoying Mitzi Shore's travails, he knew that sooner or later the mob would come for him. Several comics had told him as much, joking, "Hey, Budd, you're on next."

To which he replied, not joking at all, "Fuck you. I bust my ass to keep this place going. The comics I put on my stage at 9:00 p.m. should be paying *me*, and the day I'm forced to pay them is the day I close down and open a restaurant."

That was all bluster, of course. Friedman knew that if Mitzi made a deal to pay the comics then he would have to make the same deal, and that worried him. He was going through a divorce, and it appeared likely that he'd wind up having to relinquish ownership of the New York club to his estranged wife, Silver. New York was a cash cow; LA was barely breaking even. He'd recently opened a branch in Las Vegas, and the roof had promptly collapsed. Mitzi could afford to make a deal with the comics. He wasn't sure he could.

Still, it wasn't as if he was having a bad time. For Budd, moving to Los Angeles had been a longtime dream come true. He loved the weather. He loved his house in the Hollywood Hills with its pool and hot tub. He loved his year-round tan. And even though it didn't make as much money as the New York club, he loved his Melrose place, in no small part because it was such a great venue for meeting women. He was forty-seven, freshly single, and feeling frisky, and the club's female employees, patrons, and performers soon learned that he was something of a hound. Every night it seemed that he was entertaining another woman with bottles of champagne in his cordoned-off VIP section of the back room. He was unabashed about it and took offense whenever anyone suggested he was conducting some kind of couch-casting operation. "I would *never* put an act on my stage because I went to bed with them," he'd say, adding after a pause, "unless they were good on stage. I have too much pride in my business, and I wouldn't want to be embarrassed. I wouldn't want anyone to know I slept with a bad singer or comedienne."

A few nights after the CFC vote, Friedman took a rare night off from the Improv and went on a double date with Dottie and Tom Archibald to see Bobby Short at a club in Century City. His plan was to be back at the club before midnight to close up.

Around 11:00 p.m., a young singer named Barbara McGraw was on stage at Melrose, bantering with the midweek audience of about forty people. As she was introducing her next song, the piano player, Cliff Grisham, whispered to her, "Barb, I think I smell smoke." She went ahead with the song, but two verses into it she smelled the smoke, too. It was coming through the back wall right behind them. The audience hadn't noticed yet.

"Excuse me, everyone, but we're smelling smoke up here," McGraw said, "so we think it might be wise if we all got up and left the room until we can check this out."

The patrons picked up their drinks and calmly filed out of the room, down the short hallway and into the bar area. McGraw and Grisham were the last ones out, and by the time they got into the bar, the smoke was billowing out of the back room. They suddenly remembered that Budd had installed a new sound system a few days earlier. "We should go back and see if we can at least get the sound board," McGraw said. They went back in, but there was too much smoke to see. By the time they made their way back out to the bar, it was filled with smoke, too. The bartender had called the fire department, and people were hurrying out the front door to the street.

Several blocks away, Budd was sitting with his date in the back seat of the Archibalds' car as it inched along in oddly heavy traffic. "What the hell is this?" he asked, seconds before the smell of smoke wafted through the car windows with the answer. "Oh, my God," he shouted, "it's the club!" He jumped out of the car while it was still moving and ran down the sidewalk.

Driving down Melrose Avenue from the opposite direction, Robert Schimmel and his wife encountered the same acrid smoke and traffic snarl. Schimmel, a stereo salesman turned stand-up comic from Scottsdale, Arizona, was excited to show his wife the club where he was going to be working. He'd performed there several months before on an open mike night, prompted by a dare from his sister. It was his first time on stage. Afterwards, Budd Friedman had come up to him and invited him to "come back and play the club anytime." An ecstatic Schimmel went home to Scottsdale, quit his job at Jerry's Audio, and convinced his wife that they should sell their house and move to Los Angeles. They were just now arriving in town. He'd pulled off the Hollywood freeway to give her a peek at their bright future.

"Oh, great," she said when they got close enough to read the sign on the front of the burning building.

"It'll be okay," he said, as much to reassure himself as her. "They have to be insured."

Around the perimeter set up by firefighters, the club's performers and denizens huddled together in heartbroken disbelief as the flames at the back of the building licked the sky. Many were crying. This was the center of their lives, their family room. Their home was burning down.

Robert Schimmel parked his car a few blocks away and jogged back to the scene, where he found Budd Friedman pacing back and forth in the street, running his hands through his hair, his eyes brimming with tears.

"Jesus, Budd, I can't believe this," he said.

Friedman looked at him and asked, "Who are you?"

Schimmel reintroduced himself, explaining, "You told me that I was funny and to sign up for spots."

"Yeah, well, I'm trying to deal with this right now," Friedman said as he turned away.

By the time the firemen extinguished the blaze, the back room, more than half the structure, was gone. Few who were inside when the fire started had left the scene, as if by staying they could somehow make everything come out alright. Friedman picked through the blackened ruins, a picture of despair. He knew that his fire insurance policy wouldn't begin to cover the loss. "I'm out of business," he kept saying, "I'm out of business."

News of the fire hit the comedy community like a thunderclap. The phone lines lit up over night, and even though the blaze didn't make the morning paper, by midmorning the next day, it was hard to find a comic who hadn't heard that the fire department had ruled it arson. The fire had started outside in the rear of the building, where an alley provided easy access and quick escape for someone with an incendiary device. The question was asked over and over again in the conversations among comics: "You think Mitzi had anything to do with it?" The answer was usually, "Nah." Mitzi might be volatile and vindictive, the reasoning went, but she wasn't evil or insane. People were less sure about some of her supporters, however. Based on what Robin the waitress had told him a few nights before, Tom Dreesen would have put money on either Biff Maynard or Ollie Joe Prater as the culprit. Both had well-known substance-abuse problems and were just crazy enough to toss a Molotov cocktail onto the roof of Mitzi's main competitor in some fucked-up act of loyalty. Word from inside the Comedy Store was that Mitzi was elated about the fire, figuring it solved her problem: The comics would never strike now. With the Improv shut down, she was once again the only game in town.

With a mixture of self-interest and altruism, performers started showing up at the Improv the morning after the fire, asking if they could do anything to help. Budd Friedman put all comers to work. Things were looking better in the bright light of day, and Budd was talking about reopening. The back room was toast, but the restrooms were okay, as were the bar and restaurant. Tom Archibald, a self-taught electrician, had patched in a line from the alley to restore power to the building. Cliff the piano player was a pretty good carpenter. The comics, singers, waitresses, and bartenders were mostly unskilled, but they made up for it in determination, and by the end of the day, they had pulled off a West Hollywood version of a barn raising. They'd walled off the charred back room with sheets of plywood and fashioned a small makeshift stage on the far side of the dining room. The new configuration seated only seventy-four, the exact same number as the New York Improv back when it first opened. Rebuilding the back room was going to take time and a lot of money Budd didn't have, but he'd already received two heartening phone calls— both Robin Williams and Andy Kaufman volunteered to perform benefits for the club.

Forty-eight hours after the fire, Budd was back in business, but before he put a single comic on his new stage, he placed a call to the comedy world's newest power broker, Tom Dreesen.

"Tom, I'm really hoping you guys won't put me on the front line of this labor thing until I'm fully up and running again from the fire," he said. "If you strike me now, I'm dead."

It was a stunning turnabout: The imperious proprietor of the Improv gone supplicant before a mere comic.

Dreesen felt bad for Friedman and believed him when he said the fire had put him precariously close to bankruptcy. No one wanted to see the Improv go under, except perhaps Mitzi. The CFC needed the Improv to remain open as a counterbalance to the Comedy Store. If the Improv closed, then once again Mitzi would hold all the cards, and the newfound unity among comics would dissolve quickly as individual career concerns chipped away at their collective resolve. It all came down to time slots. The comics needed a stage where they could be seen by the people who hired them. If there were no Improv, if Mitzi owned the only stage, then they were screwed. They had to keep the Improv open if they were to succeed.

Even so, Dreesen knew he couldn't make some unilateral deal with Friedman and let him off the hook. He knew from his time with the Teamsters that when management asks for a concession, however reasonable, you don't grant it without getting a concession in return. He needed something he could take back to the membership for a vote.

"Will you agree in principle to abide by whatever deal we end up making with Mitzi?" he asked.

"Yes," Friedman replied.

"Will you put it in writing?"

"Yes."

"I think the comics will go for that," Dreesen said. He hung up elated. They had their first victory.

# The Vote

Mitzi Shore was not going down that easily. In the dark labyrinth of the Sunset Store, she was hunkered down with lawyers and loyalists, trying to figure out how to beat back the barbarians at her gate. Her enmity for Tom Dreesen knew no bounds. This was all his doing, she was convinced. Jay Leno, David Letterman, and the rest never would have done this on their own initiative. Dreesen had put them up to it, she said; he'd whispered in their ears like Shakespeare's Iago.

Shore's lawyer assured her that the comics couldn't strike because, legally, they weren't really her employees. They were independent contractors. So they could stage a "walkout," declare a "boycott," and carry picket signs in front of the club, but they could not "strike." That was cold comfort to Shore, who didn't see the difference. In either case, they could parade around on the sidewalk on Sunset, telling her customers and the world that she was unfair. After all she had done for them! She seethed at the ingratitude, ached at the betrayal.

The Comedy Store's press agent, Estelle Endler, convinced Shore to sit for an interview with the *Los Angeles Times*—something she'd never done. Shore liked publicity but hated talking to the press. She preferred to have the comics speak for her and the Store, encouraging them to plug the club whenever they appeared on TV. The gambit had worked well in the past, but it wasn't going to get her through the current crisis. As Endler explained, the *Times* was working on a story about the burgeoning labor dispute, and a lot of comics were talking, telling their side of the story, not hers. She needed to get her truth out there, to explain her vision for the Store.

So, on a midweek afternoon, a *Times* reporter was escorted down a narrow passageway and into Shore's office, where no journalist had gone before. The Comedy Store president sat at her desk with a wall full of framed eight-by-ten photos to her right: Richard Pryor, Robin Williams, Jimmie Walker, David Letterman, Jay Leno, all her favorites. "They were all born here," she said. "When Letterman came here, he was very inhibited, so I put him on as an emcee for two years because that's what his need was, to learn how to talk to a room full of people."

Over the course of nearly an hour, Shore downplayed the recent dissension over pay and made a passionate case for the purity and high purpose of her creation. "The vibes are here, the love is here, the productivity—it's just a wonderful environment," she said. "My God, the stand-up comic is the most courageous person in the whole business because he's standing out there by himself with no script, with no one to depend on but himself. It's totally courageous, and that's why I've got my guts in this business."

The way she described it, the Comedy Store was a completely altruistic enterprise. "I'm expanding because I need more time slots for comedians to work out. Any money I get goes back into the business, giving it facilities to meet the needs of the comics. I don't take trips to Europe with it, you know."

The *Times* sit-down was the first in a series of press interviews that publicist Endler lined up for Shore. Another was with *People* magazine, which had responded to Endler's pitch about the general wonderfulness of "LA's newest comics' showcase, the Belly Room."

The resultant article was a masterpiece of PR sleight of hand: It said nothing about the pay dispute while repeating the legend that Mitzi had founded the club out of love for comedians and put "all the money back into the business." It included cameos by Robin Williams (calling Mitzi "the godmother of comedy") and Jimmie Walker (hailing her as "the patron saint of comedy"). It featured a photo of Mitzi in a group hug with eleven Belly Room comediennes beaming so broadly they looked as if they might be high on nitrous oxide. And it gave no hint that seven of the eleven women—not to mention Williams and Walker—had pledged allegiance to the dissident CFC. But the biggest howler in the article, from the comics' point of view, was the photo of Mitzi in her front yard playing with sons Peter, thirteen, and Pauly, eleven. The photo caption read, "Outside her manse, Mitzi rains motherly love on Peter as Pauly wheels up [on his bicycle]." Endler was good, there was no denying it. The *People* article lacked only a quote from someone calling Mitzi "the Mother Theresa of Sunset Strip."

The CFC, meanwhile, was scrambling to counter the Comedy Store's PR blitz. The group's first official press release, issued March 12, succinctly defined the organization and the scope of its mission: "'Comedians for Compensation' was recently organized by over 120 of the comedians regularly performing at the Sunset Strip and Westwood Comedy Stores for the purpose of receiving fair compensation for their services at those locations and certain other clubs throughout the entertainment industry. The practices at the Comedy Store, however, were considered illustrative."

Noting that the club had grown from "a 150-seat local workshop on Sunset Strip to a nationally publicized nightclub with 900 seats and enforced cover charge and drink minimum policies," the release said that

> through its representatives the performers' group requested that one-half of the "covers" at the Sunset and Westwood locations be equally allocated among the regularly performing comedians

regardless of his or her industry stature or reputation. This request was rejected by Ms. Shore, who emphasized that only certain performers should be paid and that it was "inappropriate" for all of the comedians to be compensated. The performers' group described Ms. Shore's position as grossly unfair.

The release was terse, to the point, and unemotional, indicating that it had not been written by any of the comics. Indeed, the final paragraph revealed that the CFC had enlisted some heavyweight help and was now "represented by Kenneth L. Browning of the Beverly Hills law firm of Bushkin, Kopelson, Gaims & Gaines." If Mitzi hadn't realized it before, she knew it now: The comics had Johnny Carson's lawyers on their side. Things were about to get bombastic.

Over the next week, in a fevered effort to turn what had started as an impromptu bitch session among five headliners into a legitimate collective bargaining issue for more than one hundred performers, comics turned labor activists shuttled back and forth between the dual CFC headquarters at the Astrow-Lonow residence on South Spalding in Beverly Hills and Dreesen's home on Costello Street in Sherman Oaks. They formed an interim board, named committee heads, and established contact with the two major performers' unions, the American Federation of Television and Radio Artists (AFTRA) and the Screen Actors Guild (SAG). They began initial planning for a possible strike. The learning curve was steep, and their biggest fear was being seen as ridiculous. They were comedians, after all, and they knew how they would lampoon what they were doing if they were on the other side. They could already hear the punch line: "the biggest joke ever to come out of the Comedy Store" (ba-dump-bump).

For the next meeting, Jo Anne Astrow persuaded the Continental Hyatt House on Sunset to donate its large conference room on the fourteenth floor. All comics on the phone list were contacted and invited to attend, be they CFC members or Mitzi loyalists. The main issue, they were told, would be whether to authorize the leadership to call a strike. It would be put to a vote.

The turnout was the largest yet, and the mood was tense. Chairman Dreesen wore a suit and tie for the occasion. He knew Leno would mock him mercilessly, but he wanted to bring home the seriousness of what they were about. He was still praying that a solution could be found, a settlement reached short of picket lines and public protests, but he knew they were getting perilously close to the point of no return. He opened the meeting by saying that everyone would be given a chance to speak his or her mind, even if it took all night.

A few minutes into the meeting, way in the back of the room, Gallagher raised his hand and was recognized by the chair. He was a prickly personality who usually had a sarcastic word to say about everything. But as everyone turned to hear what caustic comment he might offer up, he surprised them all. "Before we take this vote, I want to remind the people in the room that we all got our start because of Mitzi Shore," he said. "She fed us, and she gave us stage time." He credited her with encouraging what had become the centerpiece of his act, the "sledge-o-matic." He'd first performed the bit at the Westwood Store on New Year's Eve, splattering the unsuspecting patrons with flecks of pulverized apple. Some club owners would have been pissed about the mess, but Mitzi thought it was a scream and urged him to go with even bigger fruit. "And after you hit it, stay in that posture and milk the laugh," she advised.

He wasn't arguing for or against a strike, he said. "I'm just begging you, no matter how you vote, to please remember one word: compassion." He repeated it solemnly—"compassion, compassion"—and then sat down. The room was silent for a long ten seconds as everyone waited for him to pop back up and say, "Nah, I was just fuckin' with you." But he didn't. Apparently he was serious.

Gallagher's sentiment did not carry the night, however, as comic after comic stood to rail against Shore and her policies.

Not surprisingly, the black performers seemed the most angered over her refusal to pay. "This is sharecropping," said Marsha Warfield, "and I just don't understand how so many smart people can fail to see the extent to which they are being exploited."

Like Brad Sanders and Jimmy Cook, Warfield regularly worked the rough-and-tumble black clubs in South Central Los Angeles— Mr. Woodley's, the Twenty Grand at Imperial and Crenshaw Boulevard—so she had little patience for the namby-pambies who were afraid of Shore's power. "There was a show business before there was a Comedy Store, and there will be a show business after the Comedy Store is gone," she said. "Mitzi Shore did not make me a comic. She did not come get me from Chicago, and she is not going to send me home." When Dave Tyree, a *brother*, spoke up in Mitzi's defense, Warfield shouted, "If you don't shut your mouth, I'm going to throw you through that window." She then made a move to make good on her threat, but other comics intervened.

Likening Shore's reasoning to "a pimp game," Brad Sanders riffed à la Richard Pryor: "Don't you tell me you're doing me a favor by selling my pussy for me. I can sell my own pussy, thank you very much." He offered a story of a club owner back in Chicago "who once put a .45 revolver on the table and told me, 'You are *not* going to get paid.' And I said to him, 'Then who's gonna clean up all the blood?' He laughed and said, 'You're a funny little nigger,' and he paid me." As for going out on strike, Sanders said, "It's a no-brainer for me. What have I got to lose? I'm broke already."

And so it went. For every person who spoke in favor of Shore and her vision of the Comedy Store as a workshop, two or three others attacked her, at times so viciously that it seemed almost as if they were more interested in punishment than fair compensation.

After several hours, a vote was taken, and it wasn't close. The comics approved a walkout at the Sunset Strip club if Mitzi did not agree to begin paying for performances in all Comedy Store showrooms. Here and there around the room, you could see angry Shore supporters, some with tears in their eyes. But mostly, there was cheering and high fives. Amid the celebration, Tom Dreesen and Jo Anne Astrow watched in astonishment as Mr. Compassion himself ran from the back of the room, down the center aisle to the front, where he raised his hands in the air and began chanting, "Kill the cunt. Kill the cunt. Kill the cunt."

# All on the Line

For the CFC leadership, the next few days were like preparing for the D-day invasion. Tom Dreesen, Jo Anne Astrow, Dottie Archibald, Elayne Boosler, Jay Leno, Paul Mooney, Steve Bluestein, and a dozen others formed the troops into committees and subcommittees responsible for everything from publicity to painting picket signs. Meetings bled into one another, and the phone calls from worried comics came in a torrent.

Mark Lonow coached the neophytes in the art of effective picketing. They would need show-of-force numbers on the line in front of the Sunset club every night from the time of the early evening newscasts until closing. On top of that, they had to have a skeleton crew of pickets present overnight and during the day so that the Teamsters who delivered liquor and other supplies would be forced to leave their loads at the curb rather than cross the line. Keeping the line manned twenty-four hours a day would require enormous effort and careful coordination. Some of the pickets would need transportation; all would require food and drink.

This was not going to be fun and games, Lonow cautioned. They were about to lay siege to a high-profile, multimillion-dollar business located on a world-famous thoroughfare. Their aim was to make it so difficult and unprofitable for Mitzi Shore to continue operating that she would accede to their demands. That could take weeks or months. Passions were likely to flare. People could get hurt. At the very least, the whole of Hollywood would be watching.

Ken Browning laid out the legalities. Officially, it would be a walkout or a boycott, not a strike, because they were considered independent contractors rather than employees of the Comedy Store. Pickets could not interfere with traffic or block the entrance to the parking lot or club, and they could not threaten, intimidate, verbally abuse, or touch customers. They could, however, be a loud, large pain in the ass. And who was better equipped to do that than a bunch of comics?

When Dreesen had time to think at all, he questioned his own sanity. *What am I about to do? Lead a bunch of performers in a labor action against a nightclub owner. And who is it that hands me the big checks that pay for the house and car and food and clothes for my family? Nightclub owners. So, why would I risk all that for this?* The answer always came back the same: *Because these are my friends, and they need my help. It's the right thing to do.*

After much discussion, members of the executive committee decided to give Mitzi a few more days to think things over, and then, if she didn't agree to begin paying for all performances in all her showrooms, they would throw up a picket line at the Sunset Store on Tuesday evening, March 27.

They didn't announce the date, but it was no secret that the members had voted to back a strike, and when a lot of headliners and regulars failed to call in on Monday with their availability for the coming week, it was clear to everyone that something was about to happen.

The potluck auditions at Sunset went on without incident on Monday night, and on Tuesday morning, the *Hollywood Reporter* ran an unattributed, two-sentence item saying the strike would begin at 6:00 p.m. that day. Early Tuesday afternoon, comics began gathering at Dreesen's house, eventually numbering between twenty-five and thirty, the committed, working core of the CFC. They went down the checklist: Pickets were scheduled in round-the-clock shifts; the signs were ready to be handed out; arrangements had been made for feeding and watering the line; megaphones and umbrellas had been donated. Everything was set. The foot soldiers were just waiting for the word.

They all crowded into Dreesen's den as he picked up the phone and called Shore to give her one last shot at avoiding the strike.

"Mitzi, it's Tom Dreesen, and I'm here in a meeting with the CFC membership."

She said nothing, just listened.

"They've voted to call a strike starting this evening if you don't agree to pay in all the rooms."

There was a brief silence, and then she said flatly, coldly, "Not . . . one . . . red . . . fucking . . . cent."

He wasn't sure what he'd been expecting, but it wasn't that, a statement so sure to inflame.

"Mitzi," he said, "they are all here with me, and I have to tell them what you say. Do you really want me to repeat that to them?"

She said it again, in the same cadence and tone: "Not . . . one . . . red . . . fucking . . . cent."

He sighed, shrugged, and addressed the group. "She says, and I quote, 'Not one red fucking cent.'" He watched as it registered on their faces—surprise at first, then anger—and held the phone out so that she could hear as they started to chant, "Strike . . . strike . . . strike!"

"I'm sorry, Mitzi," he said into the receiver. "We never wanted it to come to this." He couldn't tell if she was still on the line because the chanting was louder now and accompanied by foot stomping and pounding on tabletops and seat cushions.

"Strike . . . strike . . . strike!"

When the frenzy died down, the realization hit them like a bucket of cold water in the face: This was really going to happen.

They were about to shut down the institution that had served as their primary, if not only, connection to show business. There was nothing else they could do. Now it was, as Elayne Boosler put it, a "fight to the death." The prospect was both terrifying and exhilarating.

Within minutes Dreesen's house had emptied as all hands searched for phones to make the necessary calls to the membership. Steve Bluestein alerted the media: the *Los Angeles Times* and *Los Angeles Herald Examiner*, the AP and UPI news services, the *Hollywood Reporter* and *Variety*, and the local TV stations, where prime coverage was all but guaranteed by the weirdness factor of comedians walking a picket line. Who wouldn't want to see that? It was bound to be entertaining, and the possibilities for bad headline writing were endless: "No Laughing Matter," "Unfunny Business," "Laugh Riot, "Punch Line."

Dreesen made a point of calling Johnny Dark because he knew his pal was wavering in his support for the CFC. "We're striking tonight, Johnny, and we need you to be with us on this," he said.

Dark immediately equivocated. "But this is a woman who has done more for me than my managers," he said. "Merv Griffin saw me at the Comedy Store."

Dreesen cut him off sternly. "You are either with us, or you're with Mitzi."

In agony, Dark made a beeline for Shore's office, desperately seeking some middle ground.

"What are you going to do, Johnny?" she asked.

"Mitzi, I can't work here," he said, his eyes brimming with tears. "How can I when every one of my best friends is not working here?"

"But, Johnny, I started you."

"I know, I know. But I can't go against them. I can't work here any more until this is over. But I promise, you won't see me out there picketing. I can't cross the line, but I won't be on it. I want you to know how much I appreciate what you've done for me and Suzie."

"Well, okay then," she said, waving him away in a manner that suggested she was irritated and disappointed but not banishing him forever.

Shore had already decided to close the club for at least the first night of the strike because she didn't want any comics or customers to have to cross the picket line. She was busy making her own calls, and one of the first was to David Letterman. He'd become her favorite Comedy Store success story since his booking as guest host on *The Tonight Show*, and she didn't want Dreesen dragging him in front of the cameras to say bad things about the club on the evening news.

"David, I just wanted to call and make sure you are not going on strike," she said when he picked up the phone.

"Mitzi, I *am* going on strike," he said.

"Oh, David, I think you are making a terrible mistake."

"Well, I don't think so, Mitzi, and I hope you and I will be okay."

He could tell that she was hurt, but he didn't try to soften the blow by promising that he wouldn't walk the line, even though he couldn't imagine himself parading around in front of the club carrying a sign with some silly slogan on it. The truth was, he didn't really have his guts in the fight, didn't feel the same level of emotion that Tom, Elayne, and George Miller did. He still had a little money saved up from Indiana, and he'd managed to get on the Johnny Carson show, so the big issues of the strike really didn't touch him directly. He supported the strike because it was important to his friends. It was as simple as that, bedrock stuff. For him, friendship trumped everything.

Steve Lubetkin, too, felt bound by friendship to back the strike, but as he didn't have Letterman's stature, he was terrified that going against Mitzi might destroy everything he'd been working for the past few months. "I'm not a hero; I'm a coward," he told Susan the morning of the strike call. "I can't do this."

Ironically, the start of picketing at Sunset coincided with the start of his second five-night gig at the Comedy Store in La Jolla, which was not being picketed. He was tempted to just slip down to La Jolla and avoid taking a stand for the time being. But late in the afternoon, he announced to Susan, "For the first time in my life, I'm going to do something really courageous." His plan was to join the picketing as a show of solidarity with his fellow comics and then head down to La Jolla.

Things were just getting started when he arrived at Sunset shortly after 5:00 p.m. The TV camera crews were setting up for their live shots. Dreesen and some of the other CFC leaders were doing interviews. Tom was dressed in a three-piece glen plaid suit and talking to Connie Chung, the hot young West Coast correspondent for CBS News. Comics were arriving in a steady stream, selecting their signs and taking their places on the line. A contingent of motorcycle cops kept the traffic moving. The air crackled with excitement; the scene was heavy with portent. "This is historic, kind of like Woodstock," Dreesen told a reporter for the *Los Angeles Times*. "Ten years from now, everyone will be saying, 'Sure I remember. I was *there*.'" Lubetkin was there on the picket line for only half an hour before he set out for La Jolla.

By 6:00 p.m. the sidewalk party was in full swing. The comics carried picket signs emblazoned with slogans as marginally clever as "No Bucks, No Yucks" and "No Money, No Funny." They sang, danced, and chanted such goofy non sequiturs as "People in India are going to bed funny" and (to the amused police officers) "Use a Pun, Go to Prison." Alison Arngrim arrived in a limousine, dressed to the nines. Comedienne Roberta Kent had the presence of mind to craft a sign that promoted as well as protested. Fashioned like a theater marquee, it read, "Now Appearing on Strike: Roberta Kent." Leno worked the line as if it were a club stage, shamelessly playing to the news cameras at every opportunity, at one point stumbling out of the crowd and hollering in the thick accent of a Welsh coal miner, "I'm not goin' back in that hole 'til they Shore it up."

Every now and then a Shore loyalist arrived and hurried inside with head down and no comment. The exceptions were Alan Bursky, who crossed the picket line with a gleeful sneer, and Argus Hamilton, who played the role of courtly Southern gentleman by shaking hands and telling the picketers he loved and respected them despite their disagreement over Mitzi's pay policy.

Ken Browning was on hand as an observer, telling reporters that any settlement between the two sides would have to include a no-retaliation pledge on the part of Shore. "I think that a number of performers fear, and I don't know if it's warranted or not, that Mrs. Shore may take some action against them. If they've been playing a prime-time spot, they might feel that, by reason of their being on the picket line or being part of this organization, she might put them on at 2:00 a.m. That's part of the reason I'm involved, so that doesn't happen."

No one out front knew it, but Shore was watching intently from a spot a few feet back from the front window of the club, far enough in the shadows that she couldn't be seen. Literally and figuratively, she was in a very dark place. As the picketers passed, she said each one's name aloud and remembered the time she had made them a regular, or lent them money, or cosigned their car loan or apartment lease. She didn't see Letterman on the picket line, which was some comfort to her, but she saw Steve Lubetkin out there, and she decided to do something about it.

Fifteen minutes after his brief appearance on the picket line, Lubetkin pulled into a gas station and called the Sunset office from a pay phone. He just wanted them to know he was on his way to the gig. Of course, the line was busy because of the picketing, so he called the La Jolla club and said he would be there in about two hours, well before his 9:00 p.m. set. He was halfway there when calamity hit: His beat up 1963 Buick Skylark broke down near the city of Oceanside. In a panic, he made it to a pay phone and called La Jolla, hoping someone there could come pick him up; there was still plenty of time. But before he could say anything, he was told to forget it; word had come from Sunset that his contract had been cancelled. He tried calling Mitzi to explain, but he couldn't get through.

So, it had happened again, just when it looked like he was on the verge of a breakthrough. He had argued with his father the week before, defending himself and his dream of comedy stardom by citing the La Jolla engagement as evidence that it was all about to happen for him. Now it was gone—the gig, the $250 payday, the relationship with Mitzi, everything. He didn't have the $50 it would cost to get his car towed back to Los Angeles; he'd have to borrow it from someone. It wasn't fair. Nothing was fair.

The news that a group of comedians was picketing a nightclub on Sunset Strip didn't exactly rock the country, but the story got good play locally, especially on television. The coverage was predictably shallow, however, with most reports playing up the comedic aspects of the first night of picketing rather than the underlying issues. On day two of picketing, Elayne Boosler accosted a *Los Angeles Times* reporter on the sidewalk, poking him in the chest with her index finger as she complained about the newspaper's article that morning. "This is not a joke, and you should be ashamed of yourself for treating it like it is," she scolded. "These people are literally risking everything by being here. That's what you should be writing about."

Boosler may have been risking more than any of them. She was already on the outs with Budd Friedman, and Johnny Carson wasn't a fan of her act. So, her standing out in front of the Comedy Store talking trash about Mitzi Shore could be viewed as either extreme courage or borderline insanity. And now she was busting the chops of the reporter who was covering the strike for the entertainment industry's newspaper of record. For a moment it seemed as if the sound of the picketers was all but drowned out by the clanging of Boosler's legendary brass balls.

Steve Lubetkin was back on the picket line the second night, chanting with the zeal of the newly converted. Having spent the morning in a fruitless attempt to get Shore to listen to what had happened to his car, he decided he had nothing more to lose by throwing in wholeheartedly with the CFC. The CFC leaders were glad to hear it. In the aftermath of opening night, they were nervously eyeing the number of people on the all-comics list who had not yet signed up for picketing duties, as well as the number who had crossed the picket line. The CFC counted at least ten of the latter. They weren't technically scabs, at least not yet, because they hadn't crossed the picket line to perform, only to show support for Mitzi. In fact, Shore had placed calls to a group known around the club as "Mitzi's boys" and insisted that they make an appearance at the club. In addition to Argus Hamilton, the "boys" included Harris Peet, Ollie Joe Prater, Biff Maynard, Mitch Walters, Dave Tyree, Mike Binder, Allan Stephans, and Lue Deck. They served Shore in various paid and unpaid capacities, ranging from doorman to handyman to, in the case of Prater, enforcer. Ollie was usually the one who let a comic know when he had worn out his welcome with Mitzi either for personal or professional reasons, telling him either that he should stop trying to talk to her, or maybe take a vacation from the Store for a few months, or, worst of all, go away and never return. Prater's three hundred plus pounds proved helpful whenever they objected.

In the view of their peers, only two of Mitzi's boys—Hamilton and Binder—had acts good enough to qualify for prime-time spots. But the CFC leaders saw each of them as a threat, cracks in the dam that Mitzi could exploit, either by promoting their careers or pressing them to prevail upon others to cross the line. The more comics who crossed, the longer the strike would last, and the longer it lasted, the more likely the comics were to lose their collective nerve and vote to accept whatever crumbs Mitzi put on the table.

For anyone who doubted Shore's power, *The Tonight Show* on the second night of picketing offered a lesson in how it worked. Johnny's first guest was Mitzi's longtime friend Buddy Hackett, whose appearance had been engineered by Comedy Store publicist Estelle Endler. After some initial chitchat with Hackett, Carson turned to the audience and digressed: "You know, the young comedians out here work in a place called the Comedy Store and other places which are kind of a training ground. These places have trained most of the young comedians who start here; we get them from the Improv and the Comedy Store. And what's kind of interesting is that they are on strike because they think they should get paid." Turning back to Hackett, he then lobbed the prearranged question, "How do you feel about that?"

"Well, I think they're bananas," said Hackett. "It's very simple: Years ago AGVA [the American Guild of Variety Artists, the traditional union for nightclub performers] came down on clubs that let neophyte comics go onstage and perform after the featured acts finished; they could get up and try stuff. But the union came down on it and said they had to get paid $75, and [the clubs] all went by the wayside. Richard Pryor came out of that system, and he's now fighting for the young kids to get paid. But if he'd had to get paid in those days, then they might not have let him get up to find out if he *should* be paid. So, I think these nonpaying clubs are a necessary evil.

"They say this woman is making an awful lot of money," he continued with a straight face. "Now, I don't know the woman, and I know all the kids are going to hate me for saying this, but I am like an old father giving some advice. There is a lot of money to be made as a comedian, and once you learn your trade, you will never be without work; you will always work. There is always a place to work for a price. It might be a high price, or it might be a low price, but you will always earn a living once you learn your craft."

Turning from the audience back to Carson, he asked. "Were they going to chip in and pay for the woman's investment if she went broke?"

Carson seemed uncomfortable during Hackett's recitation of the Comedy Store talking points, making a clumsy attempt at a joke—"I could do a sketch about [the strike]. Can you see comedians on the picket line with seltzer bottles?"—and saying "I think you are making a good point; that's some good advice," while at the same time cautioning, "We don't know the depth of the situation."

All in all, it was an awkward conversation that must have seemed like a confusing non sequitur to a national audience that knew little, if anything, about the strike. But it registered with its intended audience. By the next day, the Carson-Hackett exchange was topic one among the young comics of Los Angeles, and the consensus among them was that Johnny had come down against the strike. Dreesen was concerned that Carson's stature among comics could help persuade some of the fence-sitters to jump to Mitzi's side. He was also disheartened that Hackett didn't seem to understand the plight of the young comics of the day. Hackett was right about the history of AGVA and the small clubs and Pryor, and his advice to young comics about learning their craft was solid. But the Comedy Store was a world away from the little clubs in the Catskills where Hackett had learned his craft, and it bore no resemblance to the loosey-goosey joke joint that his old pal Sammy Shore had opened on Sunset Boulevard seven years earlier.

"The little club that Buddy's talking about doesn't exist anymore," Dreesen said in an interview with the *Detroit News* that Steve Bluestein set up to rebut Hackett's *Tonight Show* comments.

"We're talking about a place that packs in 1,800 people a night on weekends at five bucks a pop and that with the bar is grossing way over $20,000 a week. All we want to do is split the door and divide our half equally among the 150 comedians who work there in a week. We wouldn't even make the lowest union scale, but getting paid would say something. It would say we're professionals."

As the dispute broke more widely in the press, Shore changed her narrative. Instead of playing up the philosophy behind her no-pay policy, she cried poor, claiming that paying the comics what they were demanding was "a financial impossibility because we have forty sets per night." "She simply can't afford to pay them," said her spokeswoman, Estelle Endler. "They're holding out for philosophical reasons; she's holding out for financial reasons."

Ken Browning immediately fired back with both barrels, claiming that Shore's most recent offer—75 percent of the door in the Main Room—was little more than a smokescreen. "The fact of the matter is, the Comedy Store derives the bulk of its income from the Westwood location, the Belly Room and the Original Room. The Main Room functions only for headliners, and it is dark most of the year. So if she offered us 110 percent of the Main Room, it would be almost valueless.

"She has also told us workmen's compensation is inhibiting her ability to afford the comedians," Browning went on. "She says it would require a $3,000-a-week expense. That is not so. We have talked with various workmen's comp carriers, and we're talking about something more like $200 to $600 a week.

"I asked for the opportunity to meet with her accountant and look at her books on a confidential basis regarding her ability to do this, but that request was rejected out of hand." Browning said the CFC's estimate that the club was grossing $20,000 a week "bears out the proposition that this is a money-making operation." The figure was based on an estimated 3,000 paying customers a week at Sunset and Westwood and was considered "quite conservative" by the CFC. "It could be twice that," Browning said.

The CFC's $20,000 estimate actually came from information provided by Shore's accountant, Helen Dornberger, who had passed it along to her son George. Mrs. Dornberger and a handful of other staffers were aware that each night's receipts were placed in a safe in Mitzi's house; then, once a week, approximately $21,000 was taken from the safe and deposited in the bank. They assumed that some portion of the receipts always remained behind in Shore's safe, undeclared. Why else would the bank deposit always be the same? Why else did the club sell unnumbered tickets? The arrangement had all the earmarks of a classic skim.

In the wake of Ken Browning's uncomfortably accurate statements about her finances, Shore did some accounting of her own: She added two and two and summarily fired Helen Dornberger. However justified, the dismissal was problematic for Shore. For one thing, Helen was an extremely popular figure among comics on both sides of the pay divide, as well as with Shore's office staff. For another, David Letterman was George's best friend, and he was upset about the firing because George was. If Dave had not been emotionally involved in the strike up to that point, he certainly was now.

Ken Browning had one strike-related discussion that he kept secret from his CFC clients. As part of his other duties at the Bushkin firm, he had to accompany Johnny Carson to Las Vegas, where the comedian was in the process of buying a TV station. Alone with Carson on the private flight, the young attorney screwed up his courage and mentioned that he was representing the striking comics. Carson took the bait, and before they landed, Browning had delivered a passionate precis on the depth of the issue. The strike would never be mentioned on *The Tonight Show* again.

On Friday, March 30, the fourth night of picketing, a dozen comics took a break from the strike to participate in the First Annual Battle of the Stars basketball game at the Forum, home of the Los Angeles Lakers. The charity benefit pitted the Comedy Store

Bombers against the Deep Pizza Celebrity All-Stars, whose only bona fide celebrity was Larry Wilcox, the costar of the hit TV series *C.H.I.P.S.* Although only one of the Bombers, Lue Deck, sided with Shore, all of them donned the uniforms she'd paid for to play in what would turn out to be their final game, which they won by a score none of them could remember the next day.

At the end of the first week of picketing, Budd Friedman met with CFC leaders at the Improv, where comics were performing nightly for free on a makeshift stage. Friedman opened his books to the group and signed an agreement to begin paying for performances when full operations resumed in six to eight weeks. The exact amount and manner of the payment was subject to future good faith bargaining.

"I agreed, in effect, to pay them *something*," he said in announcing the agreement. "Basically, I am against the strike. But if that's what they want, then maybe it's the tenor of the times. Or, as my ex-wife said, 'Maybe it's the end of an era.'"

# Dave's Big Night

After a week's shutdown, Mitzi Shore reopened the Sunset club, but it was hardly a return to business as usual. At 10:00 p.m., prime time, on Tuesday, April 3, the Original Room was only one-quarter filled, the line-up consisted entirely of amateurs culled from the previous night's potluck auditions, and admission was free (though the two-drink minimum remained in effect).

Outside, former regulars and headliners were working hard to make the media understand the issues underlying the picket signs and the slogans. "There are comedians in this town who have done all the talk shows and don't have $100 net worth," said Jay Leno. "It's humiliating after you've been on TV to have to get a job at Nate 'n Al's deli. All we want is a little gas money, just a couple of dollars, that's all it comes down to. It amazes me that it's come to this."

Elayne Boosler told a reporter that because of the Comedy Store's success, "showcase rooms are replacing paying rooms; it's sweeping the country. As it is now, you have to be a TV star like Robin Williams or you have to work for free. [Mitzi Shore] calls this a showcase when no one has been allowed to showcase [perform for agents, managers, or producers] on the weekends. And it's not really a workshop anymore. If you bomb in there, you don't continue to work in there. She recently told a comedian he was 'too experimental.'"

Tom Dreesen said that even though he was earning as much as $15,000 a week in Vegas, "I had a [club owner] offer me $250 a week recently. He said, 'Well you work for *free* at the Comedy Store.' We've got the best show in town for $4.50. We did this to ourselves; we agreed to work for free six years ago. Now we're trying to undo it."

All around them on the sidewalk, their colleagues were trying to dissuade potential patrons from entering the club, handing out mimeographed fliers that read, "Please honor the comedians' boycott. At the Comedy Store only the comedians are not paid. The people you have come to see receive nothing for their work." The picketers also provided printed directions to the Improv and the lineup of comics set to perform there that night.

At one point, a huge tour bus carrying the Canadian rock band April Wine pulled up, and the band members and their road crew disembarked. Comedian Susan Sweetzer and several others pleaded with them, "Please don't cross our picket line. We're performers, too, and we're just trying to get paid for what we do." The musicians climbed back onto the bus and left, to much cheering and praising of the Canadian people. But the bus returned an hour later, and this time those fucking Canucks, the April Winos, crossed the line and went in to watch the show.

Periodically, Shore loyalists would emerge from the club to engage the other side in debate or name calling. Harris Peet and the other doormen liked to rile the picketers up by making a show of writing down their names as if compiling a future blacklist. Argus Hamilton did his best to keep things collegial, allowing Dreesen or Dottie Archibald to complete his or her pitch to a would-be patron about not entering the club before presenting his case for crossing the line, which usually began with something like, "With all due respect to my friend and colleague, who is a very talented performer. . . . " Though he was Mitzi Shore's most ardent defender, Hamilton could not bring himself to view the picketers as the enemy. He had partied with almost every one of them, stayed up all night laughing and talking and sharing dreams. He saw them as honorable opponents who had a different view of what the Comedy Store should be. The great-grandson of a Confederate officer, he believed he was fighting the good fight for a cause greater than himself. It was a civil war, to be sure, but he was a Southern gentleman who knew that one day Arkansas and Illinois would get along again.

The war heated up as the week wore on and Shore supporters began taking the stage to perform. Argus Hamilton led the charge, urging the others to follow him into the breach. Most of Mitzi's boys did, prompting Elayne Boosler to start the sidewalk chant, "The doormen are the headliners. The doormen are the headliners."

Behind every crossing of the picket line was a story:

- When Lue Deck went over, it marked the end of the comedy team of Heck and Deck because his partner, Jimmy Heck, supported the CFC. Best friends from Houston, the pair had performed together for five years, touting themselves as "Heck and Deck, funny as a train wreck."
- Yakov Smirnoff, an émigré from the Soviet Union, was employed by Shore as the club's carpenter. Along with a handful of other strikebreakers, he was paying only a few hundred dollars a month to live in a comfortable seven-bedroom house that Shore owned on Crest Hill Drive a few blocks above the Sunset club.
- Charlie Hill had been an ardent supporter of the American Indian Movement during the bloody siege of Wounded Knee in 1973, which colored his view of the comedians' uprising: "I didn't see any of them there with me at the federal building when the FBI was killing my brothers on the Pine Ridge reservation."
- Garry Shandling was the scion of a family with manufacturing holdings and decidedly antiunion views. He had not shared the

struggling comic experience. He was a successful sitcom writer trying to break into stand-up, and prior to the strike, Shore had refused to put him in the regular lineup because she didn't think he
was good enough. Of course, that changed the minute he crossed
the picket line.

- Lois Bromfield was the only woman to join the strikebreakers.
  Naturally, a number of male comics took it as solid evidence that
  she was Mitzi's secret lesbian lover.

Inside the club, Mitzi urged her supporters to keep constant
watch on the pickets outside "because I don't know whether they
might try something violent. I wouldn't put it past them." Some
pickets delighted in playing to her paranoia by lighting pieces of
paper on fire and waving them in the air, shouting things like,
"Remember the Improv." Such antics were more inflammatory
than the pickets realized because Shore and some of her closest
cohorts suspected that Budd Friedman was behind the torching
of his club, calling it a "fire of convenience" and "a case of Italian
lightning." At one point, there appeared to be a genuine threat
to the Sunset club when two Los Angeles Police Department de-
tectives showed up with a tape of a phone call they said had come
into the precinct warning that a bomb had been planted in the
building. Upon hearing the tape, Shore blurted out, "Gee, that
sounds like Ollie." After the cops left, reassured by Shore that it
was all just a misunderstanding, a terrified Ollie Joe Prater admitted to several people that he had phoned in the bomb scare—he
just never imagined those calls were taped.

The atmosphere on the picket line was also growing increasingly tense. Whereas the first week was highlighted by such play-
ful stunts as Leno, dressed as Che Guevara, wheeling up in a
Volkswagen "Thing" painted in camouflage to resemble an ar-
mored personnel carrier, the second week was marked by angry
confrontations. In one instance, a shouting match between an
apparently unchastened Prater and Jimmy Aleck led to Prater's

chasing Aleck through the parking lot with a baseball bat, an astonishing sight given Prater's bulk and the fact that Aleck moved with a pronounced limp left behind by a childhood bout of polio. Prater had Aleck cornered against a couple of cars, and a crowd was starting to gather around them, when Dreesen pulled his car into the parking lot, jumped out, and got between them.

"What's going on, Ollie?" he barked.

"It's none of your business. Stay out of it," Prater said.

"This *is* my business."

"I'm going to break his fucking jaw."

"Then I'll have to break yours."

Dreesen was fairly confident that he could take Prater, who was heaving from the short sprint, but he was relieved when the much larger man backed off and trudged down the ramp toward the club. He shook his head in disbelief at what had just taken place. What did all this have to do with being funny for a living?

With the strikebreakers forming a semblance of a professional lineup, Shore reinstituted the cover charge over the weekend, but the mood inside the club remained as dark as the décor. Shore cycled between self-righteous rage and self-pity, with no stop in between for self-reflection. Her staff was concerned that in her pain and anger, she might do something rash. Rumor around the building had it that Glendale Federal Bank had made her an offer to buy the business. Hamilton feared they were getting dangerously close to the point at which she just might say, "Fuck 'em," and sell the place.

If Shore saw any bright spots as she stood night after night looking out the window at the picketers, it was the fact that, with the exception of Leno, none of her favorites had shown up to parade around with the others, shouting slogans and calling her names—not Robin Williams or Jimmie Walker or Richard Pryor, not Sandra Bernhard, and not David Letterman. That was about to change.

Monday, April 9, was Oscar night. Most of Hollywood was buzzing with speculation about which of the two Vietnam war dramas, Michael Cimino's epic *The Deerhunter* or the Jane Fonda vehicle *Coming Home*, would win for best picture. The comedy community, however, was focused on a sidebar story: Johnny Carson was hosting the Academy Awards ceremony, and as a result, one of their own, David Letterman, was filling in as host of *The Tonight Show*. There wasn't a comic on either side of the strike who didn't know what this meant for Dave. It made him in the business, not just as a stand-up but as a major league entertainer. It was bigger than what had happened with Freddy. Dave was being anointed as Carson's heir apparent. It was all the comics were talking about on the picket line, not just because Dave was universally well-liked but also because it gave them hope for themselves.

Once again, Dreesen accompanied Letterman to the early evening taping, but this time it wasn't solely for moral support; he was booked as a guest. A veteran of umpteen *Tonight Show* appearances, Tom was cool and calm backstage before the show, while Dave was a nervous wreck, running through his routine of self-deprecation: "This time tomorrow I'll be back in Indianapolis."

As Ed McMahon introduced Letterman, Dreesen was standing in the wings watching when he felt a presence behind him. He turned to see talk show host Tom Snyder, whose *Late Night* followed the Carson show. "I gotta see how the audience responds to this no-name," Snyder said snarkily.

Once again, Dave's jitters didn't make it past the curtain; when the cameras started rolling, he was smooth as silk. Dreesen had seen his friend perform countless times at the Comedy Store and other clubs, and he never really understood why Dave didn't feel entirely comfortable in that setting. Seeing him now in the TV host chair, he finally got it. *Oh, my God*, he thought. *This is where he belongs. He's home.*

It was a heady moment when Letterman introduced Dreesen for the stand-up segment of the show, something that neither of them could have imagined just two years earlier. "Thank you, ladies and gentlemen," Dreesen said at the top of his routine. "I always like being here on *The Tonight Show.* . . . Of course, I like it a lot better when Johnny is here." Off to his right, he heard Dave break up.

They planned to drive together to the Comedy Store after the taping. Letterman hadn't been there since the picketing started because he'd been working every night getting ready for the show. But as they were headed down the hall toward the door, Carson's longtime producer, Fred DeCordova, stopped them and told Letterman that, like all guest hosts, he was expected to attend the postshow staff meeting. To Dreesen's astonishment, Letterman begged off, saying, "I'm really sorry, Freddy, but I can't stay because I made a commitment to walk the picket line at the Comedy Store tonight."

When Letterman's red truck pulled into the Comedy Store parking lot twenty minutes later, the crowd on the sidewalk cheered. As he walked down the ramp and took his place on the line, his fellow Comedians for Compensation broke into a scat version of *The Tonight Show* theme, singing "dah-dah, dah-dah-dah-dahdah-dah."

Inside the club, Argus Hamilton watched as Mitzi looked out the window and took it all in. Her shoulders sagged, and her chin dropped to her chest. Emotionally devastated by what she could only interpret as an act of personal betrayal, she looked so small he thought she might disappear.

# The Union Forever?

The next morning, Mitzi Shore blinked.

In a hastily arranged interview with the *Los Angeles Times*, she announced, "Against my better judgment, I have conceded to pay the comics in the Original Room. It is my third and final offer to them."

Her offer was $25 per set, except for the first three acts Tuesday through Thursday nights, which would feature "beginners," who would therefore work for free. Performers in the Main Room would be paid $35 per set on Friday and Saturday nights. At Westwood, all comics would work for free except one featured performer per week, who would be paid $200.

The offer far exceeded what any of the comics had imagined back in January. For regulars, it would mean not only gas money but also a car payment, with maybe a little left over for part of the rent, a veritable windfall. But things had changed since that first New Year's morning bitch session. After hours spent together on the picket line and in CFC meetings and strategy sessions, the comics of the Comedy Store had bonded in a way that they hadn't from smoking dope in the parking lot and shooting the shit all night at Canter's deli. A group conscience had taken root, a sense of common purpose beyond being funny and making it in Hollywood.

Some of them saw Mitzi's offer as potentially divisive because paying certain performers in the Original Room and not others would ratchet up the tension and jealousy already inherent in the competition for good time slots. By the same token, the whole vibe at Westwood would likely change if one act was designated as the star and all the others were just bit players. You could kiss camaraderie good-bye. As for Shore's proposal for the Main Room, $35 a set seemed like a pittance. A full house brought in more than $2,000 in cover charges, so she was offering less than 10 percent of the door on a good night.

The CFC leaders saw something else in Shore's offer, a chink in her armor, a sign that she was weakening, maybe even scared. So, they decided to push that perceived advantage at a CFC meeting at the Improv that evening. With the media in attendance, Tom Dreesen chose not to put discussion of Shore's proposal at the top of the agenda. Instead, members first heard from a business representative from the American Guild of Variety Artists. AGVA claimed jurisdiction in the employment of nightclub performers, but since the days that Buddy Hackett referred to on *The Tonight Show*, the union's paying membership had comprised mostly performers at theme parks, ice shows, and circuses. Floyd Ackerman made a pitch for CFC affiliation with his union, noting that such an alliance would lend the support of the Associated Actors and Artists of America, or 4A, unions, which included the Screen Actors Guild, the American Federation of Television and Radio Artists, the American Federation of Musicians Local 47, the International Alliance of Theater and Stage Employees Local 33, the Screen Extras Guild, and the Actors Equity Association. He boasted that an alliance with AGVA would also lend Teamster support to their picket line. "A club can't sell liquor that isn't delivered," he said.

The room did not warm to Ackerman, however, partly because of AGVA's reputation for putting small clubs out of business in the past and partly because Ackerman came off as an old-line union hack from Central Casting. As he spoke, you could see noses turning up all around the room as if they smelled feet. After Ackerman got into a particularly heated exchange with comedian Kip Addotta, who all but called him and his union a bunch of goons, the comics voted almost unanimously against affiliation with AGVA. (Ackerman lived up to AGVA's reputation the next day when he sent a note to Dreesen that said, "You might advise Mr. Addotta that he has awakened a sleeping dragon and therein I will watch with great interest any engagement of his that is not covered by an AGVA contract.")

After Ackerman, Dreesen introduced a labor-relations attorney named Frederic Richman, who got a much better reception when he told the group, "Believe it or not, you have greater strength than Mitzi Shore does." Dreesen then read another telegram of support from Bob Hope:

Dear Fellow Comedians,
    Really, you want to be paid for your services? Hey, I don't mind working for nothing. . . . I also don't mind root canal work.

The tired old line elicited a loud groan from the crowd. Comedian Jerry Van Dyke drew a much more enthusiastic response when he stood up and pledged 100 percent of the cover charges at his recently opened club in Encino.

The meeting was two hours old before Shore's proposal came up for discussion and voting, and by that time, more than a dozen comics had left. Much of the discussion centered on Mitzi and her presumed millions, with one comic describing the Comedy Store as "a huge conglomerate bringing in tons and tons of money." Emily Levine defended Shore. "I'm in favor of a comedians' union, of comics owning their own product and getting paid for what they do, but I will not join the picket line because the Comedy Store is not a target I would pick as my main enemy," she said. "It seems to me that there is an element here that looks at it as a win-lose situation, and the only victory is to bring her to her knees. Well, I can't ally with that. She's done marvelous things for comedians, and I think her true commitment is there."

"I don't think she cares about the comics at all," countered Murray Langston, a club owner himself.

Steve Bluestein replied, "I don't know. When I was in the hospital, she sent me flowers, and no one else did."

In the end, despite some dissent, the comedians rejected Shore's final offer by a strong majority. Elayne Boosler summed it all up with the dramatic pronouncement, "The power has been broken" (a line George Miller would tease her about for the next twenty years).

In speaking to a reporter after the meeting, Dreesen made it sound as if the CFC had already moved beyond the strike. "The Comedy Store settlement is the least important thing," he said. "The organization of the CFC is the most important. What we plan to do will last forever and ever."

Among the plans he ticked off were a single booking agency for comics at all clubs in the Los Angeles area, a Hall of Fame for stand-up comedy, a comedy advisory board for the television networks, acting classes for comics, and "a central office to record and protect our material and to run charitable projects."

Of course, the whole evening—the media presence, the stacking of the agenda, the CFC plans for "forever and ever"—was part of a performance that he had choreographed to play to an audience of one: Mitzi Shore. He wanted her to read about it in the *Los Angeles Times* the next morning and conclude that the tables finally had turned and she now needed them more than they needed her. "This group of comedians has the power to make any club owner a millionaire," he said. "We did it for her, and if necessary, we can do it for someone else."

In fact, aside from the picketing, lining up new venues where members could perform was the CFC's primary endeavor. It was the comedy equivalent of keeping the kids off the street and out of trouble. The Improv was a great alternative to the Sunset Store, but it could not satisfy the demand for stage time created by the ever-growing number of comics and would-be comics. As David Letterman joked, "We now have an overload in this field. We should put some sort of patrol at the Arizona border to keep more from coming." But seriously, it was a big problem for the CFC membership committee, which was grappling with the question, How do we decide who can be a member and who can't? What if, for example, some kid fresh from Akron was the next Robin Williams just waiting to happen? Did they want him auditioning for Mitzi on Monday night?

Fortunately, the CFC's "new club committee" was having some success hooking up its idled labor force with entrepreneurs who realized that comedy was about the cheapest form of live entertainment to produce. As Jay Leno often said, "All you really need is a comic, a microphone, and a few tables and chairs. And people like to laugh as much as they do anything else. It's not like you're making them watch jai alai."

The CFC signed up the Plaza Four restaurant in Century City, which agreed to let the comics keep 100 percent of the cover charges in its newly anointed Comedians' Room. Humperdinck's in Santa Monica also pledged 100 percent of the door. Comedian Jackie Mason committed to splitting the cover charges and bar revenue on a fifty-fifty basis at a new club he was planning to open. The Continental Hyatt House, the Comedy Store's next door neighbor on Sunset, announced that it would begin featuring paid comics in the hotel's lounge on weeknights.

Jerry Van Dyke was hoping that Mitzi's problems would save him from having to shut down his San Fernando Valley club, which was featuring "name" entertainment at a cost of $8,000 a week and losing money as a result. He agreed to let the CFC set the price of admission. He asked in return only that the comics sign an exclusivity agreement not to perform at any other club within a one-mile radius. The exclusivity agreement was not aimed at Shore but rather at Michael Callie, owner of the Laff Stop in Newport Beach, who had invested $300,000 in a new club scheduled to open right next door to his in October. "So he won't have any comics, which is fine with me," said Van Dyke.

The strike was already having an unintended negative effect at one paying club in the area, the Comedy and Magic Club in Hermosa Beach, whose owner, Mike Lacey, was particularly well-liked by the comics. But Lacey had been experiencing a falloff in business since the strike began, and the only explanation he could come up with was that the public, seeing comics on the news complaining about not getting paid, assumed that he was not paying them either. "I wouldn't have been losing money for months if I hadn't been paying my comics," Lacey said in a newspaper interview. "But I don't feel you can charge a cover and not pay the performers."

Laff Stop owner Michael Callie worried about the future of clubs like his if the comics succeeded in breaking Mitzi because he used the Comedy Store and the Improv as his farm club. "I don't let anyone perform here unless I've seen them at one of those clubs first," he would tell new comics looking for a spot. "I don't like disasters on stage."

Callie counseled the comics who worked for him to be careful what they wished for, saying of the CFC, "I'm afraid they are opening up a can of worms. The idea of showcase acts being paid is an idea whose time has come, but if Mitzi has to pay all those acts, then she is going to have to run that club as a business. Before, she didn't. And if they thought she had too much power before, just wait 'til they see how much she has now. Once Mitzi has to start paying, she'll have to figure, Why should I pay some kid who has ten minutes of material? It's going to cut off the kids at the bottom, the ones that really need to work. They won't get the time slots, and they won't develop." His words would prove prophetic in the weeks to come.

In its search for new venues, the CFC approached Shore's former partners in the original Comedy Store in the San Diego area. Wayne Blackman and T. D. Hayes had operated a Comedy Store branch in the basement of their Pacific Beach restaurant from 1976 to 1978, after which they parted ways with Shore because of disagreements over admission prices and expenses. Blackman and Hayes then opened another small club, featuring one paid comic a night along with singers and magicians. Shore promptly opened the La Jolla Store and launched a campaign to run Blackman and Hayes out of business. All the comics who had signed on with them suddenly backed out, telling Blackman and Hayes that Mitzi had decreed if they worked for them, then they couldn't work for her. Shore dispatched her comics to the competitors' parking lot on opening night to hand out Comedy Store fliers. The new club quickly failed for lack of professional-grade comics.

So, when the CFC asked Blackman if he would reopen the club if they got 150 comics to work there, he replied, "Only one way: If Mitzi Shore wasn't operating in San Diego, and if she wrote me a letter giving her blessings. I don't want to compete with her," he said, "because she is tough, and we're not that tough. She is the law—judge, jury and legislature."

Shore may have blinked in her fight with the CFC, but she didn't buckle. Upon receiving the news that the comics had rejected her offer, she went to court and obtained an injunction limiting the picketing outside the club to twenty people, with no more than two picketers allowed within ten feet of the entrance. The following day, the CFC presented her with a counterproposal to her "final offer." As announced simultaneously by Ken Browning, it went along with Shore's proposed $25 per set in the Original Room but called for equal payment at Westwood, with a guaranteed eighteen paid spots and two unpaid newcomer spots on Tuesday, Wednesday, Thursday, and Sunday nights and eleven paid sets (and no unpaid sets) on Friday and Saturday nights. In addition, the comics wanted a guarantee of eight $25-sets per night in the Belly Room and 50 percent of cover charges in the Main Room. Browning said the proposal represented a "substantial reduction" compared to the comics' previous demands. For Shore, it represented a substantial increase in labor costs, from nothing to at least $3,500 a week. She wasted little time rejecting the comics' proposal. In a letter addressed to Dreesen and Leno (whom she perceived to be the strike's ringleaders) and posted on the Comedy Store bulletin board, she announced a new pay policy at Westwood and Sunset. The clubs "will remain workshops and showcases during the week," she said, but on weekends, "because of the professional levels the Stores have attained, all performers will be paid." The pay would be $25 per set. In the Belly Room, one featured act would be paid for two sets per night on the weekend, while all other performances would be unpaid. Shore invited all comedians who were willing to work under the new policy to call in with their availability. She said there would be no further negotiations with the CFC.

In announcing the new pay policy, Estelle Endler indicated that Shore felt she had been sandbagged by the CFC, which had led her to believe her previous offer would be accepted. "She made the offer to stop the dissension and get back to business," Endler said.

Dreesen was frustrated by the turn of events, which he blamed on the comics who had crossed the picket line. "If it hadn't been for those sixteen guys and one girl, this whole thing would have been over in twenty-four hours," he fumed. Now, with her new pay policy, Mitzi was going to try to break the strike one comic at a time, dangling time slots *and* money in front of them. On the picket line that night, he told anyone who would listen that the new CFC-sanctioned clubs were the best hope for the comics' future. "And all those who crossed our picket line won't be booked into Jerry Van Dyke's, Humperdinck's, and Plaza Four," he said. "I believe that our membership would walk off the stage if any of those people were placed in the line up. That's how emotional they are about it."

Through the first three weeks of the strike, Mike Binder had avoided taking sides officially, either by walking the picket line or crossing it. He was working long hours on a made-for-TV movie called *Can You Hear the Laughter? The Freddie Prinze Story*, playing the role of Freddie's good friend Alan Bursky. Most of the production was being shot on a set in a building on Doheny Boulevard, but several days of shooting were scheduled for inside the Sunset store, including a couple of scenes with Freddie and Alan interacting.

When the interior shooting got underway, Binder was able to enter and leave the club without incurring the wrath of the picketers. "It's okay; he's working on the movie," someone would call out whenever an uninformed striker challenged him. The access put him in the unique position of having a foot in each camp. At night, he was hanging out with Leno and other CFC members at Canter's or at Leno's house, where the talk was invariably anti-Mitzi, and Leno, his big brother, never missed a chance to hammer home the message, "Don't do it, Mikey. Do not cross the line, because if you do, you will regret it for the rest of your life." During the day, however, Binder was in the bunker with Mitzi and her boys, listening to the pickets shouting slogans and insults. It felt a little like being in Dr. Frankenstein's castle, surrounded by all the townspeople with their torches and pitchforks.

By all rights, Binder should have been having the time of his life. A month shy of his nineteenth birthday, dubbed "Kid Comedy" by his peers, he was being well paid to act in a movie about a Comedy Store icon, playing a fellow Comedy Store comic in the company of his Comedy Store pals. And yet, he was miserable. As the only one of Mitzi's boys who had not crossed the line to perform, he felt intense pressure to take a stand. She hadn't said anything to him about it, but he could see how sad, how really low, she was. She'd been like a mother to him, and now the CFC was talking about destroying her. They were doing a pretty good job of it, too, from what he could see. At 10:00 p.m., the place contained all the joy of a funeral parlor. There were only fifteen customers in the Original Room when Argus Hamilton came to him just as he finished his shooting for the day. "You've got to do it," Argus said for the umpteenth time. "Mitzi really needs you to go on." This time, Binder was defenseless. To ease the pressure, to please Mitzi, to hear the laughter, he agreed to perform.

Outside on the sidewalk, where pickets could see through the front window the back of whoever was performing, someone called out, "Binder's on." All eyes looked up, and sure enough, there he was doing a set, his red hair unmistakable. "That little fucker."

When he came off the stage twenty minutes later, Binder didn't feel the usual elation at having done well. Seated in her booth just inside the front door, Mitzi thanked him for what he had done and then launched into a bitter diatribe about all the ungrateful comics out on the picket line, naming Leno, Boosler, and Dreesen among those whose careers she had fostered but who had repaid her kindness with betrayal. It was a side of Mitzi that Binder had not seen before, dark and mean, and as he listened to the bile pour out of her mouth, he was hit by a sickening realization. "I've made a terrible mistake," he thought. "I took the wrong side."

There was no way out of the club but past the pickets. As Binder exited, the first person he saw was Leno, who apparently had just arrived.

"These guys are saying you went on, but you didn't, did you?" Leno said, almost pleading for Binder to say no. But Mike couldn't bring himself to answer because he could tell by the look on Jay's face just how badly he'd let him down.

"I'm sorry," he said as Leno turned and walked back to the picket line, where other comics whom Binder loved and admired were now looking at him as if he had leprosy. The shunning had already begun.

Binder called Leno at home later that night to apologize again and try to patch things up, but Jay would have none of it. He told Binder not to call or come by anymore. It would never be the same between them.

# Jay's Big Flop

Mitzi Shore's new pay policy did not produce its intended effect. Comics did not rush across the picket line to pick up their $25 checks. After Mike Binder, the number of strikebreakers held steady at eighteen.

With the injunction in effect, the picketing became less boisterous, to the point of growing almost mundane. Jay Leno, Tom Dreesen, Elayne Boosler, and George Miller were out in front most every night, but the news vans and reporters dwindled. What had started as a sidewalk celebration of comic solidarity gradually turned into a chore to check off on every CFC member's daily to-do list. For the most part, the strikebreakers came and went without provoking screaming invective. The confrontation devolved into a kind of trench warfare, a grinding stalemate.

For the CFC leaders, the work of striking became mostly drudgery. As Mark Lonow had predicted, keeping the picket line going turned out to be a Sisyphean exercise of relentless phone calling. "We need three more people at 6 p.m. Can you make it?" And the calls kept them in constant contact with the members' complaints and fears: What's going on? When will this thing be settled? Are you even talking to the other side? Have you signed up any more clubs? Why haven't I been given any time slots this week? It was hard to stay motivated in the face of such discontent.

Steve Lubetkin was one member on the executive committee whose sense of purpose never seemed to flag. His devotion to the cause at times bordered on obsession. When not on the phone or the picket line, he was putting his passion on paper in the form of manifestos, such as the one he wrote titled "What the CFC Is All About":

The CFC is an organization of comedians who have come to-gether to work for fairness.

But what does fairness mean?

There are approximately 220 million people in America. For the sake of argument let us say there are about 220 comedians. Therefore, each one of us is literally—ONE IN A MILLION. There are absolutely no restrictions as to who can become a co-median. And yet, only one in a million has had the determina-tion, the talent and the guts to do it. So how has this special group of one in a million been treated? They've been grossly un-derpaid and been so manipulated that they'll stab each other in the back for a gig while the manipulators make all the money. In any other profession, if you could do something that only one in a million could do, you would have power and protection and medical plans and dignity and respect and substantial compensa-tion. But not when there are artificial barriers.

Stand-up comedy is a profession that is so special, so market-able, so in demand that comedy clubs have had lines around the block to get in to see the performers. Why? Well, it's simple. Lots of people want to laugh. Lots of people need to laugh. Lots of people are willing to pay money to laugh. So, why aren't lots of people sharing that money. When the public lines up to see the club owners perform, then they can keep it all. Until then—share the wealth!

Our purpose is to open up the industry and resist "divide and conquer" tactics that leave us at the mercy of others. Audiences will always be the ultimate judge of talent, but people committed to fairness will now be in charge of getting the comedian and the audience together, with the comedian's best interest at heart.

Because of their strange backgrounds and influences, comedians have always been the square pegs in a world of round holes. But now, due to an exciting and unexpected series of events, all the square pegs have gotten together and the world is about to marvel at what we can do.

Privately, he was much more downbeat, telling Susan he was afraid that even if they prevailed in the strike, Mitzi would try to destroy him and prevent him from getting work. "Evil is winning," he wrote.

As the strike moved into its fifth week, Shore reopened the Main Room on the weekends, featuring a seven-member improvisational act called the Comedy Store Players. Neither the club marquee nor the press materials about the players contained any form of the word "improvisation," however, because Shore forbade its use lest anyone think she had drawn any creative inspiration from her arch enemy, Budd Friedman. In Mitzi's world, the art of improv was called "group comedy."

Shore planned to have the new group alternate weekends with the "Best of the Comedy Store" revue of comics picked from among those appearing in the Original Room. In announcing the new weekend shows, Comedy Store spokeswoman Estelle Endler acknowledged that Shore's bottom line "certainly has felt the strain of the dissenters; she wants to stay in business."

But even the loyalists gathered around her in the club wondered how she was going to manage that with only eighteen comics—most of whom did not have a polished twenty minutes' worth of material—to fill the time previously taken up by more than one hundred. It seemed like she'd need to pull off some sort of loaves-and-fishes miracle. And meanwhile, the pickets in front were handing out flyers headlined "Where Have All the Comics Gone?" listing the lineups at the competing CFC-sponsored clubs where patrons could actually see the comics whose names were inscribed on the entrance to the Sunset building.

And if that wasn't enough to worry about, on April 27, AGVA went before the Los Angeles County Federation of Labor and obtained a strike sanction against the Comedy Store on behalf of the CFC, meaning that all the 4A unions recognized AGVA's right to represent the comics in the dispute and that all their members were now prohibited from crossing the picket line. In announcing the sanction, AGVA's executive vice president, Alan Jay Nelson, said, "There is evidence that several performers working at the club are 4A members." Nelson also said AGVA had petitioned the Teamsters and the waiters and bartenders union to support the strike.

This was bad news for Shore and her supporters, but it wasn't exactly good news for the CFC, which was trying to avoid AGVA's chilly embrace. Tom Dreesen, Jo Anne Astrow, and Mark Lonow had made overtures to the Screen Actors Guild and the American Federation of Television and Radio Artists, practically begging their leadership to take the comics under their wing to give the CFC some legal standing. Both unions were sympathetic to the comics' cause but weren't sure what they could do because they lacked jurisdiction. The CFC leaders pressed for at least a public statement of support, and AFTRA responded by inviting them to address its annual regional convention on May 1 at the Hollywood Roosevelt Hotel. AFTRA also invited representatives from the Comedy Store to present their side of the dispute.

About one hundred delegates were gathered in one of the hotel's banquet rooms when Dreesen, Astrow, and Lonow arrived. They were surprised to see that Danny Mora and Biff Maynard were there to speak on behalf of the Comedy Store. They'd been expecting one of Mitzi's lawyers or maybe Steve Landesberg or Argus Hamilton. Maynard in particular seemed a poor choice because he was virulently antiunion. Dreesen and Astrow were going to speak for their side, and they were pretty sure they had an edge because AFTRA's national executive secretary, Bud Wolff, had taken a liking to Astrow, a knockout blonde who had done nothing to dampen his enthusiasm, confiding to her cohorts, including her husband, that she was "working it" for the cause.

As it turned out, they didn't need the edge. Maynard made his pitch first, and after an impassioned testimonial to all that Mitzi Shore had done for comedy and the young comedians who performed at her clubs, he told the delegates that stand-up comedians were not "workers" but "artists," drawing the distinction in a way that suggested he thought the two were mutually exclusive and that artists did not require the same sort of union protection as, say, pipe fitters. There was an audible gasp from the audience, followed by an offended murmuring that momentarily drowned out whatever else Maynard was saying. Dreesen, Astrow, and Lonow had to put their hands over their mouths to keep from laughing. Talk about misreading the room! As Maynard struggled through the rest of his presentation, they kept their eyes fixed on the floor because it was too painful to watch him dying up there at the lectern.

Dreesen had never had an easier act to follow. He delivered his well-honed spiel on the unfairness of comics working for free in a profitable club where all other employees were paid for their labor. Astrow closed with an appeal to the delegates' sense of brotherhood, pointing out that as many as ninety CFC members, herself included, were card-carrying, dues-paying members of AFTRA and therefore deserved their support and protection. After Maynard, it probably didn't matter much what they said, but as the trio left the banquet room to considerably-more-than-polite applause, they knew that they had killed. Indeed, Bud Wolff gave them a look and a nod that told them they'd be getting their statement of support. They were celebrating in the lobby when Biff Maynard banged through the double doors, scowled at them, and stomped out of the building. Giddy with excitement, they raced back to the Store, where they were regaling Leno and the other picketers with details of Maynard's epic bomb, when they heard the roar of a car engine and a squeal of tires as Maynard made a belligerent left turn off Sunset into the Comedy Store parking lot. He veered toward Leno and Lonow, who were standing in the driveway talking. They leaped out of the way of the car, but Lonow apparently leaped faster. There was loud thump, and Leno went down.

"Jay's been hit," someone screamed. Within seconds there was pandemonium as people ran over to where he lay crumpled on the pavement. "Is he okay? Is he breathing? Somebody call an ambulance." Leno's eyes were closed, and he was moaning. Astrow and several other women were in tears. "Oh, my God. Oh, my God."

Maynard didn't stop. He gunned his car to the back of the employee parking lot and ran inside the club, announcing with alarm, "I just hit Jay Leno with my car!" Dreesen started to chase after him but was restrained by others. "I'll kill that motherfucker," he raged. Leno was moaning louder now and starting to move. Dreesen knelt down and put his face close to his friend. "Jay, can you hear me?" Loud and clear, apparently. Leno immediately opened one eye and winked at him. Dreesen drew back in surprise: *Holy shit! He's faking!*

It was a brilliant bit of improv, street theater worthy of Andy Kaufman. Jay had merely slapped the side of Biff's car as it went by and executed a classic NBA flop. Realizing that no one else had seen the wink, Dreesen leaned back down and whispered in Leno's ear. "What do you want to do now? I think an ambulance is on the way." Leno moaned louder, indicating that he wanted to play it out. "We need to get him to the hospital fast," Dreesen told the others. "There's no time for the ambulance." So Leno was quickly lifted into a car, crying out in convincing agony, and was driven off in the direction of Cedars Sinai Hospital.

Dreesen immediately let Lonow in on the joke and was going to tell the others, but Lonow argued for keeping quiet about it for as long as possible. He explained that according to labor law, an employer is liable whenever a picketer is injured on the line. "If Mitzi doesn't know that, then her lawyers will certainly tell her, and she will freak. Let's see what happens."

They didn't have to wait long. Fifteen minutes after "the accident," Shore's assistant, Meg Staahl, suddenly materialized and said to Dreesen, "Mitzi would like to see you."

She escorted him into the office, where a tired-looking Shore was sitting with Danny Mora and her attorney, Steve Mason. "Let's end this whole thing right now, tonight," she said.

Dreesen was so astonished by the rapid turn of events that he was almost speechless. "Whatever you say, Mitzi," was about all he could manage to get out.

He put in a call to Ken Browning, who hurried to the club for what turned out to be a long, strange night of negotiations, with Mitzi and Mason in her office, Dreesen alone in an adjoining office, and Browning shuttling between the club and the CFC leaders— Astrow, Lonow, Boosler, Miller, and a miraculously recovered Leno—who were gathered at the Hyatt House coffee shop next door. Shore would not let Browning (whom she referred to as "that sleazy Ivy League lawyer") enter the club, so he had to confer with Dreesen out front and then return to the others at the Hyatt.

By 5:00 a.m. they had hammered out a settlement agreement that gave the comics 50 percent of the door in the Main Room and $25 per set in the Original Room and at Westwood, with negotiations regarding the Belly Room to be conducted at a later date. The six-page document was signed in Shore's office. She drew the shape of a heart next to her signature. Meg Staahl had tears in her eyes as Mitzi and Tom hugged.

"Does this mean you will finally come back?" Shore asked.

"I'll come back when the contract is honored," he said.

After more hugs at the Hyatt House, the half dozen bone-tired CFC leaders trudged up the ramp to the parking lot and drove home in the dawn light, elated by their apparent victory but not quite believing that it was all over.

Of course, it wasn't.

# "My Name Is
# Steve Lubetkin"

Much of the comedy community was awakened brutally early on Thursday morning, May 2, by excited phone calls from colleagues telling them that overnight, while they were sleeping, the strike had been resolved. Mitzi had caved! Short of a *Variety* headline proclaiming, "Nets Slate Sitcom for Every Stand-up," it was about the best news any of them could have imagined.

The surprising development seemed to render moot the morning's trade paper reports that the Screen Actors Guild and AFTRA had issued a joint statement urging their members to support the CFC and honor their picket line. "The strikers have taken a courageous step in organizing themselves and walking out without actual representation by a major union," SAG executive secretary Chester Migden was quoted as saying. "This is the sort of action that brought unions into existence in the 1920s and 1930s, and it is a rare thing today. We must commend and admire the strikers for their fortitude."

The CFC membership still had to ratify the settlement agreement, so Tom Dreesen called for an emergency membership meeting Friday afternoon at Humperdinck's, one of the three local nightclubs that had entered into an exclusive booking arrangement with the comedians' group. Only about 50 of the CFC's claimed 137 members made it to the hastily arranged meeting, but the mood was ebullient, with much back slapping and bravado, even before the agreement was read to the gathering. There was talk of printing up T-shirts proclaiming, "The CFC did it for me."

"This is *our* contract the way *we* wanted it," Dreesen told the cheering "brotherhood of stand-up comedians." In the two-year agreement, Mitzi Shore recognized the CFC as the "exclusive bargaining representative of the comedians." She agreed to a compensation formula that called for twelve paid twenty-minute sets in the Original Room on Tuesday, Wednesday, Thursday, and Sunday nights, with forty-five minutes set aside "at the beginning and/or end" of each night for nonpaid performances. On Fridays and Saturdays, there would be two shows of five paid sets per night and no nonpaid performances. Mondays would remain nonpaid "potluck" nights. The formula for Westwood varied slightly in that it called for thirteen fifteen-minute paid sets on weeknights. The Main Room was a straight fifty-fifty split of the cover charges. And the Belly Room would remain closed "until the parties shall enter into a further written agreement."

Considering that the comics had started out five months earlier talking about $5 per set for "gas money," the document read like a huge win for the CFC. The icing on the cake was paragraph 6:

Neither party (or its members, employees, officers, principals or agents) shall take any discriminatory or retaliatory action, either directly or indirectly, against the other, by reason of any of the activities, picketing, negotiations, or discussions hereto.

In laymen's language, this meant that in putting together her future lineups, Mitzi could not reward strikebreakers or punish picketers.

At 3:15 p.m., the agreement was ratified almost unanimously. Within minutes, the Comedy Store's phone lines lit up with calls from comics advising of their availability to perform over the weekend. Estelle Endler issued a statement on behalf of the club, saying, "It's back to funny business." Shore, however, made it clear that she was not happy with the agreement, telling the *Los Angeles Times*, "It is against my basic philosophy and the principles of the Comedy Store that this settlement was made. You might say I was unionized into a corner."

In a victory statement to reporters, Dreesen said, "Mitzi Shore is a formidable opponent, but we won the battle because our cause was honest, fair and just. I think what we've done is a nice legacy for the young kids coming up. Maybe they won't have to go through what we went through."

Perhaps no one was happier than Dreesen to see the strike end. He'd dropped more than twenty pounds since January and had endured a recurring, sweat-drenched nightmare in which the strike dragged on for four years, leaving him as the last lonely picketer standing in front of the Comedy Store, refusing to give up the fight. He'd also lost a small fortune in bookings that he turned down to attend to his CFC duties. With the agreement ratified, he joked, "Now I can get back into show business."

Before the champagne corks were popped and the celebrating of the armistice could begin, however, Floyd Ackerman of AGVA threw a wrench in the works by announcing that the strike wasn't over until he said it was. "AGVA does not recognize any agreement made by the dissident comics short of a union contract between AGVA and the Comedy Store," he said in a statement, "because the CFC is not certified by the U.S. Department of Labor as a bargaining unit. We're the only union that's chartered to handle a situation like this."

What's more, Ackerman claimed that an invisible picket line still existed around the club and threatened to reactivate a "physical" line with AGVA members unless the Comedy Store came to as yet undefined terms with the union. "Walking into that club constitutes crossing the line whether there's a physical line there or not," he said. "We expect and assume that our sister unions will enjoin their members from crossing the line or working there."

Ackerman went so far as to claim credit for the settlement agreement that, in his opinion, had not ended the strike. Noting that the Federation of Labor sanction AGVA had obtained against the Comedy Store caused the club to be placed on the AFL-CIO "Do Not Patronize" list, Ackerman said, "Only then did Mitzi Shore return to the bargaining table."

Ackerman's aggressive stance stunned AGVA's sister unions. Spokesmen for both SAG and AFTRA stammered that they were unaware of AGVA's invisible picket line and therefore could not say whether they would enjoin their members from crossing it. "That would have to come from our national office," said Allan Davis, director of AFTRA's western region. "We'd have to determine whether AGVA really represents the CFC and whether it's a legitimate AGVA picket line. If it is, then that's another matter. It's a delicate situation. We do have an obligation to support our sister unions' efforts to organize their legitimate areas of jurisdiction. But I don't know if that's the case here."

Ken Browning advised the CFC leadership to ignore Ackerman and proceed under the terms of the agreement while the big unions worked out their jurisdictional issues. But the prospect of AGVA's reasserting itself in the comedy club business unnerved Budd Friedman. "Once the unions are involved, they can kill everything," he said. "If I have to start dealing with them, it will become no fun. I have alternate plans. Maybe it's time for me to move on to something else. I never really got rich in this business anyway."

The following week, the CFC executive committee met at Dreesen's house to deal with myriad poststrike issues. They didn't have to worry about manning a picket line anymore, at least not a visible one, but that headache had been replaced with the equally grinding task of enforcing the new contract and making sure that people got paid properly. Not surprisingly, there were a lot of bugs in the new system, and grievances were coming in from the membership.

The meeting was to be Dreesen's swan song, his farewell to the troops. He was resigning as chairman and handing over the reins to Jo Anne Astrow, who would serve as acting chair pending the election of new officers. Dreesen was set to go on the road with Sammy Davis Jr. in a few weeks, and he was definitely looking forward to the trip after five months in the pressure cooker. At the same time, he'd grown close to the twelve people on the executive committee. They had been through a strange boot camp together, and he knew he was going to miss them.

"I just want to congratulate you guys," he said at the end of the meeting. "I am so proud of you all. Because of the great job you did and how hard you worked, comedians all over the country are now going to be paid fairly for their performances. You have done a wonderful thing for your fellow comics. But I'm out of here now. You need to elect new officers, and I need to move on and get back to my career."

He kept his comments uncharacteristically short because he was already late for a meeting with the producers of a new TV show called *Real People*. As he was hurrying for the door, Steve Lubetkin intercepted him.

"Tom, please, can I talk to you for a minute?"

Dreesen resisted the temptation to glance at his watch and beg off. Something in Steve's voice, a kind of desperation, made him stop and listen.

"What's up?"

"I called in to the Store this week, and Mitzi did not give me any time slots, and it's happened to other people, too," Lubetkin said. "I'm afraid that if you and the other big guys leave the group, then she's going to retaliate against all us little guys who were active in the strike."

Dreesen smiled. "That's not going to happen, Steve. She can't retaliate. It's right there in the contract, and she signed it."

Lubetkin nodded but he didn't look reassured.

"Okay, I'll tell you what," Dreesen said, looking him straight in the eye. "I promise I won't go back to the Comedy Store until you go back, okay?"

That seemed to help. They hugged, and Dreesen rushed off to his appointment confident that everything would work out fine for Steve.

A couple nights later, Lubetkin phoned Richard Lewis at home, where he was watching a boxing match on television. After some small talk about the state of the fight game, Steve said that he was seeing faces in rugs and carpets. The statement was such a wild non sequitur that Lewis sensed it was the real reason Steve had called.

"We can all do that," Richard responded. "If you stare at something long enough, your mind starts playing tricks on you. Remember that bit I used to do in my act about seeing my dead uncle as a cloud in the sky?"

"Do me a favor," Steve said. "Go into your bathroom and stare at that little rug you have there and tell me if you see anything."

Lewis couldn't tell if Steve was goofing or not; he sounded curious more than anything else. Playing along, he put down the phone and went into bathroom and checked the rug.

"Okay, fine," he said, back on the phone. "I think I can see the outline of a face, but I can't tell if it's Theodore Roosevelt or Thurman Munson."

Lubetkin chuckled and then let the subject drop. They talked a little more about sports before hanging up. Lewis was puzzled that Steve seemed so serious about something so silly, but he shrugged it off as Steve just being weird. He was a comic, after all—weird was a prerequisite for the job.

Susan Evans had been hearing about the faces too. Steve told her he was seeing them in trees as well, and he speculated that they were the faces of dead spirits, of all the people who had ever lived on earth. She was concerned, but not alarmed, because he invariably defused his remarks with a joke, so she didn't know if he was being serious or working on a concept for his act. His humor always tended toward the far-out and absurd.

He had scared her once, however, back in February, when she accompanied him down to La Jolla for his first paid gig at the Comedy Store branch there. They stayed in one of the condos Mitzi provided for the comics, and one morning he told her that he had gotten up during the night convinced that they were supposed to go to another planet and start a whole new civilization together, like Adam and Eve. So, he had gone to the kitchen to turn on the gas to help them get to that other place more quickly.

"But apparently God didn't want that to happen," he said, "because the oven turned out to be electric." It was his light, laughing delivery of the last line that pulled her back from feeling utterly horror-struck. Again, she managed to dismiss the episode as Steve's trying out some new material, which bombed badly as far as she was concerned.

It quickly became apparent that the CFC's settlement agreement with the Comedy Store had not settled much of anything. With the Belly Room still dark and the Main Room still featuring improv performers, Shore abruptly closed the Westwood club on Tuesday, Wednesday, and Thursday nights, claiming she was losing money due to small crowds. That reduced the number of Comedy Store time slots to 70 a week (from a prestrike high of more than 250). The closure was a flagrant violation of the agreement, according to the CFC, which also accused Shore of retaliating against the strike leaders by denying them stage time. In the two weeks since the settlement, eight or nine members of the executive committee—including Steve Lubetkin, Jo Anne Astrow, Dottie Archibald, and former headliners George Miller and Elayne Boosler—had not been given any time slots.

To make matters worse, a club that the CFC had touted as one of its saving alternatives to the Comedy Store, Jerry Van Dyke's, closed due to financial difficulties. Humperdinck's, too, was strug-gling. The comics had won their battle to be paid, but apparently it was a pyrrhic victory.

The deteriorating situation coincided with a downward spiral in Lubetkin's mental state. As he saw it, his worst fear had been realized: He was broke, blackballed from the Comedy Store, and effectively banished from the business of comedy. Over and over he told Susan and his CFC brethren that his career was finished, that Mitzi was going to make sure he never worked in LA again. It didn't help his frame of mind when, on May 20, the *Los Angeles Times'* Sunday Calendar section ran a big spread headlined "The Diary of Four Young Comics" that profiled Richard Lewis along with Jay Leno, David Letterman, and Elayne Boosler as the "hottest stand-up comics to recently emerge from the comedy club system." He was happy for Richard but sad for himself. He sounded listless and despondent when he called his brother, Barry, that week. "Something's not right. He wasn't making much sense; he was not himself," Barry told his wife, Ginny, as he packed for a flight to Los Angeles the next day.

In LA, Susan told Barry about the faces and confirmed that Steve had gone into an emotional tailspin since the strike ended. A practicing psychologist, Barry spent the next few days hanging out with Steve and casually probing for clues to what was going on with him psychically. Steve wasn't hallucinating, hearing voices, or using drugs (other than his usual pot), but he was clearly depressed, en-veloped in sadness, particularly about his sundered relationship with Mitzi Shore. He talked constantly about losing the gig in La Jolla and how unfair it was. He talked about how much he loved Susan and his fellow comics. For the most part, he was rational, but at times his conversation consisted of a flight of ideas that would suddenly shift to something entirely unconnected. At one point, Steve broke down sobbing, hugging Barry closely and saying that he "would give anything if I could just talk to Mom one more time."

Barry arranged an appointment for Steve with a psychiatrist he knew who practiced out of Veteran's Hospital in West Los Angeles. He drove Steve to the appointment and nervously read magazines in the waiting room while Steve talked to the doctor. During the drive home, Steve said the doctor thought he was depressed for all the obvious reasons, and he'd set up another appointment for the following week on May 31, but he had prescribed no antidepressant drugs. Over the next few days, Steve's outlook seemed to improve, and Barry flew back to New York cautiously hopeful that a crisis had been averted.

On Friday morning, June 1, Steve and several other CFC executive committee members met with AGVA's business agents at the union's Hollywood headquarters. They didn't like AGVA, but it appeared to them that Mitzi had no intention of living up to the agreement, so they wanted to see if the union had any ideas for helping them. They came away after an hour convinced that an affiliation with AGVA was not a solution to their problems.

Late that afternoon, Jo Anne Astrow convened a meeting at her house. Lubetkin attended, along with Astrow's husband Mark Lonow, Dottie Archibald, George Miller, Elayne Boosler, and CFC secretary Susan Sweetzer. The situation was worse than ever, with a rash of complaints coming in from members freaked out about the dearth of time slots. The brand-new brotherhood of stand-up comedians appeared to be bombing, with comics bickering among themselves and threatening to break ranks. Some wanted to return to working for free at Westwood if Shore would reopen the club. In the battle for stage time, it was beginning to look like every comic for him- or herself. The committee tried to reach Shore by phone but was told that she was out of town. They wished that Tom Dreesen and Jay Leno were there with them—Tom for his cool in the midst of crisis and Jay for his leavening sense of silly. Lubetkin remained uncharacteristically calm during the sometimes chaotic meeting. At one point, he seemed to be filling in for

Jay when he executed a series of pratfalls off the couch, doing goofy shoulder rolls onto the floor.

The committee members were commiserating about the fact that for the third week in a row none of them had been given any time slots when Steve suddenly stood up and announced that he "had an appointment." On his way out the door, he stopped and turned to them. "I want you all not to worry anymore," he said. "Everything is going to be fine. I'm going to take care of it." When he was gone, the others exchanged looks and shrugged. *Whatever.*

Lubetkin drove to the Sunset Strip and parked his Buick on Queens Road, around the corner from the Comedy Store. Leaving the keys in the ignition, he walked east on Sunset and passed right in front of the club, where he ran into comic Mitch Walters, who greeted him warmly and wanted to chat. Lubetkin said he needed to take a walk up the street but would be right back. "You look terrible," Walters said as Steve walked away. "Is everything alright?"

A few minutes later, at approximately 6:40 p.m., Kent January looked out the window of his apartment at 8440 Sunset, across the street from the Comedy Store, and noticed a man on the roof of the Continental Hyatt House. Then, as January watched in horror, the man suddenly leaped off the building.

Segio Sais and Julie Abarzu were walking together about fifty feet from the Hyatt when they heard a scream, turned, and saw a body hurtling down from the roof, head first with arms spread out, toward the concrete parking lot.

The body hit with such impact from the 105-foot drop that it sounded like a small explosion to Robert Delagran, who was staying in Room 926 at the Hyatt. He heard someone screaming, looked out the window, and saw a woman pointing to where a body was lying on the pavement. He called the lobby and said, "I think somebody just jumped off your building."

Donald Hicks, the hotel's chief maintenance engineer, bolted out the front door of the hotel and around the side to where a man was lying about twenty feet from the building on the ramp leading to the Comedy Store parking lot. Blood was flowing from the man's nose and ears, and he had a gaping wound in his forehead. Hicks felt the man's left wrist for a pulse but couldn't find one.

Paramedics arrived within few minutes but were unable to revive the victim. They were followed an hour later by four police investigators, one of whom pulled a handwritten note from the left hip pocket of the dead man's faded blue jeans.

My name is Steve Lubetkin. Call Susan Evans at 403-7861.

I used to work at the Comedy Store. Maybe this will help to bring about fairness.

To Barry—I love you. You've been generous and good to me always.

To Dad—I love you for raising me and giving me my sense of humor.

To Susan—I love you but it would have been hell for us to continue.

To Mom—I'll be joining you soon. I love you.

To Ginny—I love you, beautiful sister-in-law. You're terrific.

To Rich Lewis—You're the best blood brother a man can have. I love you.

To the CFC—I guess nice guys do finish last.

To the world—Fairness, fairness, fairness, please, before it's too late.

To all comedians—Unite, it's in your best interest.

Suze—Play my "dum dum dum last set in Westwood" cassette at the funeral in LA. Bury me next to Mom in New York.

No revenge, please, only love.

Lubetkin's body lay on the concrete covered by a police tarpaulin for more than two hours before an investigator from the coroner's office arrived to examine it. He noted "multiple crushing wounds to chest, face and head." A hundred feet away, the show was going on at the Comedy Store, where the comics and staff were buzzing with macabre jokes about "the jumper" next door. No one thought to connect the grim scene outside to their world until a police detective walked up to the front entrance of the club and asked if the owner was present. Lue Deck, who was working as the night manager, told him that Mitzi was in La Jolla. The officer wrote down her name and telephone number and then told Deck it appeared the "decedent" may have been a Comedy Store employee. He handed Deck a plastic baggie containing Lubetkin's driver's license.

"Did you know him?" the detective asked.

Deck recoiled. The license was smeared with blood. He confirmed that Lubetkin had worked at the club on and off for the past several years, but he refused the detective's request that he walk over and identify the body.

"I can't," he said. "I don't think I could handle it."

As the word of the jumper's identity ricocheted around the club, Susan Evans arrived home from work to find two policemen waiting by her door. "We need to talk to you," one of them said. She listened to what they said but could not speak a word in response. Neither could she cry. She was numb, in shock.

When the police left, she called Barry in New York. "Steve's dead," she told him. "He jumped off a building next to the Comedy Store." She couldn't bear to stay in the apartment, didn't even want to look around. She walked out in a daze and sometime later found herself wandering the second-floor back hallways of the Comedy Store. In an empty room, she came upon a framed poster from *Dante Shocko* leaning against a desk. She and Steve had one hanging on the wall in the hallway outside their apartment, but she was surprised to find one in the Comedy Store. She could hear muffled laughter from a show downstairs, but it was all very strange and quiet around her. She picked up the poster and took it into Mitzi's office, propped it up on a sofa opposite the desk, and wrote on the wall above it in Magic Marker, "Got the message."

Lue Deck walked into the office at that point and thought at first that he was interrupting a burglary. But he realized who and what he was dealing with when the apparently disoriented woman said softly, "Mitzi killed Steve." He led her gently by the arm out the back door of the club and turned her over to a group of comics who seemed to know her.

Richard Lewis arrived at the Improv that night already distraught because he had broken up with Nina the day before. She was now on a plane back to Copenhagen, and he was feeling more alone than he had in his entire life. He hoped a couple of drinks and a good set would help fill the void. But as he crossed the room by the bar, a comic he barely knew called out to him, "Hey, Lewis, did you hear about Lubetkin? He jumped off the Hyatt House and killed himself." In an explosion of rage at what he thought was some sort of sick joke, Lewis grabbed the guy by his shirt front, slammed him up against the wall, and screamed, "If you're fucking with me, I will fucking kill you."

The two were quickly separated, and others present said that they, too, had heard that Steve was dead; apparently, the police had confirmed it with the Comedy Store. In a state of shock, Lewis asked a friend to drive him to Steve's apartment. He knocked and called out, but Susan was not home. He was wracked with guilt because he hadn't told anyone about Steve's seeing faces in the rug. Maybe if he had, then Steve could have gotten help and would still be alive. So I'm responsible for my best friend's death, he thought.

Back at the Improv, he sat down at the bar and started in on a bender that would last fifteen years.

Shortly before midnight, Tom Dreesen was in his dressing room getting ready to go on stage at Harrah's in Lake Tahoe when the phone rang. It was Leno, mistakenly thinking he was calling just as Tom was coming *off* stage.

"Did you hear?" Leno asked. "Steve Lubetkin committed suicide by jumping off the Hyatt House."

"Oh fuck, please don't tell me that," Dreesen replied, flashing on his last conversation with Steve.

"He left a note about not being allowed to work at the Comedy Store anymore," Leno said, his voice quavering.

Dreesen's mind reeled. "Fuck, fuck, fuck," was all he could think of to say. Then came the knock at the door.

"Two minutes, Mr. Dreesen."

Later that night, after the most difficult performance of his career, Dreesen sat on the bed in his hotel room blaming himself for what had happened: If I had just left the fucking thing alone and not jumped up to chair that first meeting, then Steve would still be alive. Once again, he thought of the promise he made: I won't go back until you go back.

He was going to keep that promise. Since Steve was never going back to the Comedy Store again, neither was he.

# A Standing Ovation

Barry and Ginny Lubetkin arrived in Los Angeles the next day, having left New York without even telling Jack Lubetkin that Steve was dead. They weren't sure the seventy-six-year-old patriarch was strong enough to hear the news that his youngest son had died in such a manner. They needed time to think, and the circumstances did not allow for that.

During the flight, Barry could think only about how he had let Steve down. He was a mental health professional, after all. He was supposed to be able to anticipate such things. How could he have missed it? What had blinded him to the fact that his little brother was in danger of taking his own life? If only he'd stayed longer or taken Steve back to New York for treatment. He knew he was going to regret his decision to leave for the rest of his life.

The trip to LA was supposed to be a private family matter to finalize Steve's affairs and escort his body back home. The couple wasn't expecting to land in the middle of a publicized show business controversy. But by the time they reached their hotel room, the wheels were already in motion for a bizarre and unseemly display of competitive mourning.

On Saturday, Steve's name suddenly appeared where it never had before—on the Comedy Store marquee: "In Memoriam, Steve Lubetkin." Under normal circumstances, it would have seemed only fitting for the club to mark the passing of a performer who had been part of its tight-knit creative community for nearly six years. It stood to reason that Mitzi Shore would be shocked and saddened by the sudden death of a young man whom she had invited into her home and whose career she had promoted. And anyone who knew Steve might imagine that he was smiling down from Comedy Heaven at the sight of his name in lights on Sunset Strip (with single billing to boot). Given the events of the past few months, however, the marquee and Shore's announced plan to hold a memorial service for Steve at the club the next day drove CFC members into paroxysms of rage. *How dare she!*

As the CFC saw it, Lubetkin was theirs. He had worked and died for the cause. Mitzi had blackballed him. He had killed himself because of her unfair system and intransigence. She had no right.

The CFC began arrangements for its own memorial at Humperdinck's in Santa Monica. Barry Lubetkin tried to get the two sides to hold a single service on neutral ground, but Shore refused to cancel her plan. The way she saw it, she had *every* right.

So, despite Steve's hope that his death would bring the two sides together, the dueling memorials went off as planned. No strikebreakers attended the one at Humperdinck's, and none of the CFC leaders appeared at the Comedy Store. The Lubetkins attended both, but Barry took pains to point out that his presence at Shore's service was dictated by the fact that, unlike the CFC, she had thought to have a rabbi present. "I went to the Comedy Store simply out of respect because my brother's body was lying in a funeral home, and no rabbi had prayed," he said. "I was in no way supporting Mitzi Shore or the Comedy Store. I want that made clear."

At Humperdinck's, Barry addressed a packed house of Steve's friends and fellow comics from the stage where he'd watched his brother perform two weeks before. "I'm not a comedian; I'm a psychologist," he said. "This has hurt me deeply as a brother and as someone who is sworn and trained to prevent this kind of thing from happening. Well, I couldn't. I didn't."

He told them he planned to initiate a program at his psychology center in New York "to develop free counseling services for comedians, where they can go and share their pain and their hurt and frustrations, so that this never happens again. It's a lonely plastic town out there. We're all a little bit fragile, a little bit on the brink. Steve just went over."

Susan Evans did not speak at the memorial. She had not returned to the apartment she shared with Steve and had spent two nights sleeping on a friend's couch with her head between two pillows, crying and, at times, screaming. To get through the memorial, she had calmed her grief and rage with a large dose of valium borrowed from Ginny, which left her feeling as if she were wrapped in cotton.

Ashen-faced and hollow-eyed, Richard Lewis wept uncontrollably through most of the memorial but managed to pull himself together somewhat when it came time to deliver the keynote eulogy. He talked about the "blood brother" days and nights in Greenwich Village when he and Steve dreamed of stardom and promised to help one another no matter what. "And I know Steve would have achieved those things that he wanted and he would have been on all those panel shows that he always talked about, because he was good and because he deserved it," he said. For ten minutes, he paced the stage, running his hands through his shoulder-length hair, sobbing with grief, talking about his dead friend, and getting laughs. The connection between pain and laughter was never more tangible, causing more than one person present to wonder if providence hadn't created humor and comedians for this very purpose.

The service closed with the recording that Steve requested in his suicide note: his final set at Westwood on March 24.

You know what I was thinking the other day? Wouldn't it be wild if they made men's contraceptives in sizes? Imagine the ego trips guys would go on. Can you see a guy swaggering into the drug store? "Wanna give me a dozen Trojan Big Boys and a handful of Moby Dicks?" Of course, the ego trip is shattered the minute he gets back to the car and the girl friend says, "Did you get your Tom Thumbs and Gherkin Pickles?"

I've been a little depressed lately because a comedian friend of mine had a nervous breakdown. . . . He had to go up against the Ayatollah Khomeini on *Make Me Laugh*.

You really have to love LA because they have so many weird people out here. I read about a guy who died the other day and his family put out a statement saying that in lieu of flowers they would appreciate . . . stereo equipment.

On tape, the Westwood crowd roared its approval; at Humperdinck's the audience wept as well and gave him a standing ovation.

The next day, Barry and Ginny, Susan, Richard, and Steve flew back to New York. Richard crashed at the apartment of his childhood friend and fellow stand-up, Larry David, while Susan stayed with Ginny and Barry, who took on the excruciating task of telling his father about Steve. As a precaution, Barry first called Jack's next door neighbor, a cardiologist, and asked him to be present.

"Dad, I have terrible news," he said after Jack invited them into his apartment. "Steve has passed away." The elder Lubetkin did not collapse as Barry had feared, but he was rocked to his core and reacted with stunned disbelief. Barry instinctively withheld the fact that Steve had taken his own life. Instead, he told his father there had been an "accident" and that Steve "fell off a building," which caused the old man to wonder aloud, "Why would he fall off a roof? Was it drugs?"

At a memorial service for family members the next day, Richard found himself sitting next to Susan. For three days, he'd been carrying around the crushing burden of a guilty secret; now he couldn't hold it in any longer. "I know something important that no one else knows," he told her, as the story of Steve seeing faces in the weeks before his death poured out of him. When Susan responded that both she and Barry knew about the faces, too, he almost wept with relief. It wasn't all on him after all.

Steve was buried next to his mother at Wellwood Cemetery in Pinelawn, Long Island. Later in the afternoon, Barry and Richard walked to the East River a few blocks from the Lubetkin's apartment and sat on a bench for several hours talking about the brother they had shared.

Back in Los Angeles, the hostilities between Mitzi Shore and the CFC (now calling itself Comedians for Comedians) continued unabated. On June 6, the CFC took out a half-page in memoriam ad in *Daily Variety*, choosing to quote not a sampling of Steve's humor but rather an excerpt from the essay he wrote titled, "What the CFC Is All About." Shore responded by having the city of Los Angeles proclaim June 6 "Comedy Store Day." Written in flowery script with wording provided by the Comedy Store, the official proclamation was stamped with the seal of the city and suitable for framing:

WHEREAS June 6, 1979 will mark the 6th anniversary of The Comedy Store and,

WHEREAS the primary purpose of The Comedy Store is to develop new comedy talent through a graduated process, which starts on Monday nights when anyone who wants to is invited to experience five minutes in front of a mike; and

WHEREAS The Comedy Store is frequented by managers, agents, casting directors, producers, talent coordinators, network

executives and studio executives and is a showcase and springboard for the comedians who play there; and

WHEREAS, a creative consultant for ABC-TV, Mitzi Shore
is the innovator of every new program that The Comedy Store
offers; and in order to encourage the growth of women in comedy
she opened The Comedy Store Belly Room last season for female
comics, and her latest innovation is Video Workshop sessions
where growing comedians will work out in front of a camera in a
classroom environment;

NOW, THEREFORE, I, TOM BRADLEY, Mayor of the City
of Los Angeles, on behalf of its citizens do hereby proclaim June
6, 1979 as "The Comedy Store Day" in recognition of its sixth
anniversary and commend the many talented comedians for
sharing their unique ability to make people laugh; and

FURTHER, I congratulate Mitzi Shore for her outstanding
contributions and wish her continued success in her future
endeavors.

Not content to hang the proclamation on her office wall,
Shore had the document reproduced as a full-page ad in *Daily Variety* at a cost of nearly $1,500, which would have covered a
week's worth of paid time slots.

The week after Lubetkin's death, Shore appeared exhausted
and on edge during a set-the-record-straight interview with the
*Los Angeles Times*. "I loved Steve Lubetkin, and I wouldn't have
done anything to hurt him ever," she said. In her view, Lubetkin
was the victim of the agreement "that was forced on me by the
CFC." The agreement had compelled her to cut back time slots
at Westwood, and Steve was among the comics affected. It was as
simple as that. There was no retaliation; it was merely "arith-
metic." She said she would gladly renegotiate the agreement "because this one is not working. I knew it wouldn't."

The subject of the CFC quickly set her off. "I'm getting pissed
off that I'm being blamed for someone else's inadequacies," she

said, banging her desktop for emphasis. "This system works. If you've got it, then you'll make it and become a star. Not everyone is going to become a star, and those people who are angry and blaming me are probably aware that they are not going to become a star. So, they can't lay that on me or the Store. It's totally unjust and unfair. You're dealing with a bunch of children.

"Steve was a clever writer, but he had trouble as a performer," she said, softening slightly. "He was a person who wanted to be a superstar and didn't have the ingredients. He killed himself because he could not handle his life." While there was undeniable truth to her words, in the end, of all the people who knew and loved Steve Lubetkin, only Mitzi Shore denied any responsibility for what happened to him.

Ten days after his best friend's death, Richard Lewis looked wan and disheveled as he sat with a reporter who had covered the strike from the beginning. The reporter had come armed with a list of questions, which became superfluous the second Lewis started talking.

"I think it got him off the hook," he said of Lubetkin's suicide. "After trying so desperately and so hard and so long for some kind of recognition in this business, I think he was exhausted, tired of expecting rewards.

"No one should ever chalk this man up as just another crazy performer. I'm not defending his final act—I am bitterly angry and will feel his loss forever. But he was Steve Lubetkin to the end and only the last second seems crazy. In his head, he was giving at the end, just like he had thousands of times before in front of thousands of people. Only this time he wanted nothing in return—no laughs, no applause, no promises of gigs, no auditions. He purely just wanted to leave a message that things should be fair. To point a finger seems to demean what that moment meant to him. To point to some situation or person and blame them is the very nature of the sickness that's in this town. It makes them bigger than life. And it's the thing that killed Steve.

"I feel sorry for all the Steve Lubetkins who are not thinking past that one night at the Comedy Store, that particular night when they are indeed making people laugh and being an entertainer in the grandest sense. But they shouldn't make the Comedy Store bigger than it is. Don't make it Vegas, because it isn't. Don't make it a series or a tour or a screenplay, because it isn't. It's just tables and chairs and a stage where you can go work and be seen and maybe make some pocket money. Mitzi Shore is not a psychiatrist. Neither is she their mother. I never wanted to give her that much responsibility for me.

"People in this business give too much power to those who judge them, and it is so damned destructive. It keeps you from doing what you can do. Granted, it's a bitch to work for free and be a piece of meat, which is generally what you are in this business. But it's a choice that actors and comedians have made, and the best way to deal with it is to work on your craft, surround yourself with good friends, be able to love people and get love back, and keep your fingers crossed.

"But if you depend on the business people—the agents, managers, producers, the Improvs, the Comedy Stores, the Budd Friedmans and the Mitzi Shores—to give you credence and sustenance, then you are in big trouble. I think Steve Lubetkin was in this kind of trouble for a long time. Perhaps it was in his nature to have this happen to him. He thought these people cared more than they do."

He sighed. "The business, by and large, is made up of wallets, not hearts."

# Epilogue:
# The Prisoner of Memory

For the stand-up comedians who migrated to Los Angeles in the mid-1970s and participated in the strike, Steve Lubetkin's suicide serves as a sad signpost, like a classmate's fatal car crash on graduation night, marking an end to their innocence.

"We were just young kids trying to be funny, and all of a sudden, it wasn't about making people laugh anymore," Tom Dreesen recalled nearly thirty years later. "It wasn't even about making a living. There was something deep and dark and scary, and all the fun was out of it."

"It colored everything," said Dottie Archibald. "It made it bigger than it was, bigger than just a bunch of people trying to get paid. It made people reflect more on what happened."

"After Steve's suicide, it was never the same," said Jay Leno.

Lubetkin's desperate last act did not accomplish what he had hoped. There was no coming together of the two sides in its wake, no fairness finally codified. The strike settlement agreement didn't last the summer. The Comedians for Compensation renamed themselves the more union-sounding American Federation of Comedians (AFC) and filed charges of unfair labor practices against the Comedy Store with the National Labor Relations Board (NLRB). Mitzi Shore responded by rescinding the contract and reducing the per-set payment to $10 on weeknights. The AFC sued to force her into arbitration; she countersued, challenging the AFC's right to act as a collective bargaining agent. The comics turned to SAG and AFTRA for help and were told there was nothing that could be done unless they affiliated with AGVA, which had jurisdiction in nightclubs. So, in January 1980, the AFC reversed its previous stance and voted unanimously and apprehensively to affiliate with AGVA, which, sure enough, did little more than collect dues for the next two years. After months of hearings, the NLRB finally ruled in January 1982 that the comedians who worked at the Comedy Store were independent contractors rather than employees and, as such, were "not qualified for NLRB protection." By that time, the AFC was broke and owed its lawyers nearly $40,000. It struggled on for more than a year after that, with Chairman Susan Sweetzer and a handful of other unpaid officers spending the bulk of their time dealing with grievances and complaints from a dwindling and increasingly unappreciative membership. But the movement to unionize the stand-up comics of America ultimately proved to be an insurrection of the moment, and on some unremembered date in 1984, the organization that Steve Lubetkin died trying to save simply ceased to exist.

The principal lasting effect of the 1979 strike is that it ended the era of comedians working for free. Even though Mitzi Shore repudiated the contract and reduced the amount per set, she continued to pay the comics who performed on her stages, to the extent that a regular could earn as much as $200 to $300 a week. Budd Friedman and the owners of Catch a Rising Star and the Comic Strip in New York grudgingly went along with the new reality, and purely "showcase" clubs disappeared from the entertainment landscape.

The end of the strike coincided with an explosion in the popularity of live comedy around the country. By the dawn of the new decade, new comedy clubs had opened in San Francisco, Chicago, Detroit, Cleveland, Boston, Toronto, Vancouver, and Edmonton. Southern California soon boasted a total of sixteen paying clubs, including the Laugh Factory, located less than half a mile down Sunset Strip from the Comedy Store. The Laugh Factory was launched shortly after the strike by a nineteen-year-old wannabe comic named Jamie Masada, who had walked the picket line. On the club's opening night, Masada charged fifty cents at the door and divided up the proceeds among the performers. But the first performer to take the stage, Richard Pryor, refused his share and instead handed Masada a $100 bill and said, "Pay your rent."

Within a couple of years of the strike, there were an estimated three hundred comedy clubs in the United States. Seventeen of those were branches of the Improv, licensed by Budd Friedman and his new one-third partner Mark Lonow. That many clubs created an unprecedented demand for talent, which put comics with diplomas from the Comedy Store and the Los Angeles Improv in a previously unimaginable position of power, able to command what they started calling "stupid money." As Lonow explained, "A new club would open with a neophyte owner that the comics knew didn't know anything, and a comic making $2,500 a week would ask for $10,000, and they'd settle for $8,000, and six months later the club would be out of business."

"The strike was a great lesson for how to conduct your career, in terms of being a business person and learning how things work, and getting a little gumption to stand up for yourself and knowing what things are worth, and how to put a contract together and negotiate," said Elayne Boosler. "It was sort of a jumping off point."

It wasn't just the headliners who did well. Lesser-knowns such as Jo Anne Astrow, Dottie Archibald, Susan Sweetzer, Jimmy Aleck, Ollie Joe Prater, and Lue Deck joined the legion of stand-up "road warriors" who spent the 1980s making a damn good living telling jokes in water-tank towns across America.

It wasn't all good times, of course. Some of the new club own-ers made Mitzi and Budd seem cuddly in comparison. "There was a club in Tempe, Arizona, where the owners were all drug dealers, and no one ever got paid because their checks always bounced," recalled Elayne Boosler. "I was determined to get paid, so when the guy said, 'I'm going to announce you now,' I said, 'But I haven't been paid yet.' He said 'later,' and I said, 'No, now, or I don't go on. Or maybe I'll just go out there and tell them *why* I'm not going on and what you do to comics, and I sure hope you have fire insurance.' He said, 'Just a minute,' and he came run-ning back in a few minutes with a vial of cocaine and said, 'Can I pay you with this?' I said, 'Only if you buy it back from me after my set.' He said, 'I don't have the cash.' I said, 'Well, go get it.' And he got it and gave it to me, and then he said, 'Don't you want me to put that in the safe while you go on?' I said, 'How stu-pid do I look?'

"I realized then why Henny Youngman always stood with his hand on his side—to make sure the money was still there," she laughed. "I became notorious for not going on stage without first getting paid in full in cash. It all went back to the strike."

The major downside of the strike was that it killed the cama-raderie that had characterized the LA stand-up community for at least half a decade. "That was all gone," said Argus Hamilton.

Tom Dreesen never went back to performing at the Comedy Store. Neither did Elayne Boosler, Dottie Archibald, Jo Anne As-trow, Marsha Warfield, Bill Kirchenbauer, or Murray Langston, the Unknown Comic. In some cases, the choice was theirs; in others, it was Shore's. For Richard Lewis, the idea of returning to the ground where Steve died was just too painful. George Miller went back only once: He stopped in for a drink on Halloween night 1979, and Shore immediately dispatched Ollie Joe Prater to throw him out. David Letterman, who had been performing at Sunset sporadically, never returned after that. Jay Leno continued to work at Sunset for some months after the strike, but it wasn't like the old days. "I just go in, do my job, get my money, say thank you, and leave," he told the *Los Angeles Times* in February 1980. "I used to hang out, but I don't anymore. I try not to associate." The *Times* quoted a "source close to Shore" as saying, "David and all those people are missed. They all used to hang out in the hallway, and Mitzi would sit back there talking with them. It used to be a lot of fun to come to work. But it's so different now. It's really a shame. This used to be the greatest place in town."

The Improv became the hangout of choice for the comics who had sided with the CFC, and the two clubs turned into mutually exclusive encampments. The strikebreakers were not welcome at the Improv; the same held for the strike leaders at the Comedy Store. Only Robin Williams and Andy Kaufman felt free to float between stages without fear of offending either Budd or Mitzi, whose animus toward one another increased after the strike. Shore bitterly resented that Friedman had managed to come off as a hero to the striking comics at her expense. "I don't like the man," she told the *Los Angeles Times* in 1982, at the same time admitting that they had never even spoken. "I don't think we are potential friends," he responded dryly.*

Shore was also rankled by the fact that Friedman and Lonow had leapfrogged her by launching the successful cable series *An Evening at the Improv* in 1980 (it would run for eleven years and help make both men rich). Despite her early jump into the medium—via her consulting deal with ABC and the club's hosting of HBO's *Young Comedians* specials in 1979 and 1980—in the decade following the strike, Shore had a hand in producing only two Comedy Store "anniversary" specials (the eleventh and fifteenth)

---

*"Did You Hear the One About Budd and Mitzi?" *Los Angeles Times*, October 31, 1982.

on HBO and one four-episode series, *The Girls of the Comedy Store*, for the Playboy Channel. Associates blame her difficult personality and "control issues" for the fact that she was not able to capitalize further on her access to the world's best stand-up comics. "She wanted to produce, but the networks didn't want her to produce because they saw her as a nightclub owner," said Mike Binder. "So instead of becoming a great nightclub owner, she became a really pissed off failed producer."

Binder's own experience is indicative. In 1985, when he was still working as a regular at Sunset, he made an independent film called *The Detroit Comedy Jam*, which he sold to HBO. Shore was "livid" that he hadn't involved her or the club, he said. "She thought I had no right doing that. She wanted to control me. So she fired me from the club, even threatened to call the police if I didn't leave immediately." And so ended their relationship. "Mitzi's talent was creating an environment that nourished this new comedy, but she wasn't able to adapt and let [the comedians] go and not own them," Binder said. "She felt like she wasn't getting her piece."

Although the Westwood Comedy Store closed on January 1, 1984, the Sunset club continued as the dominant venue for stand-up comedy in the Los Angeles area into the early 1990s, helping launch the careers of Louis Anderson, Jim Carrey, Roseanne Barr, Paul Rodriguez, "Bobcat" Goldwaith, Pee Wee Herman, Whoopi Goldberg, Andrew "Dice" Clay, Sam Kinison, and, of course, Pauly Shore.

Meanwhile, success, the road, and time gradually took a toll on the club's 1970s graduates. Letterman and Leno remained friends for a dozen years after the strike, albeit at a distance since the old gang didn't go to Canter's anymore, and Dave had moved out to Malibu for a couple of years before relocating to New York to host *Late Night* on NBC. Prior to *The Tonight Show* imbroglio in 1991, their get-togethers were pretty much confined to Leno's appearances on Letterman's show, which were notable for their apparent mutual affection. If they have talked since, none of their friends are aware of it.

Richard Pryor nearly burned to death while free-basing cocaine in June 1980, suffering third-degree burns over 50 percent of his body. He made a triumphant return to the stage in 1982 in a performance filmed at the Hollywood Palladium and released on video (and later DVD) as *Richard Pryor Live on Sunset Strip*, but he never again reached his previous creative heights. Diagnosed with multiple sclerosis in 1996, he gave a handful of alternately brilliant and heart-wrenching performances at the Comedy Store in the late 1990s and died in 2005.

Robin Williams's drug use became public in 1982 when it was revealed, in the course of a police investigation, that he had visited John Belushi's bungalow at the Chateau Marmont on Sunset Strip the night the *Saturday Night Live* star died of an overdose. Williams was not accused of any wrongdoing, but the incident was a major personal and professional embarrassment for the then star of a PG-rated network TV series. He later admitted that he was addicted to cocaine and alcohol during those years and went through twenty years of so-called white knuckle sobriety (meaning without professional help) before entering rehab for treatment of alcoholism in 2006.

Several other regulars in the late-night parties at Mitzi's house subsequently saw their lives and careers affected by substance abuse, including Mike Binder, Biff Maynard, Ollie Joe Prater, and Argus Hamilton. Following the strike, Hamilton commenced a three-year romantic relationship with Shore that Comedy Store insiders characterized as volatile due to drug and alcohol use. Shore eventually helped him get sober, and in 1998 she announced the foundation of the Comedian's Drug and Alcohol Abuse Foundation, "a nonprofit charitable corporation formed to provide counseling, medical care and financial assistance to aspiring young comedians who are trying to overcome drug and alcohol abuse problems." Shore and Hamilton were on the board of directors, and among the twenty-five members of the "honorary committee" were, ironically, George Miller and Ollie Joe Prater. The latter died of a massive stroke in 1992 at the age of forty-four and weighing a reported four hundred–plus pounds. A joke often repeated by his fellow comics and attributed to Charlie Hill goes, "What did Ollie Joe die from? Room service."

As the 1980s wore on, the vibe at the Sunset Store grew louder, darker, druggier, and more dangerous, thanks in no small part to the influence of the club's resident muse, Sam Kinison, whose appetite for guns and cocaine led to instances of shots being fired in the Main Room, the lobby, and the comics' house on Crest Hill Drive. Kinison was famously quoted as saying of his favorite drug, "There is no happy ending to cocaine. You either die, go to jail, or else you run out." In April 1992, he was driving his supercharged Pontiac Trans Am to a sold-out gig in Laughlin, Nevada, when he was killed in a head-on collision with a pickup truck. He reportedly had cocaine, prescription tranquilizers, and codeine in his system when he died.

Kinison was the last big star born at the Comedy Store. After his death, the club went into a long, slow decline artistically and financially. According to the *Los Angeles Times*, in recent years, Shore has borrowed money against the club as well as her house to meet operating expenses, and she has experienced "persistent problems with delinquency on tax and mortgage payments."*

Today, the Laugh Factory stands in stark contrast to Mitzi Shore's crumbled comedy empire. The West Hollywood club is a favorite among comics because owner Jamie Masada pays far more than anyone else—$60 per set, compared to the Improv's $17.50 and the Comedy Store's $12.50—and claims no credit for any comic's success. "For me to say that someone wouldn't have

---

*"Echo of Laughter," *Los Angeles Times*, June 22, 2003.

made it if not for me would be like saying that if I hadn't given you this pencil then you would never have been able to write," he said. "I haven't 'made' anyone. I've made money from them.

"Most of what I learned from Mitzi about being a club owner was what not to do, and one thing you cannot do is hold the talent down," he said. "I think the reason so many people did not want to go back there is that she tried too much to control it. She wanted them to be *her* comics."

The Laugh Factory was George Miller's principal performing home during the final years of his life, so it was fitting that his memorial was held there. Many of the comics present had attended the sixtieth birthday party Elayne Boosler threw for him the year before. (George didn't show up for that gathering either, but he did call Elayne in the middle of it to see how things were going.) Some, however, had not been in the same room together since before the picket lines went up, and there was some initial uneasiness as former strike leaders and strikebreakers paid their respects to Miller, if not to one another.

After the memorial, Mike Binder acknowledged the hard feelings some still held. "Crossing the picket line is definitely a dark mark on my life," he said. "I never should have done that." He has tried to make amends. A few years ago, he ran into Tom Dreesen in a club, and according to both men, they went outside to talk. "I said, 'Tommy, I was wrong. I made a mistake. I should have been in your corner.' I saw on his face it was over at that moment. I've said the same thing to Jay, but I think he still harbors some resentment. We're friendly, but we've never been good buddies again. I used to be good friends with Elayne Boosler, too, and we haven't said five words to one another since."

"I have no problem with Mike because he came to me like a man and said he made a mistake," said Dreesen. Nor does he hold a grudge against Argus Hamilton "because he was always a gentleman, and he was in love with the woman, so what was he going to do." Regarding Garry Shandling, the only strikebreaker who went on to achieve bona fide stardom, Dreesen said, "I wish him all the success in the world. He's a funny guy and a good writer, but as a human being, as a man, I don't have any respect for him."

For Richard Lewis, the scene at the Laugh Factory called to mind the memorial for Steve Lubetkin at Humperdinck's in June 1979. "If it makes Steve's soul feel any better, his last act wasn't heroic, but what he stood for was unbelievably heroic because he believed so deeply in the journey of an artist," he said. "And he is now forever linked to us as a symbol for this struggle. It's bigger than any three-year sitcom run he might have gotten. Steve symbolizes the journey of an artist and how hard it is for everybody. Steve is forever linked to us who knew him in a more powerful and important way than he ever dreamed he would be."

And, of course, the Miller memorial sparked considerable conversation among his peers about the owner of the club down the street who once had him escorted off the premises and banished. "I don't hold any bad feelings, just disappointment and sadness," said Jay Leno. "And I don't dislike Mitzi. I just don't understand what made it go bad. It wouldn't have taken much to hold everybody's heart. I would have loved to be able to go back to the Comedy Store, but it's like that old saying, 'You can do anything for the person you used to love except love them again.'"

"In retrospect, as much as I think Mitzi mishandled it, she did say, 'Money is going to fuck everything up for you guys,' and she was truly not wrong," said Mike Binder, who has written and directed several critically acclaimed feature films, including *The Upside of Anger*, starring Kevin Costner and Joan Allen. "When we were working for free because we loved it and wanted to be good, it was wonderful. It wasn't until we realized that she was making a lot of money and we could, too, that everything changed."

Not everything. After a recent taping of *The Late Show*, David Letterman was eating pizza in his lawyer's office and reminiscing with Tom Dreesen, who had appeared as he does frequently, not as a stand-up guest but rather as an "old friend of the show," much the way Leno did in the 1980s. Dreesen was still dressed in the elegant gray suit and tie he'd worn on camera, while Letterman had changed into a baggy sweatshirt, gym shorts, and sneakers with no socks. Notoriously press shy, Dave had agreed to sit for his second press interview in nearly a decade only because Tom had asked him to.

"How long has it been since we've seen each other, Bill?" he inquired of the interviewer.

"Twenty-eight years, Dave," came the reply.

Another old friend from the Comedy Store days, Johnny Dark, had stopped by the Ed Sullivan Theater earlier to tape a comedy segment for an upcoming *Late Show*, on which he appears frequently in the character of "the oldest CBS page," a dimwit whose career spans thirty-nine years. "You know, if George were here, he'd have left fifteen minutes ago," Dave joked.

Even though Letterman is now the alpha dog careerwise by dint of hosting a network show continuously since 1982, his relationship with Dreesen remains remarkably the same as when they were young pups shooting hoops at the San Fernando Valley YMCA, with Dave still deferring to Tom as a kind of wiser big brother. At one point in the discussion, they disagreed about an incident during the strike.

"With all due respect, I don't think that happened," Letterman said.

"I swear on my children it did," Dreesen responded.

"Well, I don't recall it exactly that way," Letterman said to the interviewer, grinning sheepishly and only half joking, "but I'll go with whatever Tom says."

Dreesen looks back on the comedian's strike as perhaps his greatest career achievement, his professional legacy. "I'm proud of what we accomplished," he said. "Young comics have come up to me over the years and said, 'Somebody told me you used to work for free. Is that right?' I say, 'Yeah, that's right.' And they say,

'Man, the first time I ever went on stage I got paid.' I say, 'Really? That's great.' And they don't know what happened."

Letterman, typically, downplays his own role in the events. "I wanted to do what my friends were doing," he said. "I thought my friendships were more important than the other issues, so I could not *not* support the strike. I thought this is what you do. It's part of being an adult. You see the way the landscape is, and you embrace it."

As for Mitzi Shore, "I was in awe of her and still am to this day by virtue of the operation she ran, the fact that she could build this machine, this retail comedy establishment," he said. "If I were to put together a list of the people who have helped me, it would be a very long list, but she would certainly be at the top of it. But as good as she was to all of us, the world is a two-way street, and I would hope that she doesn't harbor any bad feelings.

"I have undying affection for those times and for all those people," he said, "because the older I get, the more I realize that they were the best times of my adult life."

It's a sentiment shared by nearly all the people who were interviewed for this book. In the rosy glow of remembrance, they see the latter part of the 1970s in Los Angeles as their version of Paris in the 1920s, a time of astonishing creativity and unprecedented camaraderie in the singular world of stand-up comedy. "People helped each other," recalled Jamie Masada. "I remember working at the Blah Blah Café with Robin Williams and David Letterman, and when I came off the stage, Robin sat me down and gave some notes, and Letterman started fixing my jokes. You don't see that anymore."

As TV, movie, and nightclub performers in the latter part of the twentieth century, they have traveled the world performing in front of untold millions of people and lived, by most accounts, colorful, eventful lives. And yet, an odd little woman who ran a dark little nightclub on Sunset Strip when they were young remains perhaps the most indelible character in their collective memory bank.

Why? The answer may be buried deep in the sixty-page National Labor Relations Board ruling that sounded the death knell for the comedian's union. Noting the Comedy Store's "dominant position as the best-known purveyor of comedic talent" at the time and Shore's personal control over "the greatest number of performance opportunities" in the marketplace, the administrative law judge in the case cited as "persuasively descriptive" the testimony of hearing witness Mark Lonow:

When you are beginning a career in which every fiber of your ego, your self-esteem, your entire fantasy life of who you are and who you are going to become is involved, and there is only one path—one way—to make it, in your mind, and that is through the Comedy Store, then the person who owns the Comedy Store becomes an all-encompassing dictator. Whether or not it is true is almost irrelevant to a person trying to become a regular at the Comedy Store to fulfill their fantasy of being a great star. What Mitzi Shore says is the law. It isn't that she requests or indicates. The mere fact that the thought passes through her mind, in ninety-nine percent of the cases, becomes the law in your life. It is very hard to explain what an entertainer goes through; what an artist whose emotional life is totally involved with the need for success, what goes through their being when someone who they believe controls their destiny says something to them.

Apparently, once you are placed at the mercy of that level of personal power, it is difficult, if not impossible, to forget it.

If it's any comfort to comics who labored in her service those many years ago, Mitzi Shore is the prisoner of her own memories. Several months after George Miller's memorial, she sat in the dining room of the storied house on Doheny Boulevard where she'd hosted coke-snorting sessions with Richard Pryor and Robin Williams nearly three decades before. She was now in her midseventies, and the years had not been particularly kind. She moved slowly, and her hands were palsied. A 2003 article in the *Los Angeles Times* had portrayed her as "the Norma Desmond of Comedy," living like the faded silent screen star in the film *Sunset Boulevard*, alone in her rundown mansion and lost in reverie about her glorious past.*

"She's in declining health and full of hope," said Argus Hamilton, who had smoothed the way for the interview. "She survived an aneurism ten years ago, and she has increasing tremors, but they are non-Parkinson's, according to her doctors at UCLA." In the *Los Angeles Times* metaphor, Hamilton would be cast in the role of Norma Desmond's loyal butler, Max, who was also her ex-husband. Shore continues to employ Hamilton as the permanent emcee and comic emeritus at Sunset, and his admiration, loyalty, and faith appear to know no bounds. "She's definitely not finished with Hollywood," he said. "She is a true artistic genius, and a cash cow that the networks have not finished milking yet if they are smart."

Despite her physical infirmities, Shore seemed in full control of her mental faculties as she spoke about the past. Photographs, press clippings, and mementos of those times were arrayed on the table for her reference. Chief among them was a limited-edition, self-published, hardcover book commemorating the club's fifteenth-year "class reunion" TV special. Basically a professionally produced scrap book, it contains an idealized history of the Comedy Store from 1972 to 1987, along with yearbook-type photos of what appears to be every performer who ever took the stage at any of the clubs—more than three hundred of them, including such obscure practitioners as Fred Asparagus and Glenn Super—but not Tom

---

*"Echo of Laughter," *Los Angeles Times*, June 22, 2003.

Dreesen, whose name is nowhere in the text. Jay Leno is not mentioned either. In contrast, Letterman is among the few—Richard Pryor, Andy Kaufman, Robin Williams, Garry Shandling, and Sam Kinison—who merit a two-page spread. The story about his Comedy Store emcee duties paving the way for his subsequent talk show success appears twice in the book, and Shore repeated it again to the interviewer, relating how at one point "David was ready to give up and go back to Indiana, but I talked him out of it."

The mention of Steve Lubetkin's name drew a misty-eyed smile. "A soft sell," she said of his performing style. "He didn't come at you hard. He sort of snuck up on you, softly. He was a good writer," she said, adding wistfully, as if savoring a distant memory from the table where she now sat. "His favorite meal was roasted leg of lamb."

Lubetkin is pictured in the commemorative book, along with an oddly truncated entry in the historical chronology: "June 1979. An uneasy peace prevails. Steve Lubetkin dies tragically, separate services are held by differing comics." There is no further explanation.

Shore said she thought Steve committed suicide because the CFC had put him in a difficult leadership position for which he was emotionally unprepared. "The job was too much for him, and they should have known that." So, despite all evidence to the contrary, including his suicide note, in her mind the striking comics were to blame.

In 2003, Shore told the *Los Angeles Times*, "I won the strike, but I made it that they won. That movie should be done because I was like Ruth, being stoned to death. I didn't deserve what they did to me."*

---

*"Did You Hear the One About Budd and Mitzi? *Los Angeles Times*, October 31, 1982.

Asked more recently if, looking back, there was anything she wished she had done differently during the dispute, Shore said no, there was nothing. "The Store worked," she said. "The Store was the light. And if they couldn't see that the Store was the light, well, then fuck 'em."

# Index

**William Knoedelseder** has been a journalist with the *Los Angeles Times*, executive producer of Fox Entertainment News and of the *Philadelphia Inquirer*'s hour-long nightly television news program "Inquirer News Tonight," and vice president of news at USA Broadcasting. He is the author of *Stiffed: A True Story of MCA, The Music Business, and the Mafia* and *In Eddie's Name: One Family's Triumph Over Tragedy*. Born in St. Louis, Missouri, he lives near Los Angeles, California.

PublicAffairs is a publishing house founded in 1997. It is a tribute to the standards, values, and flair of three persons who have served as mentors to countless reporters, writers, editors, and book people of all kinds, including me.

I. F. STONE, proprietor of *I. F. Stone's Weekly*, combined a commitment to the First Amendment with entrepreneurial zeal and reporting skill and became one of the great independent journalists in American history. At the age of eighty, Izzy published *The Trial of Socrates*, which was a national bestseller. He wrote the book after he taught himself ancient Greek.

BENJAMIN C. BRADLEE was for nearly thirty years the charismatic editorial leader of *The Washington Post*. It was Ben who gave the *Post* the range and courage to pursue such historic issues as Watergate. He supported his reporters with a tenacity that made them fearless and it is no accident that so many became authors of influential, best-selling books.

ROBERT L. BERNSTEIN, the chief executive of Random House for more than a quarter century, guided one of the nation's premier publishing houses. Bob was personally responsible for many books of political dissent and argument that challenged tyranny around the globe. He is also the founder and longtime chair of Human Rights Watch, one of the most respected human rights organizations in the world.

·   ·   ·

For fifty years, the banner of Public Affairs Press was carried by its owner Morris B. Schnapper, who published Gandhi, Nasser, Toynbee, Truman, and about 1,500 other authors. In 1983, Schnapper was described by *The Washington Post* as "a redoubtable gadfly." His legacy will endure in the books to come.

Peter Osnos, *Founder and Editor-at-Large*

CPSIA information can be obtained at www.ICGtesting.com
Printed in the USA
LVOW05s2020150514

385860LV00003B/7/P